TRIUMPH OF THE THIRD REICH

BY A. EDWARD COOPER

Triumph Of The Third Reich
By A. Edward Cooper

© 1999 by A. Edward Cooper

ISBN 1-888106-99-9

Library of Congress Catalog Card Number: 99-60980

Cover Design: Bryan Baker

Agreka™ LLC
800 360-5284
www.agreka.com

Chronology

TRIUMPH OF THE THIRD REICH

PROLOGUE

On Monday, the 11th of November, 1918, the Great War ended with the signing of the Treaty of Versailles. However, the War to End all Wars, was soon to prove to be just the forerunner of another longer and more terrible war.

In 1931 Japan seized and occupied Eastern Manchuria turning it into the puppet state of Manchukuo. The next year Japanese troops crossed into China. Despite United States condemnation, the Japanese advanced swiftly and penetrated deep into China.

Realizing the League of Nations was not willing to take action against the Japanese aggression, Germany repudiated the Versailles Treaty in 1935 and reincorporated the Saarland back into Germany. In the same year Mussolini invaded helpless Abyssinia (Ethiopia) whose troops attacked tanks with spears. Despite Emperor Haile Selassie's personal appeal to the League of Nations, only sanctions were imposed on Italy, and Abyssinia became an Italian Colony.

In 1936 Hitler occupied the Rhineland, unopposed, although facing a much larger French Army which did nothing to oppose the occupation.

By 1937 Japan had occupied the major Chinese cities of Peking, Tientsin, Shanghai, Nanking and Hangchow. Seeing the success of the Japanese, Hitler occupied Austria in March of 1938, and seven months later moved into the Sudetenland of Czechoslovakia.

Not to be outdone, Mussolini sent his troops into Albania on the 7th of April 1939. Still, the Western Democracies failed to act.

In August 1939, Russia and Germany signed a nonaggression pact, freeing Germany to invade Poland on September 1, 1939. Now at the worst possible time under the worst possible circumstances, unprepared France and England were committed to come to the aid of Poland. The Second World War had begun.

In 1940, Germany invaded Russia in violation of their nonaggression pact and swiftly advanced deep into Russia.

On December 7th, 1941, the United States entered the war, when Japanese Naval forces attacked Pearl Harbor and the Philippines, and began their sweep through the Far East.

In 1942, the German advance into Russia was finally stopped at the gates of Moscow and at Stalingrad. In North Africa Rommel's advance was stopped at El Alamein. Prime Minister Churchill in referring to these successes, stated in a speech, "Now, this is not the end. It is not even the beginning of the end. But it is, perhaps, the end of the beginning."

By the spring of 1944, the Allies had completely regained the initiative. The Japanese were being driven island by island back toward the Home Islands. The Germans and Italians had been cleared out of Africa and American and English troops were advancing up the Italian Peninsula. In the East the Russians were driving the Germans back along the entire twelve hundred mile front. It was now time to strike the blow that would be "The beginning of the end."

ENGLAND, 5 JUNE 1944

The wind drove the rain in horizontal sheets against Southwick House in southern England, the headquarters of Admiral Sir Bertham H. Ramsey, the Commander of the Allied Naval Expeditionary Force. Group Captain John Stagg, chief meteorologist of operations, was slowly and intently reviewing the latest weather maps.

The wind whipped to a new fury, more like a storm expected in mid winter, than in early June. The storm had broken twenty-four hours before, causing General Eisenhower to postpone the scheduled June 5, 1944 invasion of France, *Operation Overlord.*

The wind rattled the windows, causing several to look up from the table, Captain Stagg with an air of confidence, explained that the worst was nearly over. Reports from as far away as Greenland and from convoys in the mid-Atlantic reported the storm had passed. From the northern Shetland Islands came reports that the barometric pressure was rapidly rising.

Starting tomorrow morning, the 6th of June, Captain Stagg predicted fair weather for at least two days. There would be an early morning overcast of 1000 feet and two to four foot waves off the coast of Normandy but conditions would improve throughout the day.

Eisenhower solicited opinions from around the table. Admiral Ramsey responded, "General, I think we had better go. The troops have been cooped up on the ships for at least 24 hours and some for many more. The wait is consuming great quantities of food and fuel for the ships."

"Marshall Mallory?" Ike asked.

Sir Trafford Leigh-Mallory, commander of the Allied Air Forces, responded, "I agree with Admiral Ramsey. Although the ceiling is somewhat low most of the initial air support will be from low level fighter aircraft anyway. Heavy gun fire from our ships will fill the gap until our heavy bombers can be used against targets farther inland."

Turning to Field Marshall Sir Bernard Montgomery, Ike knew what the Field Marshall's opinion would be. Commander of all of the Allied ground forces, Montgomery had been the only one eager to proceed with the invasion as scheduled this morning in spite of the storm. To the thinking of Montgomery the surprise of an invasion in such weather would outweigh the lack of full air support for his ground troops.

"Yes! Of course, by all means!" exclaimed Monty, "Let's go!"

Glancing around the room at the other senior officers, Ike received a nod from each one. "O.K. We'll go," he said.

The room quickly emptied as the officers left for their respective offices to get the largest invasion in the history of the world underway.

Ike looked at his watch. It was 0415, June 5, 1944 and he had just made the most momentous decision of his life and perhaps one of the greatest in the annuals of war.

Turning to an aide, Eisenhower said, "Please see the President is notified by encrypted message."

"Yes, sir."

Picking up Admiral Ramsay's white phone, Ike placed a call to the Prime Minister. As the phone rang, Ike suddenly realized what the hour was, but on the second ring the familiar gravelly voice came on.

"Yes?"

"I am sorry to trouble you at this hour, Mr. Prime Minister, but we have just decided to initiate *Operation Overlord* tomorrow."

"Wonderful! Is there anything I can do for you?"

Ike was about to say yes, but decided against it. "No sir, but should something develop, I will call."

"Please do, and God be with you."

"Thank you sir, and goodnight."

"Get some sleep General, you are going to need it."

Ike had wanted to ask if Churchill was still planning on accompanying the invasion fleet as he said he was, in spite of objections from all of his military advisors and cabinet members. Ike wondered if the Prime Minister actually realized his value to the war effort and what a boost it would be to the Axis if he were to be killed during the invasion.

It had worried Ike so much that he had sent a personal letter to the King requesting his assistance in keeping Winston at home until the invasion forces had at least secured the beachhead. The

King had written back that he would take care of the problem. But there had been no conformation from the King and Ike knew that the King could not technically order Winston to stay home. He, too, could only recommend and hope that Winston's loyalty to his sovereign would overcome his desire to be in the thick of it.

Riding back to his quarters, Ike couldn't help but notice that the rain seemed to be slacking off. He also thought back to the 27th of March 1942, when the Allies were still being pushed back, and yet military planners had presented to President Roosevelt an outline of a plan to invade Europe in the spring of 1943. At the time the English had been very hesitant to invade Europe across the English Channel. They had, of course, made their own plans on how to repulse a German invasion from across the channel, which they had expected in 1940. They had felt confident that they would succeed in crushing the German plan, *Operation Sea Lion*. If the Germans were as well equipped and determined in defending Western France, the cost of the Allied invasion would be exceedingly high as well.

For that reason the invasion was postponed and instead Italy had been invaded to provide a second but limited front. Churchill, always suspicious of the intentions of the Soviet Union, also saw an advantage to an invasion through Greece and into the Balkans to cut off the Russian onslaught before they could sweep into the heart of Europe. He, in fact, still believed deep down that was the most prudent thing to do. But that was all behind them now.

The success of the next few days was now essentially out of Ike's hands and in the hands of the various on-site commanders at the front. With that thought, he undressed and climbed into bed and drifted off into a restless sleep.

H-hour was 0130 on the sixth of June for the approximately thirteen thousand paratroops to be dropped behind the German lines to seize certain key positions. Consequently, at 2215 on June fifth, more than 900 transport planes began to take off from some 25 different airfields in southern and eastern England.

By 0230 over 5000 war ships, troop ships, tankers, freighters, and 4000 landing craft weighed anchor and fell into long columns following the mine sweepers across the channel. Meanwhile, at airfields all over the British Island, air crews were making their final inspections on the more than 11,000 aircraft scheduled to support the troop landings.

0900, 5 JUNE, BERCHTESGADEN, GERMANY

The German High Command and other invited quests began arriving at 0800 to enjoy a buffet breakfast that had been prepared in the grand dining room at Berchtesgaden, Adolf Hitler's mountain retreat in Bavaria. First to arrive were *Oberst General* Alfred Jodl and *Feldmarschall* Wilhelm Keitel of the Oberkommando der Wehrmacht, or Armed Forces High Command. They were soon followed by Feldmarschall Gerd Von Rundstedt, Supreme Commander of the West, and *Feldmarschall* Erwin Rommel, Commander of the western defenses. Gross Admiral Karl Doenitz, Commander of the *Kriegsmarine*, walked in with General Walter Dornberger, head of the Vergeltungswaffe or Vengeance Weapons Development Section. All of the officers were accompanied by their aides and senior staff officers, making a total of thirty officers, the elite of the *Reich Wehrmacht*.

Promptly at 0900 the doors from Hitler's private office swung open and in swept *Reichsmarschall* Herman Goering, supreme commander of the Luftwaffe. Touching his swagger stick to the brim of his hat he greeted his associates.

"Pompous *Schweinehund*," Von Rundstead whispered to Rommel who was standing on his right. Rommel smiled and nodded his head in agreement.

The *Reichsmarschall* positioned himself behind the chair to the left of the *Führer's*, as usual. Following Goering's lead, the Senior Officers all took their positions standing behind their chairs at the table in the established pecking order. The aides and staff members took positions around the sides of the room in no particular order.

At 0910 Hitler walked in, accompanied by Heinrich Himmler, head of the Secret Police and the elite S.S. Storm Troops. Following behind was an *Oberleutnant* whom no one in the room recognized.

All present in the room came to attention and in unison clicked their heels and gave the Nazi heil Hitler salute.

With an uplifted hand, Hitler acknowledged the presence of all in attendance.

Von Rundstedt couldn't help but notice the change in Hitler's appearance. Just four days before when they had last talked, Hitler had been obviously depressed as he was being briefed on the progress of the war. On the Russian front the Red Army had reclaimed almost all of the previously captured homeland and was well into Poland. The Anglo-American forces in Italy were slowly but surely advancing northward. The Fatherland itself was being pounded by day by the U.S. Eighth Air Force in England and the Fifteenth from Italy and by night by the British Bomber Command. However, today Hitler not only had a spring in his walk, but he was actually grinning.

"*Mein Herren*, please be seated," said the *Führer* as he took his seat. "As you all know, things have not been going well for the Third Reich for some time now and we are now anticipating an invasion of France. But today we have some good news and I want to assure you the tide is about to change again in our favor."

"How many times have we heard this?" Von Rundstedt thought.

"Yesterday," Hitler continued, "We made an extremely important discovery. Let me introduce *Oberleutnant* Helmut Meyer, the intelligence officer of the Fifteenth Army, which as you know, is positioned along the French and Belgian border."

"*Oberleutnant*, inform this group what you have been doing and what you have found out."

"*Jawohl, Mein Führer.*"

Somewhat intimidated by his audience, Meyer spoke softly and slowly but became more animated as he noticed out of the corner of his eye that Hitler was actually beaming at him.

"For the past year or more, we have been assembling the most sophisticated electronic equipment that can be produced and have had this equipment trained across the channel. With our equipment we actually have been able to listen to radio transmissions between military police vehicles directing traffic. In addition, we have been successful in breaking several codes the Allies use to contact the resistance forces in France. We even discovered what the message would be to alert the resistance forces of the time of the invasion. Yesterday, at 2100 over the BBC came the strains of "*Les Sanglots Longs Des Violons de L'automne.*" This alerted us that an important message was soon to follow. Within five minutes came the first and second lines of the nineteenth century French poet, Paul Verlaine's poem, "*Chanson d'Automne.*" The first line was word the invasion was on, the second meant it would begin in forty-eight hours starting the day following the transmission. I am confident the invasion is scheduled for the morning of June sixth, the day after tomorrow."

Instantly there were a dozen conversations going on at once.

Raising his hand, Jodl silenced the babble, and pointing to the window asked, "*Oberleutnant*, how could that be possible? Look out of the window. There is a fierce storm blowing in right now. It must be even worse over England. No one in his right mind would launch an invasion across open water in weather like this."

"You're quite right, *Feldmarschall*. This bad weather even took our meteorologists by surprise. No one thought a spring storm would be so fierce. I suspect it caught the Allies by surprise as well."

"No doubt," agreed Jodl.

"If it did," interjected Rommel, "they probably would have their ships loaded, and rather than disembark, they would sit tight to see what will happen in the next day or so. Do we have any forecast for the seventh or eighth?"

"*Ja*," responded *Admiral* Doenitz, the Commander in Chief of the *Kriegsmarine*. "One of our U-boats on patrol southeast of Iceland reported this morning that the weather was clearing and the barometric pressure was rising."

"There you have it," said Hitler. "Probably on the sixth or eighth at the latest, they will attempt the great invasion, and we will be ready for them!"

"Attempt," thought Rommel, "what is to stop them? Not the defenses we have in Normandy, around Calais perhaps, but not Normandy."

"*Danke Oberleutant*, for your diligent and magnificent work. You may now be seated," said Hitler. Turning to Rundstedt, he went on, "*Feldmarschall*, see that the *Oberleutnant* is given proper recognition for his accomplishment."

"*Jawohl.*"

With that, Meyer returned to his seat amidst a brief round of applause.

"Now," said Hitler, "we have half of the puzzle solved. But unfortunately the coded message did not say exactly where the invasion will take place. Any new ideas?"

Again Jodl spoke up. "*Nein, Mein Führer*, but it is the general consensus that it will be somewhere between Dieppe where the English and Canadians made their futile attempt on August 19, 1942 and Calais the narrowest point across the channel."

"I agree," interjected Rundstedt. "And for that reason we have made formidable defenses in that area."

"Also, let us not forget that the latest intelligence informs us that the American General, George Patton, is still at his headquarters near Dover with a large Army and many landing craft are positioned in the Thames," added Keitel.

"*Herr* Himmler, what else does your intelligence agency know?" asked Hitler.

We have caught a number of the French, Belgian, and Dutch underground leaders, some even on their actual return from England. Under, shall we say, intense interrogation, to a man they all confessed that the invasion was to be near Calais where the Allied troops would be exposed on the sea for the minimum distance. Also this being the shortest route to the Fatherland, the damage to France and Belgium would be minimized during an advance on the Fatherland.

Everyone in the room nodded in agreement with the exception of Erwin Rommel, who alone among the men in the room would be in the thick of the battle to come.

Hitler, noticing Rommel's lack of agreement, turned, "You disagree Erwin?" calling him by his first name.

"*Mein Führer*, I have personally gone over every inch of our defenses from the Spanish border to Denmark. The fact that we have so heavily fortified the Dieppe/Calais beachhead is the very reason I do not think the Allies will land there. Their losses would be too high and they know it. With their ability to reconnoiter our entire fortifications at will..." Rommel hesitated and glanced at Goering whose Luftwaffe was supposed to prevent this. Goering showed no sign of offense. "Well, in any event they probably know our strong points and weak points as well as we do. The Netherlands are out, as we could flood the lowlands too easy. The French-Spanish border is too far away and the Diepe/Calais area is where we are the strongest. No, I think Normandy is the place. The British, and Churchill in particular, are steeped in tradition and history. Just the fact that the Norman invasion of England in 1066 originated in this area would be sufficient for Churchill to insist the invasion be at Normandy."

With that, everyone except Rommel laughed.

"If I may continue, the fact that the underground leaders confessed that the Diepe/Calais area is the invasion point, may be to mislead us. It is possible that the Allies deliberately gave the underground leaders misinformation knowing that some of them would be caught and would be, ah, shall we say persuaded to tell what they know. As for General Patton, I agree that he will be involved in the invasion but it would be very easy to transfer him at the last minute, while using him as a decoy in the meantime to mislead us."

No one said anything for a few minutes. Finally Hitler spoke, "Your arguments are very logical, *Feldmarschall. Ja?*" as he looked around at the others for comments.

"Possibly," acknowledged Von Rundstedt, Rommel's immediate superior.

Several others nodded in agreement, however none was willing to fully support the proposition.

"Well," said Hitler, "let's put that aside for the moment. What is the status of our forces? *Admiral* Doenitz, let's start with you."

The Admiral rose from the plush chair and walked over to an easel upon which an aide placed several large charts and maps.

"At the present time," the Admiral began, "we have 3 destroyers in the Bay of Biscay. They are very well camouflaged and so the Allies are not aware of them. In addition we have 5 of our large one thousand ton torpedo boats. In the various small channel ports, and at Brest, we have 30 of our smaller E-boats, including the one that is very badly damaged. At your direction,

Mein Führer, that one is still in a covered repair facility at Le Havre."

"*Ja, Ja*, go on," responded Hitler with a wave of his hand.

Also in Brest, we have 36 operable U-boats, 8 of which have been refitted with snorkels. There also are 2 damaged U-boats in repair"

Turning to a map of the North Sea, he went on.

"Our Battle Cruisers, *Scharnhort, Gneisenau* and *Prinz Eugen* and their escorts are safely hidden in the fjords of Norway. The pocket battleship *Scheer* is hidden in the Baltic. Although our capital ships are no match for the far superior Allied forces with their aircraft carriers, we believe just the threat of our ships coming out of port is to our advantage. It has forced the Allies to tie up several of their capital ships, including all of their aircraft carriers in the Scotch ports, thus reducing their forces that could otherwise support the invasion. Any questions?"

Before anyone could respond, Hitler said, "That will do *Admiral*."

Turning to Keitel, he asked, "Who will brief the army's status?"

"*Feldmarschall* Von Rundstedt, *Mein Führer*."

"*Gut*."

Stepping to the lectern, with his aide at the easel with the charts, Von Rundstedt began. "*Mein Führer*, at the present time, north of the Seine, where we expect the invasion to occur, we have the Fifteenth Army comprised of 19 infantry and artillery divisions and 6 armored divisions. These are joined by approximately 900 of our tanks and another 200 or so, captured French and Russian Tanks.

"South of the Seine, we have *Generaloberst* Dollman's Seventh Army made up of 13 infantry and artillery divisions. Only one is armored, the 21st *Panzer*, with 200 *Mark* V Panthers, our most powerful tank."

"Where are the other Panzers?" inquired Hitler.

"About 500 of them," interrupted Himmler, "are under the command of the SS and are equally dispersed along the North side of the Somme to repel an attack on Calais and along the south side to support the defense of Dieppe should it occur there."

"Is that their proper position, taking into account Rommel's opinion that Normandy is the target?"

"It may be prudent, *Mein Führer*," replied Von Rundstedt, coming around somewhat to Rommel's thinking, "to shift the Panzers south of the Somme to about here." He pointed to the north bank of the Seine, inland from Le Havre. "That would place them approximately halfway between the two invasion possibilities."

"And still too far away to be of much value to turn the tide on the first day," thought Rommel. He believed that the only way the invasion could be defeated was by not allowing the Allies to establish a beachhead to start with. Still it was much better than before.

Rommel could see that this was as far as his immediate superior was going to support his theory, so he said nothing as the other Senior Officers agreed. As he thought out how he would plan the invasion if in Eisenhower's position, Rommel blotted out Von Rundstedt's briefing on the mine fields, tank traps, and barbed wire entrapments, both on the beach and under the water at high tide, all of which he was very well aware of.

When Von Rundstedt had concluded, Hitler again cut off further discussion and turned to Goering. "Next."

With some effort Goering raised his bulk from his chair and walked to the podium. As he did so all of the Army officers couldn't help but wonder why Hitler put up with this imposter. Here was the man who once boosted that his Luftwaffe would prevent a single Allied bomb from ever falling on Germany. He had been quoted as declaring, "If an enemy bomber reaches the Ruhr, my name is not Hermann Goering: you can call me *Meier*!" Now there was not a day in which bombs were not falling somewhere on Germany. And then there was his miserable failure at Stalingrad, where he had convinced Hitler that even if the Red Army surrounded the German Sixth Army his Luftwaffe would be able to supply them by air. Barely thirty percent of the supplies required to support the army were actually delivered. Consequently, on January 31, 1943 *Feldmarschall* Friedrich Von Paulus had to surrender the 90,000 remaining men of his once proud 350,000 man strong sixth Army. It was the greatest defeat in German history, and it was all due to this incompetent man's boasting.

Most leaders present thought that deep down Goering was Hitler's hero. While he, Corporal Hitler, was groveling in the mud of France amid the squalor of rats and the death of the Great War, Goering was soaring high in the sky, one of the modern knights of the skies flying with the great air ace, Manfred Von Richthofen, in his renowned Flying Circus. When Richthofen was shot down and killed the day after his eightieth Allied kill, Goering was chosen to lead the Flying Circus and went on to claim twenty two kills himself before the war ended. Although the German Army had been defeated on the ground, the German Air Force had not been defeated in the air. This undefeatable attitude, personified by Goering and his Flying Circus, evidently remained with Hitler and encouraged him to restore the glory of Germany in the Third Reich.

Gripping the lectern with both of his massive hands, Goering began, much to the dismay of all present, with a history of the growth of the Luftwaffe and its past glories. Even Hitler was taken by surprise by his rambling.

Rommel leaned over to Rundstedt. "How many planes do you think he has?" he whispered.

"My sources tell me about 480 which includes about 100 first line fighters, and 60 reconnaissance planes."

"*Mein Gott!*" exclaimed Rommel, a little too loud causing several others to look his way. "The Allies are probably figuring on losing half that many in establishing a beachhead!"

Sensing he was losing his audience, Goering looked pleading at Hitler. Hitler also recognized the situation and said, "All right *Reichsmarschall*, it is time to reveal our success with the ME-262 program." Beaming, Goering came to life.

"*Herren*, as most of you are aware, for several years my friend, Willy Messerschmitt, has been working on a revolutionary type of aircraft. Instead of being powered by a reciprocating engine turning a propeller it is powered by a turbine type engine which is called jet propulsion. With this new engine our new ME-262, has a cruising speed of over 150 kilometers per hour faster than the top speed of any existing Allied aircraft. What's more, it doesn't burn precious high-octane gasoline but uses simple kerosene. I have personally taxied one down the runway, but since my reflexes are not what they used to be I did not actually attempt to fly it. However, I can assure you that when we hit the Allies with this new development we will sweep them from the skies."

Everyone present had heard of this project but very few actually knew its status. Goering liked to spring his little secrets every now and then.

"How many of these ME-262s do we have ready for action *Reichsmarschall?*" asked Rommel.

"As of this morning, 237."

"But," interjected Albert Speer, the Reich Arms Production Minister, "we are producing ten a day in each of our two plants."

"We also have 198 of our *Dammer* AR-234s," continued Goering, "which are also powered by jet propulsion. They are medium bombers almost as fast as the ME-262 but with twice the range. They are capable of carrying more bombs than our regular medium bombers.

Anticipating the question, Speer added, "By special order of the *Führer* we are producing ten of these a day. Although they are bombers they are more than capable of handling any existing enemy fighters in aerial combat."

"May we now have the room darkened please?" asked Goering, obviously annoyed by Speer's interruptions.

A screen had been set up at the end of the room.

"Some of you may wish to move your chairs so you can see better."

There was the scraping of chairs as everyone moved to a better viewing position.

The men sat enthralled watching some twenty minutes of movies showing both aircraft taxiing on the ground, and flying doing extraordinary maneuvers. Several scenes showed them rapidly accelerating away from ME-109 chase planes.

It was unlikely that these new aircraft would turn the tide, or so everyone else thought, and the Allies were bound to seek out the factories and place them as prime targets once they went into action. But still it was something.

"And that is just the beginning," interjected Hitler.

"Thank you *Reichsmarschall*. Now let me introduce you to someone that probably only a few of you have ever met. General Walter Dornberger of our *Vergeltungswaffe* Weapons Development Section, based mostly at our top secret facility, *Peenemünde*, on the Baltic Coast.

Everyone turned and nodded to acknowledge this visitor that many had heard about.

"General, tell them about our first two Vengeance weapons that we are about to unleash on the Allies."

"*Jawohl*, lights and film please."

The first scene was looking down a long rail where at the end several people could be seen working on what appeared to be a small aircraft. A side view now showed the small winged aircraft sitting on the rail and the workers walking away from it and taking positions behind a barrier. There was a flash and the small aircraft could be seen hurtling down the track and lifting into the air accompanied by a roar. In just moments the aircraft was only a dot in the sky. The next scene was taken from the window of a chase plane looking back out of the canopy at a dot that was growing larger by the moment. In a few minutes the same small winged aircraft could be seen passing the aircraft from which the picture was being taken.

"*Mein Herren*, these movies are being taken from a stripped down ME-109 flying at top speed. Notice how the small aircraft quickly pulls away from the chase plant."

"That small pilotless aircraft is our V-1. It is capable of carrying a 250 kilogram bomb at over 800 kilometers per minute. It has a range of approximately 200 kilometers, but can be programmed to dive onto its target at any range thereunder."

"With what accuracy?" someone asked out of the dark.

"That is a slight problem. While our cross range accuracy is less than 20 meters, the down range impact area may vary up to 150 meters." Anticipating the response, Dornberger quickly went on. "As you can see, this is not good enough for a specific target like a ship. But, can you imagine the devastation an attack of several hundred of these would have on a thin beachhead for example?"

"Very effective, I would think," responded Hitler, "and we now have almost fifteen hundred of these produced and waiting for use."

"But there is still more." prodded an excited Hitler. "Tell them about the V-2, General!"

Everyone turned and faced the screen again. They were now looking at the largest rocket they had ever seen. It was sitting on what Dornberger explained was a launch pad. Some wires were seen to be pulling away from the rocket at the same time it ignited. The film, being run in slow motion, showed the rocket slowly lifting off of the pad, and in a cloud of smoke disappearing into the sky. The next scene was taken from an aircraft flying high above the launch site and to one side. The rocket was seen rising toward the plane, then passing it continued to climb until it was out of sight.

"Now *Herren*, we shall see the same scenes in real time," explained Dornberger. This time, after ignition on the launch pad the rocket climbed out of sight so rapidly there were a number of loud comments from the startled group.

"This is our V-2 ballistic missile. It is forty six feet long and has a gross weight of four metric tons when fully loaded with fuel and warhead. It will reach a maximum speed of a little more than 6400 kilometers per hour and reach an altitude of about 100 kilometers. It can carry a 1000 kilogram bomb up to 325 kilometers. At the present time, we can program a target into the guidance apparatus and we will hit within in a quarter kilometer of the target. Our next generation guidance apparatus, which is now in development should cut this margin of error in half."

Anticipating the questions, Dornberger when on, "At the present time we have 2200 of the V-2s ready for launch and are producing twenty a day."

"Would it be possible to launch either of these weapons from a ship?" asked Admiral Doenitz.

"Yes, but knowing the precise location of the ship is very important. Otherwise, you could miss the intended target by that error in addition to the V-1 or V-2s own margin of error."

"I was just thinking that with either of these weapons aboard a ship we could carry the war to the American homeland."

There were a number of small conversations going on all at once as the officers discussed among themselves what they had just seen and heard.

Taking advantage of the confusion, Himmler leaned over to Hitler and quietly asked, "Are you going to tell them about the V-3? *Herr* Heisenberger assures me all is well and waiting."

"*Nein*, I think we best keep that a close secret for security reasons. But we will hold Doenitz over to inform him of our plan since the Navy will be involved."

"A wise decision, *Mein Führer.*" responded the ever accommodating Himmler.

"*Herren*, may I have your attention?" asked Hitler, pulling the meeting back together. "We have covered a number of issues in this meeting. I am convinced the invasion will occur as soon as this storm passes. The location is still an unknown, but, I can assure you, it will make little difference."

"Little difference?" thought Rommel.

"There is one very important thing I wish to tell everyone present," continued Hitler, "and this is, regardless of where the invasion takes places, twenty four hours after it starts, you will all receive word that I am about to make a special announcement. You will then have fifteen minutes to make and hold contact with all of your field commanders. I will then give you some special instructions which must be relayed to all units as quickly as possible. Is that clear?"

Everyone nodded in agreement.

"Thank you for all coming on such short notice. And, in light of what is about to happen on the beaches of France, I suggest that all of you get back to your commands as soon as possible. Since it is still storming, and the Allied fighters are probably still grounded, I have made arrangements to have several aircraft at your disposal at our local airfield for those of you who have a long way to travel and do not mind a bumpy ride."

"Thank you again and good luck. *Ach, ja*, Admiral, would you please join us for a few minutes in my office?"

With that, Hitler and Himmler, followed by Admiral Doentiz, rose and walked out of the room.

Turning to Von Rundstedt, Rommel asked, "Any ideas on

what the *Führer's* special announcement is about?"

"*Nein*. But perhaps he is going to propose some accommodation with the Americans and English, if, and *Gott* forbid, they actually establish a beachhead."

"If they land at Normandy, as I think they will, and the armored *Panzer* divisions are not quickly released to me, I am afraid there is a strong possibility that they will establish a beachhead. After which, it will be almost impossible to dislodge them."

"Don't underestimate the value of the new ME-262 fighters we have been informed of this morning," replied Von Rundstedt, trying to encourage his finest field commander.

"I hope you are right."

"Are you flying or driving back to France?"

"I think I will fly. In this weather if we stay low we should be able to avoid any enemy fighters that may be prowling around."

"I think you are right, Good luck. We are probably in for a rough seventy-two hours."

The two officers exchanged the universal military salute, rather than the more political correct Nazi salute, and walked to their respective Mercedes sedans.

0330, 6 JUNE 1944, NORMANDY

Three American battleships, the *Nevada,* the *Texas* and the *Arkansas* pulled in an east-west line parallel to the Normandy beach at a range of 10,000 yards and dropped anchor. To the west of the *Nevada* the U.S. Cruisers *Quincy* and *Tuscaloosa* took up their positions. Guarding their west flank was the British Cruiser HMS *Black Prince*. To the east of the Nevada were the US Cruisers *Hawkins* and *Enterprise,* and the Dutch Cruiser *Soimba*. Next came the Battleship *Texas*, while east of her were the British Cruisers HMS *Glascow* and *Montcalm* and the French Cruiser, *George Leyques*. The U.S. Battleship *Arkansas* was next in line, with the US Cruiser *Bayfield* which was the U.S. Command ship to its east. These ships would provide the heavy gunfire support for the American beachheads designated as Utah and Omaha. Farther to the East, supporting the British Sector, the three Royal Navy battleships, HMS *Nelson, Ramillies* and *Warspite* also pulled into their positions at a range of ten thousand yards directly out from the designated Gold, Juno and Sword Beaches. The U.S. Cruiser *Augusta* took up a position between the American and British Sectors, while another thirteen British, Canadian, and French cruisers filled in on the flanks and between the battleships. The British ships included in this group were the HMS *Ajax*, HMS *Rodney*, HMS *Nelson*, HMS *Arctlusa* and the British command ship HMS *Largs*. Slightly farther east was the French Cruiser *Montcalm*. From this most eastern position the *Montcalm* could not only support the landings on Sword Beach, but also engage any Germany land or sea forces that might come down from LaHavre or the Seine estuary.

At some 12,000 yards two Royal Navy Monitors, or heavy cruisers were held in positions from which they could quickly move to any position along the coast to provide additional fire support. They could also replace any of the battleships or cruisers that might be disabled during the action.

By 0400 thirty one USN, 37 Royal Navy and Royal Canadian Navy, 1 Dutch and 2 French destroyers had moved to within 5000 yards of the beach and were more or less equally spaced along the entire beach. All were almost dead in the water so as to be able to provide more accurate fire.

Hundreds of smaller vessels were ready to move in to the beach and support the actual landing crafts while providing a watch for German submarines that might try to attack the heavier ships.

In his bunker Major Werner Pluskat, a German battery commander, was almost halfway thru his watch. He had received several reports that enemy paratroops had been sighted but no actual fighting had occurred. Although it might have been a false report, everyone was jumpy after having received word that an attack was very likely to occur in the next seventy two hours. The fifth was now history and the eastern sky was beginning to lighten as the dawn of the sixth rapidly approached. Even if it was not a rumor, the paratroops would in all likelihood be a diversion. Pluskat listened as a low rumble indicated another formation of enemy aircraft was passing over in the darkness. It sounded like many more than usual. Since the bad weather had probably kept the enemy aircraft grounded the past thirty-six hours, they were likely coming out enmasse to make up for it.

Every few minutes Pluskat scanned the sea with his glasses. "Still too dark to see anything," he said to *Kapitän* Lludiz Wilkening and Leutnant Fritz Theen, the other officers that shared the bunker. The three officers made small talk for perhaps ten minutes and then Pluskat walked back to the small aperture in the bunker and looked out. The sky was lightening by the moment and the mist over the sea began to lift. Again raising his glasses, Pluskat began scanning the horizon from as far west as he could see through the small opening. As he reached the point directly out from his bunker Pluskat stopped scanning, and adjusted his glasses. There, right in front of him, a vast naval armada appeared through the mist. Quickly scanning the entire horizon he could now see what appeared to be thousands of ships, spread from as far west to as far east as he could see.

"This is the end!" he sadly exclaimed.

His two follow officers looked up.

"*Kommen und sehen*. It is the invasion."

As Wilkening and Theen looked on in disbelief, Pluskat picked up the phone and called the 352nd Division headquarters where Major Block was on duty.

"*Herr* Major, this is Pluskat, the invasion is here! There are thousands of ships right in front of me!"

"Thousands? That is impossible. Which way are they headed?"

"Right towards me."

Unknown to Pluskat, his bunker was situated right in the midpoint of Omaha Beach.

"I can see the flashes from their guns!" yelled Theen. In a few minutes the entire beach below the bunker erupted in countless explosions.

Pluskat looked at his watch; it was 0550.

At 0630 the first wave of what was to total two divisions of American troops came ashore at Utah and Omaha Beaches. The first wave of three divisions of British, Commonwealth, and French troops poured in at Gold, Juno, and Sword beaches.

In his armored trailer, which served as his sleeping quarters and office when in the field, Erwin Rommel was awakened by the distant rumblings at the same instant his aide knocked on the door.

"*Ja?* Come in."

"*Herr Feldmarschall*, the invasion has begun."

"Where?" asked Rommel as he pulled on his pants.

"The heaviest fighting seems to be along the Normandy beach."

"Just as I thought. Get me Von Rundstedt while I dress."

Always an early riser, Rommel looked at his watch, and thought, "What a day to oversleep."

In less than a minute the telephone rang and Rommel grabbed it. "Rommel here, *Feldmarschall*, what is happening?"

"There are reports of heavy enemy attacks from the Carentan Estuary on the west to the Orne River on the east, with scattered paratroop and glider landings throughout the coastal regions."

"Has the *Führer* been notified?"

"I don't know but we just placed a call through to the High Command."

"I am going forward to see the situation myself. I'll call you back in an hour."

"Good. And be careful Erwin."

"I will."

Rommel could hear the engine of the *Mark* V tank that pulled his command trailer running. Jumping out of the trailer Rommel climbed up into the turret of the tank and yelled down to the driver, "Head towards Ouistreham."

Throughout the day the Allied naval forces continued to pound the German positions. Some of the destroyers had pulled into the coast so close that they could direct their fire by watching where the ground troops were firing. This type of heavy gun fire was entirely new to the *Wehrmacht*. They had never been exposed to heavy naval firepower before.

As the day wore on, Rommel realized he was losing his chance of defeating the Allies on the beach. The *Panzer* armored divisions were too far away. Although Hitler and Himmler had released them at mid-day and they were moving toward the attack area, they would never arrive until after the Allies had established a firm beach head.

"If only they had listened to me," thought Rommel over and over.

All day long some of the most ferocious fighting of the war took place on the beaches of Normandy. As darkness settled over the lines, Rommel and his staff reviewed the reports from the various commanders. It appeared that the deepest penetration was by the British who had established a line some six kilometers from the coast. However, a Canadian armored patrol had reached a point on the Caen-Bayeux highway, 18 kilometers from the sea, but they were under heavy attack and had been forced to pull back.

"Where is Goering and his ME-262s?" thought Rommel. His field commanders had reported that only two planes of the Lufftwaffe had been seen over the entire front all day.

Ensign Leland Lewis was in the final hour of his four hour watch on board the HMS *Swift*, one of the Destroyers guarding the left flank of the British Sector. All through his watch, there had been a steady stream of landing craft moving onto the beach with new troops and returning a few minutes later loaded with wounded being evacuated to the hospital ships safely located behind the cruisers and battleships. Lewis and two other officers on the bridge provided lookout for any signs of threatening enemy activity. Three other officers on the aft deck provided the same coverage from that vantage point. Although the night had been uneventful aboard the *Swift*, now that it was getting light, Lewis felt more comfortable and secure. In front of him the two forward turrets with their five inch guns both fired almost at the same instant. Lewis swung his glasses to the shore in an attempt to view the target that was being pounded, but the mist rising from the sea made it impossible to see the coast in this area even though it was only two thousand yards away. He kept his glasses trained on the area he thought was the target, thinking he might be able to see the flash as the shells exploded. He saw a dim red glow quickly followed by a second one. But before he shifted his gaze, he saw a small boat slowly moving out of the mist.

Instinctively he stiffened as he recognized it to be a German E-Boat. These fast boats carried two forward facing torpedo tubes and two facing aft in addition to two turrets with twin twenty millimeter cannons. As he was about to sound the general alarm, he noticed the E-Boat signaling them with its semaphore. Decoding the message as it came in Lewis wrote it down. "Please hold fire. We have a captured E-Boat carrying wounded men. Radio out. Please give us heading to nearest hospital ship." Lewis quickly walked over to Captain Percil Shelley and handed him the message as he pointed to the boat. Shelley, Lewis and the two other observers studied the boat. "It certainly is an E-Boat, but it is flying the Union Jack," noted the Captain.

"And badly damaged too, I would say," responded Lewis. "Look, both port torpedo tubes have been blown away and the other two are pointing up at an abnormal angle."

"I would say that at least one of her gun turrets is also out of commission," added the second observer.

"What do you think, Captain?" inquired Lewis. "should we challenge them or give them a heading to the hospital ship?"

Shelley studied the boat for a few more seconds and then observed, "Well she certainly isn't a threat to anyone. She is riding so low in the water that even at her slow speed the waves are breaking across her bow. Go ahead and notify the signalman to give her directions."

As soon as the directions had been given, the E-Boat made a slight change in course. One which caused it to pass within two hundred yards of the bow of the *Swift*. As it slowly plowed past in the water, Lewis could see the helmsman who waved, while on the aft deck a nurse was seen working among the men, several of whom raised up on one elbow and waved. In five minutes the E-Boat was just a small speck.

The Battleship HMS *Rodney* had pulled in from 10,000 yards off the western end of the British beachhead designated as Gold to support the US battleship *Arkansas*, which was about to commence firing on a tank convoy moving up the road toward the town of Bayeux. It was hoped that the Germans not realizing they were within range of the newly positioned battleships could be caught in a massive surprise bombardment and that many of the tanks would be destroyed before they had time to disperse.

Aboard the HMS *Rodney*, Winston Churchill was cooling his heels. He had always planned to go ashore on the afternoon of the invasion, in spite of advice to the contrary from all of his staff. But yesterday, as he was about to depart for Portsmouth to begin his trip across the channel, he had received a phone call from the King himself.

"Mr. Prime Minister, what may I ask are your personal plans for observing the invasion?"

Thinking fast for fear the King had heard of his plan and was about to interfere by requesting him to reconsider, Churchill responded, "Well, ah, I was about to depart for Portsmouth and be ferried to the HMS *Rodney* where I will personally observe the situation and then make plans for going ashore."

"Splendid! Just splendid! I would like to join you."

"My Dear Majesty, you do realize there is some element of danger to this venture?"

"Of course and I promise not to go ashore until you assure me that it is reasonably safe. But keep in mind there has been a precedent of the King leading his troops into battle," joked the King.

"Without a doubt, but that was so long ago I can't even remember the battle, let alone the date."

"Thank you Winston, I'll see you aboard the *Rodney*."

That was some eighteen hours ago, and now the Prime Minister and his sovereign stood side-by-side watching the battle from the bridge of the HMS *Rodney*.

"I wonder who put the King up to this little trick?" thought Churchill. "Eisenhower is probably the only one that would dare approach the King on this matter, so that's who it must have been." But before he could get very upset, he stopped and thought, "I have to admit it was a brilliant maneuver on his part. No direct order from the King not to go and yet he knew I would never take the slightest chance with the King's life or even my own thanks to this little game. A very smart move on his part and one the King himself is probably enjoying immensely."

The King and Prime Minister watched as the two forward

turrets each with three, 16 inch guns swung towards their newly assigned target. The two leaders could see the US *Arizona* already in position about two miles to the west.

"Time to put in our ear plugs," advised Admiral Ramsey, the commander of the combined naval task force. "We are about to fire. As soon as we fire the Americans will do likewise. However, since we are farther from the target the American shells will get there first. The American spotter aircraft which detected the tanks will then be able to discern where we are hitting as compared to the Americans, and then he can direct each of us how to adjust our targeting."

The three men suddenly pitched forward as the great ship rolled back from the recoil of the nine guns firing in unison.

"Sorry I didn't warn you to hold on," apologized the Admiral.

"Exhilarating!" exclaimed Churchill, who suddenly felt back in his element. He had been First Lord of the Admiralty in both the First World War and in the opening days of this one. No one had ever held the post twice with such a large interval between.

As the guns fired again, hurling their two thousand pound shells almost twenty miles, Churchill turned to the King. "Your Majesty, if you watch carefully a little way out past the end of the barrels, you can sometimes see the shells actually moving through the sky."

Both men carefully watched the forward battery which again fired a salvo.

"Yes! yes! I see them." responded the King.

"You may be interested in this story which came in late yesterday afternoon," offered the Admiral. It seems one of our destroyers, the HMS *Swift*, on station at the eastern most end of the fleet, had been called upon to shell a very strong German fortification which was holding up the advance of some Canadian troops. The destroyer was very close to the shore, and began pouring in devastating five inch fire on the German position. Within minutes the spotter, Ensign Lewis, saw a white flag being waved out of one of the portals. Lewis called to cease firing, and the German troops began filing out of the bunkers. The *Swift* signaled by semaphore, "If you are surrendering, file down to the beach two abreast." The Germans complied and were taken captive by the Canadians on the beach, but these ground troops actually surrendered to our destroyer.

"A very interesting development indeed," noted the King.

As they had been listening to the story, Churchill noticed a small craft on a course that would cut across their bow. Suddenly, he recognized it and excitedly pointed. "Look! A German E-boat!"

"Oh," explained Captain Jones, "don't be alarmed, we have been advised of its presence. It seems it was captured near the beach earlier and is now being used to transfer some wounded back to a hospital ship."

"I sincerely hope it can make it," observed the King, "look how slowly it is moving through the waves. It looks like it could be swamped at any time."

As if in response to the very suggestion, the E-boat started signaling again in Morse Code. Proud that he could decipher the message, Churchill began mouthing the message as it was being sent. "Sinking...please...send...assistance...immediately."

Others on the *Rodney* had seen the message too, and there was an immediate response as several seaman began preparations to launch two of the ships long boats. Within two minutes the first boat was in the water with two medics aboard, along with the helmsman and an Ensign.

Major Kurt Kuntz was in the forward Panther tank leading the first fifty five tanks arriving from their northern position near the Seine River. It had been a wise decision to relocate half of the tanks from north of the Seine to the south. Otherwise, Major Kuntz wondered how he would have crossed the river since in the first half hour of the invasion all of the bridges in the immediate vicinity had been destroyed by Allied air attacks. They had refueled just before dawn. and were now only two miles from where they would fan out and move to take their positions along the front lines.

The Major heard a sudden whistling sound and instinctively looked up, thinking he was under attack from high flying enemy bombers. But the sky was clear, except for a small observation plane that was flying to the south of him, well out of range of their guns.

The first sixteen inch, 2000 pound shell from the *Arkansas* hit to the right and in front of Kuntz's tank, approximately one hundred meters away. The tank was rocked so violently Kuntz had to grab the side of the turret to steady himself. Within seconds the other 8 shells from the *Arkansas* exploded across the tank column at a very shallow angle. The last shell exploded in the field approximately 100 meters to the left of the middle tank in the column.

From its position the *Arkansas* had fired its broadside at the tank column almost head on. The guns were all on the same bearing but set at slightly different ranges. On the other hand, from its position, the HMS *Rodney* was firing almost perpendicular to the column. As a result the *Rodney's* guns were all targeted for the same range but at slightly different bearings so as to fan out the coverage.

Before the smoke had cleared enough to allow him to assess the damage to his column, Kuntz, to his horror, heard a second salvo coming in. The *Rodney's* attack was even more devastating than the *Arizona's*. All nine shells fell within fifty meters of the column, which due to the variations in the guns and powder loads, caused some to fall on the near side and some on the far side of the column. Two right on the road itself.

Never in his military career had Kuntz experienced such an intense attack. A veteran of the African Campaign under Rommel, Kuntz and been on the receiving end of 155 millimeter artillery attacks, and once had even experienced a bombing attack from an English Halifax bomber which had dropped a string of one hundred kilogram bombs on his position. But never had he experience anything like this.

"Damage assessment." he called down to his radio man.

As the dust and smoke cleared, Kuntz could see the attack had been devastating. Everything was over so quickly that none of the tanks had even had time to turn off the road. The remaining tanks were now doing so in anticipation of another attack. The reports were all in within a minute. Twelve tanks along with their crews destroyed, 13 badly damaged and 9 slightly damaged for a total of 34 out of his 50 total. The shells were now coming in again, but only in salvos of three, as each turret aboard the two battleships had been given the order to fire at will.

Frantically, Kuntz made contact with a mobile anti-aircraft battery. "*Mein Gott*! Get that observation plane before he redirects the fire to hit all of the tanks that can't move," he barked.

"It is coming through *Herr Feldmarschall*," the radioman called out. "It is the notification that the *Führer* will make an announcement in a few minutes. Shall I get all units on the line?"

"*Ja*, go ahead," responded Rommel."Those are our instructions, although for the life of me, I can't understand how a message could be so important as to tie up all of our communications at a time like this."

"Does anyone have any idea what he is going to say?" inquired one of Rommel's aides.

"I am not sure, but evidently even *Feldmarschall* Von Rundstedt is in the dark."

"Maybe he is going to propose a cease fire to the Allies," ventured another.

"From the beating we are taking, that would probably be a good idea," responded Rommel. Now, it was out in the open. Even the great Desert Fox thought the situation was hopeless.

Everyone was engaged in small talk until the radioman brought them back to the situation at hand. "All units on line, *Feldmarschall*."

"Thank you, Sergeant."

In another minute the favorite German march "*Alte Kameraden*" came over the open radio lines, followed by the announcement, "*Kameraden*, our glorious *Führer*." The men all stood at attention as if in the presence of Hitler himself.

"Attention, all officers and men of the *Wehrmacht* in and around Normandy," began Hitler. "In precisely five minutes, at 0550, all hostilities on our part are to cease, except in immediate life or death situations and all personnel are to hunker face down in their respective bunkers or foxholes with their backs to the coast until further notice. I am about to make an important announcement to the Allies. That is all."

Immediately, the march resumed.

"Turn it down but not off," ordered Rommel.

All the men in the bunker looked at Rommel as if for further directions.

"It would be presumptuous on my part to have to approve orders from the *Führer*."

"But," interjected General Herman Parduhn, "this is so extraordinary!"

As Rommel pondered the situation, the radio man spoke up, "Another message coming in over another line, *Feldmarschall*. It is from *Feldmarschall* Von Rundstedt."

"Turn it on the speaker so that we all can hear."

"Attention all units, this is *Feldmarschall* Von Rundstedt speaking. This is to confirm the instructions you have just heard from our *Führer*. It is not an Allied trick. I repeat it is not a trick. All units are to comply with the instructions given unless your life is in immediate danger. You are allowed to protect yourself if need be."

"That's it then." said Rommel.

"It sounds like a unilateral cease fire to try and entice the Allies to do likewise," someone volunteered.

Within a minute the sounds of nearby firing ceased. Only the distant firing of the Allies could be heard, followed by the explosions of the incoming rounds.

"I hope we don't have to wait too long under these conditions," General Parduhn ventured.

"I agree," responded Rommel.

Eisenhower had traveled from his office to Portsmouth, where he was greeting some of the wounded already being returned from the beaches. As he walked among the stretchers, he stopped and took the hands of the injured men. "Thank you for what you have done," he repeated over and over.

A Major walked up to him and quietly said, "I am sorry to interrupt you General, but there has been an important development."

Thinking the worst, Eisenhower led the Major to a corner where they could talk privately.

"General, we just overheard a radio message from Hitler himself over an open radio line. He has ordered all German forces, in France at least, to cease fire at 0550."

Eisenhower looked at his watch, "That's in just a few minutes."

"Yes sir."

Though perplexed by this change of events Eisenhower couldn't resist spreading the good news. Turning back to the wounded men who had all been looking in his direction he announced, "Men we have just received notice that Hitler has ordered his troops to cease firing." The room erupted into cheers and applause.

"I'd best leave and see what is happening." With that, Eisenhower and his aides walked out into the sunshine and stood looking across the channel towards Normandy. The sea was still full of ships coming and going.

"Get me the Prime Minister."

"Yes, sir; he is still aboard the *Rodney*."

Eisenhower smiled, his little trick had worked.

On board the *Rodney*, the radio operator also had picked up Hitler's orders to his army.

"Can you believe this?" he asked handing a copy to the courier, who glanced at the message and then offered, "I guess they have had enough." With that he dashed towards the bridge where the King and Prime Minister were still watching both the gunfire from their battleship and the long boats as they approached the disabled E-boat.

"Mr. Prime Minister," blurted out the courier, forgetting the proper protocol, "look at this message." Churchill frowned at the intruder, but grabbed the message from his hand. "I can't believe it," he responded as he handed the slip of paper to the King.

"Nor can I. It is almost too good to be true," agreed the King. "What do you think Admiral?"

Glancing at the brief message, Ramsey replied, "It is the best news we have had in almost five years, if it is really happening."

"I must get in touch with General Eisenhower immediately so we can reach a general agreement on how to handle this unexpected turn of events!" exclaimed Churchill.

As the Prime Minister turned to leave the bridge, he glanced once more at the E-boat. The others turned to follow his gaze.

"Strange, there is no one on the deck save the wounded."

The first longboat was pulling along side of the E-boat, when four men were seen emerging from the cabin. All were dressed in the officer dress uniform of the SS.

"What is this?" exclaimed Churchill.

The corpsmen aboard the longboat were all unarmed, but as the Ensign in charge of the longboat started to draw his side arm, the four SS Officers faced the *Rodney* and gave the Nazi salute.

It was the last image formed in Churchill's, or any of the other men's eyes. The E-boat vanished in a brilliant flash, far brighter than the sun itself.

In his command bunker behind a hill which overlooked the beach, Rommel and his staff saw the flash as it lit up the inside of the bunker through its small aperture ports.

"*Ach, mein Gott!*" exclaimed Rommel, and he turned and ran out of the bunker. Towards the sea, and behind a small hill, there was a brilliant ball of light that forced the men to shield their eyes. The small group broke into a run up the side of the hill, and dropping down, crawled to the top of the hill to cautiously peer over. The brilliant ball of light had now faded and the men watched in awe as a large peculiar shaped cloud began forming over the sea.

"It looks like a giant mushroom," ventured one of the staff officers.

"*Jawohl*," the others quickly responded.

"I wonder if this is related to the *Führer's* message to the Allies?" wondered Rommel thinking out loud. "*Schnell*, we must get back to the radio for further information and instructions."

General Theodore Roosevelt, Jr. had set up his command post in a captured German bunker on Pointe du Hoc, which was a triangular cape rising an almost vertical one hundred and seventeen feet above the beach. The cape had been taken the day before by two hundred U.S. Rangers who had scaled the cliffs in what was one of the most difficult assaults in the annals of military history.

Bending over the table spread with maps, Roosevelt suddenly stood straight up as the flash illuminated the bunker. Thinking one of the ammunition ships tied up at the floating docks had exploded, Roosevelt rushed out, only to be almost blinded by the fireball off the coast. Quickly turning his back to the flash he rubbed his eyes, which felt like they were full of sand. Gradually the flash subsided and Roosevelt again turned toward the sea.

"What happened General?" asked one of his aides.

"I have no idea! Have you ever seen such a sight and look at that cloud forming."

Suddenly Roosevelt was aware of an immense, rapidly expanding bubble in the air itself. The shock wave from the explosion was rapidly moving out from the center in all directions. In horror, Roosevelt watched as the bubble expanded toward some aircraft that were flying past it. As the bubble enveloped the planes they instantly burst into flames. Likewise did the ships which were in the path of the wave. Suddenly the group of men were almost blown off their feet as a violent wind whipped past them. Things were now happening so fast that it was difficult to keep up with everything taking place before their eyes. Aircraft further away from the cloud were not bursting into flames but were breaking apart in midair. Large and small ships engulfed by the blast were capsized and in some instances, snapped in two like a dry twig. As the noise of the blast rolled past the men they were forced to cover their ears with their hands, in hopes of protecting their ear drums from the sound.

Just as they thought the worst was over, one of Roosevelt's aides pointed to the sea. "Look what is coming!" Racing toward them at the speed of an express train was a wall of water over forty feet high. "It looks like it will roll right over us," wailed someone.

"Get hold of yourself," said another, "no tidal waves are ever that high."

"The men, the men on the beach!" exclaimed Roosevelt, as he looked down on the thousands of troops coming toward the beach in landing boats as well as those already on the beach. "We must warn them!"

But the men on the beach had seen the approaching danger themselves. Some were frantically trying to scale the cliff with their bare hands, while others were running up the beach past others running down the beach. Boat after boat was engulfed by the wave and disappeared. What looked like a destroyer could be seen rolling over and over along the crest of the wave. The men on the piers were running toward the shore, glancing over their shoulders at the approach of doom. With a terrific roar the wave hit the cliff below Roosevelt and his group, causing the point itself to tremble. As the water rolled back to its previous level, a deadly silence fell over the beachhead. Not a man, nor anything man made remained on the beach in either direction as far as could be seen. The only sound was the sobbing of a group of war hardened U.S. Officers.

In his command post, General Eisenhower was getting the opinion of his staff on how to respond to the surprise cease fire.

"I think it is a trick to stall for time and give themselves a chance to reinforce their position," stated General George Patton. Patton had recently completed his duty as a decoy and was preparing to go to Normandy and take over the U.S. Third Army now being formed on the beaches of England.

"Since there is no evidence that the same cease fire order went to the eastern front, it could be a plan to drive a wedge between us and the Russians," continued Patton.

At that moment the outside door was flung open and one of the Military Police guards broke in. "Come, look at this!" he yelled, pointing towards Normandy. Surprised at the rude interruption, the officers all looked toward the door which was illuminated by a brilliant sky. As the men stood looking to the southeast, a large mushroom shaped cloud could be seen rising from the sea. In another minute a distant explosion could be heard.

"My God," said Eisenhower, in a quiet, reverent manner. "They did it. They developed it before we did."

"Did what?

"Developed what?'

The questions were now coming thick and fast at Eisenhower.

"It was a top secret. Only a few of us were informed. But I guess it is not a secret any more after that," responded Eisenhower, pointing to the rapidly growing cloud. "Our top scientists have been trying for several years now to develop a weapon of enormous power. It is based on deriving that power through the changing of matter into energy. All of you remember from your college physics Albert Einstein's famous equation, $E=MC^2$? It is not a theory, but a reality if a way to accomplish it can be found. The Germans have undoubtedly solved the problem. General Bradley, get a call through to the President. In the meantime I'll call the Prime Min..," Ike stopped in mid sentence. "Churchill, he's out there!"

"Aboard HMS *Rodney*," offered General Peay, the British liaison officer, "and the King is with him."

"Oh! no!" exclaimed Eisenhower, holding his head, "and I am responsible for the King being there."

"No, you're not, sir, they are both where they each wanted to be. Remember, that this is one of the most glorious days in our history," offered General Peay.

"Or was supposed to have been," countered Eisenhower.

As the group walked back to the command post, Eisenhower turned again to General Peay. "General, in America, if our President dies while in office our Vice President automatically becomes the new president. My knowledge of your parliamentarian form of government is not detailed enough. Who will be your new Prime Minister, if...if Churchill, God forbid, is dead?"

"Well, the Tories still control Parliament and will quickly select a new head of their party. But in this situation, I think I would call the Foreign Secretary, Mr. Eden, Anthony Eden."

"Thank you. If you know how to contact Mr. Eden for me, would you please do so?"

"I do and I will," responded General Peay.

BERCHTESGADEN

Hitler was receiving a moment by moment assessment of what was happening off the coast of Normandy. Unbeknown to General Theodore Roosevelt and his staff, almost sixty feet under the captured German bunker in which they had set up their command post, SS *Oberst* Ludwick Melching was peering out of a small reinforced portal. With him were a radio operator and an aide fluent in English. At the start of this plan, slave laborers had dug and blasted out of the solid rock a four by eight meter cavern set five meters in from the face of the cliff. A one meter wide Z-shaped passageway led to the face of the cliff where the small portal was cut, and then covered with a six centimeter thick glass plate. Another Z-shaped passageway led to the surface and a well hidden entrance. Sufficient supplies were in the cavern to last the three men up to thirty days, if they were conservative.

With Hitler were Alfred Jodl, Wilhelm Keitel, Karl Doenitz, Herman Goering, Heinrich Himmler, and Walter Dornberger. From the time the E-Boat had left its hiding place, *Oberst* Melching had been giving the group a running narrative of what was happening, using a secure underground cable running back from the coast to a relay station.

Following the explosion, Melching at times was so overcome with the events unfolding before his eyes that he had to be prompted to relay back what he was seeing.

"Are you still there *Oberst*?"

"*Ach, jawohl*, sorry for the break there. A huge wave is now racing towards us. It looks like it could come up to our window."

There were some murmurs among the listeners.

"All of the enemy ships in its path are being capsized and swamped."

Hitler stood smiling and rubbing his hands together. "*Wunderbar! Wunderbar*! This is even better than we had hoped for. Right Walter?"

"*Jawohl, Mein Führer*. Our scientists had calculated that the explosion would be equivalent to at least twenty thousand kilotons of TNT, but since there has never been such an explosion before, other than volcanoes, we had no idea of what..."

Dornberger was interrupted as *Oberst* Melching came back, "The wave is now moving across the tidal flats...it is hitting the cliff below us! I am now looking out across the water which is just a few meters below the window. Now it is receding. *Mein Gott*! There is nothing left behind it. Everything has been carried away!"

"I wonder what Churchill and Eisenhower think of my little announcement?" asked a triumphant Hitler.

NORMANDY

Aboard the *Swift*, everyone saw the flash aft of the destroyer. Captain Shelley, not immediately realizing that the blast was very large and far away, thought another ship had exploded and that meant men would be in the sea. "Flank speed and hard port rudder," he automatically ordered.

As the engines began to come up to speed, Ensign Lewis ran to the side window of the bridge and attempted to look aft towards the bright flash which was even now beginning to diminish in intensity. Not being able to see to the rear he opened the door and stepped out onto the deck. The sky was rapidly changing colors and a large cloud was rising out of the sea. As the destroyer picked up speed the bow began slowly turning out to sea and toward the cloud. The port side deck was now crowded with sailors watching the strange formation with fascination. The ear shattering roar that followed caused the men to flinch and cover their ears. At the same time, the shock wave hit the men causing them to grip the rail to steady themselves. From its position, the *Swift* was one of the ships farthest from the blast. Yet the destroyer rocked as the shock wave hit almost broadside as it continued to turn.

Nearly everyone saw it at the same instant - a huge wave appearing out of the cloud and racing toward them. The destroyer continued to slowly turn toward the approaching wave. As the size of the wave became apparent, everyone realized that their only hope of not being capsized was to hit the wave head on. Those who did not have life jackets on instinctively began grabbing them off the hooks along the wall. Captain Shelley raced back onto the bridge where he quickly realized the helm was hard over, and although the engines were not yet up to full speed, they were winding up. It was going to be a close call. A deathly silence fell over the destroyer as the wave swept on toward them. The death wave was only two hundred yards away when the *Swift* completed its turn, and with the rudder returned to its neutral position the *Swift* started to pick up speed. As it did so, the bow started to rise just as the wave hit them. The bow heaved upward as the Swift attempted to climb the wave. As the vertical angle of the ship approached forty-five degrees, the men clung to anything at hand to prevent being thrown over the stern. A shudder of fear ran through the men as it appeared the ship would actually flip over backwards. On the bridge Captain Shelley braced himself with his back against the bulkhead, while the helmsman stretched out at a ridiculous angle, held onto the wheel. Suddenly the top of the swell was under the bow which now extended up out of the water. As the swell passed amidship, the bow came down and for a brief moment the *Swift* was essentially balanced on top of the swell, with both the bow and stern of the ship out of the water. Captain Shelley heard the engines immediately turn up to a high-pitched scream as the twin screws, now clear of the water, rotated in the air under no load.

"Ahead one quarter!" he yelled at the helmsman, hoping to reduce the speed of the engines before they tore themselves apart. The Swift now pitched sharply down the back side of the swell, hitting the level water at such an angle that the bow of the ship now plunged into the water, burying itself up to the forward gun turret and sweeping twelve men who were forward of the turret overboard. Then it was over. Captain Shelley said a silent prayer of thanks that he had responded so quickly in the turning of the *Swift*. If he had been indecisive for five seconds...he shuddered thinking of what would have happened.

What he failed to consider was the huge wave that would soon be surging back to fill the large depression in the water the blast had initially created.

"*Oberst* Melching?" inquired Himmler. "Are you still there?"

"*Ja*, I am still here. The prevailing wind has now moved the cloud to the south and the sight in that area is unbelievable."

"*Ja*? Go on."

"Across an area, of what I would estimate at that distance to be five kilometers, there is nothing, absolutely nothing, not a ship on the sea nor an aircraft in the sky. Another three kilometers farther out, all of the ships are on fire."

"Is there any gun fire from any of the remaining enemy ships, *Oberst*?"

"*Nein*."

Everyone turned and looked at Hitler. This had been such a

closed secret that very few outside of those in his presence knew about the plan. And since no one was sure it would even work, they had, incredibly, not been informed to make plans of what to do next.

Hitler answered the question on the minds of all those present, "We shall now wait and see what the Allies will do."

"Other reports coming in," responded Jodl, "indicate that all fighting in and around the invasion area has ceased, at least temporarily."

"*Gut, gut*," responded Hitler gleefully. "Keep the V-1s, V-2s and jets on alert."

"General, Mr. Eden is coming to the telephone now," said General Peay, handing the handset to Eisenhower.

"Eden here, General. Is what I hear really true?"

"I am afraid so Mr. Eden. Have you any word on the Prime Minister and the King?"

"One of our gun boats dashed into the cloud as soon as things had settled down a bit. They report that there was not one ship to be seen within a circle about three miles across."

"Good Lord! Are you aware of what it probably was, Mr. Eden?"

"Yes, I helped contact a number of our top scientists that we sent over to help your folks master the problem. We had our own program, under the code name of *Tube Alloys*, going on as well. But it was agreed that the work would progress more quickly if we combined our efforts."

"Good. I didn't know how many in your government were aware of the effort. But any secrecy is moot at this time, I suppose."

"Probably so. By the way General, I have placed a call to Washington and expect to hear from the President at any time now. We will patch it through to you on a conference call, now that we know where you are."

"Good. We are starting to get some reports in from Normandy. I'll take them while waiting."

"Good idea."

"General," said General Bradley, "we diverted some aircraft to scout the area and report their findings. It is all very bad. Two of battleships, the *Rodney* and *Texas* are–well just gone as are at least four of the cruisers and both of the monitors. Two more battleships and at least ten cruisers are apparently burning out of control. Of the 75 destroyers we had, there appears to be only 17, that are not on fire, capsized, or simply gone. On the other ships no one can be seen on the decks and all efforts to contact the ships have been futile. General Roosevelt reports that all of the smaller landing craft, as far as he can see, are gone or capsized and..and..," Bradley's voice trailed off.

"Yes General, go on," encouraged Ike, placing his hand on the shoulder of his close friend.

"The beaches have all been swept clean. The..the thousands of men on the beaches..all swept away." With that, General Bradley broke down and began sobbing, as did most of the others.

Eisenhower turned away and wiped his eyes as General Peay beckoned him to come to the phone.

"This is the President, Mr. Eden. What can I do for you? Good news from France I presume?"

"I am afraid not, Mr. President. I have General Eisenhower on the line with us. Perhaps it would be best if I let him apprise you of the situation. General, are you there?"

"Yes." answered Eisenhower. "I am here. Mr. President, I have the worst news our country has ever heard. Less than twenty minutes ago we suffered the most devastating calamity ever to befall an army in the annals of history. Mr. President, the Germans evidently exploded a nuclear device of some sort in the midst of our invasion force."

"Are you positive, General?"

"There can be no doubt Mr. President. The reports coming in all indicate that is what happened."

"*Mein Führer*, we simply must make plans for our next course of action," prodded Jodl. "We can wait for the Allies to respond in France, but what about the campaign in Italy?"

"And the entire Eastern Front," added Keitel.

"We will continue the struggle in Italy as it is for the time being," responded Hitler. "But as for the Eastern Front...Where is the second V-3, Heinrich?"

"East of Warsaw and ready to be moved into position at your order."

"And the third?"

"On U-168 which has rounded the horn of Africa. It is about to rendezvous with the *Atlantis*, one of our raiders in the Indian Ocean, to make the transfer."

"You see *Herren*," boasted Hitler, "I have not been asleep. Plans have been made." He winked at Himmler.

"The Russians love their massive attacks, and are about ready to make a push on into Poland and capture Warsaw. Zhukov has been boasting that he can take Warsaw in two weeks after he launches his massive attack. Well, when he does we will fall back and let them sweep past our little secret. And then no more Zhukov and his great Red army."

Much to the surprise of those in attendance, Hitler, who was a teetotaler, poured himself a glass of wine, and continued. "We know the Americans are also working on a nuclear device and probably will have one soon. It is one thing to use our V-3 to destroy their army attempting to take from us what is rightfully ours, but quite another to destroy one of their cities or one of their English comrades. For if we did, when they succeed in developing their own, they will no doubt respond in kind and we may be helpless to prevent them. No, we will let our Japanese Allies handle the surprise on the Americans. They are very good at that sort of thing, as we all know."

"What is the status of the fourth V-3, General Dornberger?" asked Himmler.

"We have been working on it day and night, and it should be ready by the fifteenth."

"Good, we can bluff them for that long. Of course if the Russians attack in the meantime, we will have no reason to bluff. Is that not correct *Herren*?"

"*Jawohl, Mein Führer*," confirmed Jodl, "quite correct."

LONDON/WASHINGTON

As Eisenhower and Eden finished briefing President Roosevelt on the disaster, the President asked, "Mr. Eden, is the reason you are on the line rather than the Prime Minister because he was at or near the front when this happened?"

"That, I am afraid, is the case. Both he and King George were aboard the *Rodney*, which was destroyed in the blast."

"Both leaders were lost at the same time? Excuse me for a moment."

Roosevelt turned to his advisors that were with him and explained the recent events at Normandy and added, "Please convene a meeting of the National Security Council as soon as possible."

Turning back to the telephone, Roosevelt regained some of his composure, and asked, "What is the current status of the invasion? You were saying that there has been an unofficial cease fire on the Normandy Front?"

"That is correct," responded Eisenhower. "Shortly before the blast, we picked up a message from Hitler ordering his military forces, in France at least, to cease firing until further orders. And that order evidently is still in force. Our own forces were so overwhelmed by the blast they just quit fighting. We are now being bombarded with questions from our field commanders as to what happened and what they are to do under the circumstances."

"I can understand their actions. Do we have any report from Italy?"

"Yes, we have contacted General Mark Clark's office. There evidently was no cease fire order given to the enemy there and action is still underway."

"I see. I must get in contact with our military and civilian leaders as soon as possible as well as General Groves out in New Mexico. Mr. Eden, may I suggest you do the same on your end. Let's have each group come up with several possible courses of action and get back together as soon as possible to compare ideas. Shall we say two hours from now?"

"I think that is a good idea, Mr. President," agreed Eden. "We will have General Eisenhower meet with us, of course."

"Fine. But in the meantime keep us informed on any new developments and any estimate you may receive on casualties."

"We will, Mr. President."

"Mr. President," asked Eisenhower, "what are you going to tell the Russians?"

"A good point, General. I better place a call to Stalin to apprise him of the situation and the possibility they may be on the receiving end in the immediate future too."

By the time the conversation ended, several members of the Joint Chiefs of Staff had arrived at the White House along with several cabinet members. They were quickly ushered into the Oval Office, where they waited for the President. Meanwhile, more of the invited officials arrived. Ten minutes later the President, now dressed, was wheeled into the room.

"Gentlemen, I know you are curious as to why you have been called here out of your beds. Time is of the essence, so rather than explain to you now, I'll simply ask you to listen in on a phone call that I am just now putting through to General Groves, who is in charge of the Manhattan Project." Quickly looking around the room the President added, " I believe all of you are aware of the Manhattan Project?"

Everyone nodded in the affirmative.

"Well," began the President, "less than an hour ago I received a phone call from General Eisenhower and Anthony Eden..oh excuse me, I see my phone flashing. My call to General Groves must be coming through now. Hello, General Groves? Not very well, I am afraid General, I am not very well at all."

As the President explained what had just happened, everyone sat horrified at what they were hearing.

"No, General Groves, we are not sure how the weapon was delivered. But it was probably not by aircraft, as I understand there was no enemy air attacks on our fleet whatsoever. I guess it is possible that it was previously planted in position or a miniature submarine suicide attack."

"Yes, I agree if it was delivered by an aircraft, it would have even further serious implications."

"Tell me General, how close are you to having your device ready?"

"Mr. President, while we have been talking, Dr. Oppenheimer just walked in. Perhaps I better let him answer that question," replied the General Groves.

"Mr. President, I walked in just in time to get part of the story. You said the Germans actually exploded a nuclear device over the Normandy beachhead?" asked J. Robert Oppenheimer, the chief scientist of the Manhattan Project. "We had no idea they were even close to mastering the problem."

"Well, Doctor, we don't know if they exploded it over, in or under the fleet. But it was evidently off shore a couple of miles in the midst of our invasion fleet."

"I see. But to get back to your question of how close we are to mastering the problem, I wish I could give you a definite answer. However, it is very difficult to estimate how long it will take to do something that you have never done before. However, after several false starts I am sure we are now on the right track of how to hold what we call the critical mass together long enough for the chain reaction to commence. If our new method proves out I think we could have a device in six months."

"Six months!" exclaimed the President.

"I am afraid so, and that would only be what you noticed I referred to as a device. Our goal is to be able to build this weapon into a bomb which can be dropped from a B-29 bomber. Our first device will be much too large I'm afraid, for a B-29 to carry. To get it down to bomb size will probably take another three to six months."

"Doctor, in six months we could be reduced to ashes."

"That is why it is important to find out how the Germans delivered the bomb into the middle of the fleet. If it was in a bomb or even a torpedo from a mini-sub, that would be very bad news indeed. But, if it was a mine previously placed on the floor of the channel. It was probably a crude device, like our first one will be, and they probably can't produce them very fast."

"What is very fast?" asked the President.

"Well, I would think one a month would strain their resources."

"One a month would still give them a chance to explode six of them before we are ready," observed General Marshall.

Hearing the comment, Oppenheimer went on, "That is correct, but with just six devices they could wreak havoc on the European mainland and even England. But fortunately, with what I know of our defenses we should be safe until we are ready. May I make a recommendation, Mr. President, that I believe we should follow through with as soon as possible?"

"Of course, go ahead," responded Roosevelt.

"The key ingredient to a nuclear weapon is Uranium 235, an isotope which is very rare in nature. The Germans, like us, are probably separating it from Uranium 238 which is far more plentiful. The most likely sources of their U-238 are from mines in Czechoslovakia. Now, to get enough U-235 to build a nuclear weapon you must obtain a very large amount of pitchblende ore, refine it, and then separate the types of Uranium. This requires, as some of you know, a large facility. And since I assume we are bombing their railways very heavily, they must have these processing plants near the mines themselves. Find the mines and facilities, and bomb the hell out of them."

"A good point, Doctor."

"Any other targets that we should be concentrating on Doctor?" inquired Air Force General Hap Arnold.

"Well, the location of the facility in which the devices are actually being built is probably impossible to determine from the air. But in the processing of the U-235 it takes what we refer to as 'Heavy Water.'"

"Heavy water?"

"Yes, D_2O, deuterium oxide, actually. Ordinary water is H_2O, two atoms of hydrogen combined with one atom of oxygen. But one molecule in about every 5000 molecules of water is D_2O, two atoms of deuterium combined with one atom of oxygen. Deuterium is a heavy isotope of hydrogen weighing about twice as much as ordinary hydrogen. We are using it as a moderator to control the energy of the neutrons in a chain reaction."

"We know," said General Marshall, "from the British that the Germans are extracting this heavy water from sea water at a fairly large facility near the Norsk hydro electric plant, which is up a deep and narrow fjord on the west coast of Norway. In fact they've made several attempts to disable the plant, but unfortunately, were unsuccessful each time."

"That is a place that also must be destroyed," responded Oppenheimer.

"Thank you gentlemen," said Roosevelt. "Keep pushing out

there, and we will keep you informed of any new developments."

"Very good, Mr. President," responded Groves and Oppenheimer simultaneously.

Turning back to the men who now almost filled the Oval Office, Roosevelt said," Before we go on gentlemen I had better inform 'Uncle Joe' in Moscow of what has happened."

"I took the liberty of initiating the call, Mr. President," offered special assistant Harry Hopkins.

"Thank you, Harry. Now while we are waiting, have any of you had time to consider what our course of action should now be?"

"Mr. President," offered General Arnold, "we have had some reports of large plants near some mines in Czechoslovakia but they were thought to be coal mines and so were not a priority target. I'll order immediate strikes on these facilities from the Fifteenth Air Force in Italy. In fact we ought to be able to give them a double whammy. After six months of negotiations, we finally have consent from the Russians to let our bombers land at several of their forward airfields to refuel and reload, rather than flying back empty to their home bases which are twice as far away from some deep targets."

"You have been trying for six months to get the Russians to let us use their bases?" asked the President. "Why wasn't I informed?"

"Well the truth is, Mr. President we thought we had everything worked out several times and at the last minute, when we informed the Russians when we would be coming, they always had an excuse for why it couldn't be at that time."

"Damn!" responded the President hitting his fist on the table. "Sometimes I wonder whose side they're on."

"Mr. President, the call is going through now," said Hopkins, handing the phone to the Russian interpreter who was standing by.

After a brief exchange the interpreter looked at the President. "It seems the Premier is indisposed at the moment. But they are attempting to locate the Foreign Secretary, Molotov."

"Indisposed!" said the President growing more upset by the minute. "I don't think Stalin has ever answered one of my calls personally. Trying to control himself he said, "I should be more like Winston. He was the most vocal opponent of Communism in all of England before the war. However, after becoming Prime Minister and following the Nazi invasion of Russia, Churchill informed Parliament that he was immediately initiating supplying the Russians with whatever supplies Britain could spare. When one of the opposition members asked him how he could do that after all he had previously said about the evils of Communism, Churchill stood up and said, 'Gentleman, if Hitler invaded hell, I would feel obligated to stand before Parliament and say a few words in behalf of the devil, himself.' "

The laughter that followed was interrupted by the interpreter. "Mr. President, Mr. Molotov is coming on the line."

Looking quickly around the room, Roosevelt said, "I am going to tell him exactly what we know so far, any objections?"

There were none.

"Mr. Foreign minister, this is President Roosevelt. I am calling you to inform the Soviet Union of what has happened during our invasion of France." With that, Roosevelt proceeded to tell Molotov what had happened. At the end he added, "Mr. Secretary we can only warn you to be careful and not present any choice targets, like we did, that could entice the Nazis to expend one of the atomic weapons on you. No, like I said we don't know at this time how it was delivered. But the general consensus is that it was probably planted before hand."

"Thank you Mr. President, I will see that the Premier gets the message as soon as possible." And with that, Molotov ended the conversation.

As he set down the receiver, Stalin asked, "Well, what did our 'Little Allies' want now?"

"Comrade Stalin, it was both good news and bad news for us."

"Oh, in what way?"

"This morning the Fascists detonated a nuclear weapon in the middle of the Anglo-American invasion fleet off the coast of France. The losses, although not yet completely compiled, were evidently enormous. Shortly before the explosion, as we know, Hitler ordered his forces to cease fighting. Because of the shock of the atomic explosion the Anglo-American forces also quit fighting. So at the present time, there is a mutual cease fire which the President assured me is temporary on their part, until they can better assess the situation."

Stalin half smiled. "I see why you said you had both good news and bad news. Maybe you should have asked Roosevelt how soon his atomic weapon will be ready."

"I was tempted, but decided it best not to let the Americans know we are aware of their little project - what is it called - Manhattan, I believe. Anyway, it will be interesting to see if and when they inform us on their own."

"Quite right," mused Stalin. "This turn of events in France could work to our advantage. The invasion forces are still engaging several Fascist armies that would otherwise be facing us. The setback to the invasion will mean the Anglo-American forces will not penetrate as far east as they otherwise would and we will be able to advance farther west until we meet them. Also, it is about time they learned a thing or two about huge losses like we have suffered so far."

Molotov nodded his head. "I agree wholeheartedly, but what shall we tell our field commanders? Marshall Voroshilov has informed us that Marshall Zhukov has his forces all ready for the spring offensive as soon as the fields dry out a little more. Field Marshall Model has been probing our lines for several days in order to keep us off balance, but to no avail."

Stalin thought for a few minutes and then responded, "We won't say anything about this to our military leaders. We have momentum and I don't want anything to adversely affect our men's morale. So the Fascists have a big bomb."

"Not a bomb. A large device, capable of causing a very large explosion," interrupted Molotov.

"So much the better. Large explosive devices that are difficult to move into position. And how much more powerful can it be than our 1000 kilogram blockbusters? Ten times, a hundred times? Suppose they do manage to detonate several of these devices along our entire front. So it kills fifty thousand or even one hundred thousand troops. What is that compared to the ten or more million we have already lost. It will just further infuriate our fighting men to press their attack even more furiously."

"Still, would it not be prudent to at least get an estimate from our own scientists on just how large an area such a blast could affect?" inquired Molotov.

Totally underestimating what the magnitude of an atomic explosion could possibly be, Stalin ended the conversation with a wave of his hand and walked out of the room.

The President and his advisors had been discussing the situation, but decided until they had further information from Normandy it would be difficult to make any firm plans. They placed a call back to the residence of Mr. Eden who also had his office full of advisors.

"Mr. Secretary," began the President, "I have been in contact with our scientific community working on the Manhattan Project and have been given some disappointing news, I'm afraid. It is their opinion that we will not have an atomic device for at least six months."

"That is disappointing and may I add, alarming, Mr. President."

"Yes it is. We have been unable to reach any ideas on this side until we have additional information on the extent of our losses. Any more news on that?"

"Yes, I'll let General Eisenhower advise you of what we know so far. General?"

"Mr. President, this is the most difficult report I, or perhaps any military leader in history, has had to give his commander-in-chief," said Eisenhower.

"Go ahead General. Dr. Oppenheimer has informed us of the probable magnitude of the explosion. But the numbers are really beyond our comprehension."

"OK, here are the numbers. The battleships *Rodney, Texas, Arkansas, Nelson* and *Ramillies* all utterly destroyed, with approximately 1500 officers and men aboard each one. The cruisers *Glasgow, George Leyques Montcalm, Augusta,* and *Ajax,* and *Largs,* the British Command ship, all destroyed with approximately 1000 officers and men on each. The cruisers *Bayfield,* our command ship and the *Enterprise* were capsized with few survivors found so far. At least 23 destroyers caught between the blast and the coast were also capsized or broken in two."

"My God!"

"And even worse. There were at least five troop ships fully loaded that were capsized. Since their men carried full packs, most were probably drowned. The beaches which were full of men were swept clean. The total estimated number killed stands at least 50,000 with an additional 20,000 wounded, mostly from very serious burns," concluded Eisenhower.

"Mr. President, I must inform you that all of the hospitals in Great Britain cannot possibly treat this number of burn victims," added Eden.

"What about the men on the shore, beyond the beaches?" inquired the President.

"Fortunately there were a limited number of deaths, but many cases of blindness among those who happened to be looking out to sea at the instant of explosion. That probably explains why Hitler ordered his troops to cease fire and take cover just before the blast. They would have all been facing the sea, of course, while our backs were towards it."

"Yes, you are probably correct."

"Mr. President," went on Eisenhower, " we have discussed the existing cease fire and it is our opinion that in light of the fact that all of our supplies that were stock piled on the beach are gone, we should maintain the cease fire, if possible. At the rate we were expending ammunition before the blast our troops will be out of ammunition in less than four hours if new supplies don't reach them. In addition, they will be out of rations within seventy two hours."

Roosevelt placed his left hand to the side of his head and said, "I have a terrible headache," and with that, the phone fell from his hand. Grasping his head with both hands he collapsed forward, his face striking the table. His physician, Surgeon General Ross McIntyre was immediately at his side. After checking the President's vital signs, he looked up. "Gentlemen, I believe the President has had a cerebral hemorrhage, but is still alive. Someone call an ambulance. I think it would also be wise to notify the Vice President."

Eisenhower heard the phone drop and the confusion that followed over the phone. Turning to the others in the room he quietly said, "I am afraid something has now happened to the President."

"General Eisenhower? This is Secretary Stimson. It appears that the President has just had a stroke."

"Good Lord!"

"He is unconscious, but still alive according to Dr. Gordon, who was here with us. General Marshall was on the extension phone as you talked to the President, so we do have your report. He is briefing the others now. Please stand by."

"Of course, sir."

After a few minutes, Stimson came back on the line. "General, in spite of the President's condition, it is the consensus here that we are still facing essentially a military situation in Normandy and not a political one as we have not heard anything from the other side. We, therefore, are asking you to lay out your plans and let us know what they are as soon as possible."

"I think that is the correct assessment of the situation too. We'll be back with you shortly," he explained.

Turning back to the group, Eisenhower relayed what had happened to the President and that the military decision was back in their own hands.

"General," ventured Eden, "you asked me how we will handle the death of our Prime Minister. Now may I ask you how the United States handles a situation where the President, though alive, is totally incapable of running the affairs of State?"

"I can answer that," interrupted pale Joseph Kennedy, the U.S. Ambassador to England, who had arrived during Eisenhower's report to the group. "We, unfortunately, are not as prepared as you are Mr. Eden for this type of eventuality. The last time this happened was during the final few months of Woodrow Wilson's administration when he was almost totally disabled. Essentially his wife ended up running the country. We have no laws or regulations to handle such a situation. For that reason, the health of our President should always be taken into consideration before he runs for the office."

The Americans present all knew what the Ambassador was referring to. He had wanted to be President for years and thought he stood a good chance of winning the Democratic nomination in

1940 at the end of Roosevelt's second term. But when Roosevelt chose to run for an unprecedented third time, Kennedy lost the chance. Then again in 1944, when the health of the President was obviously failing, Kennedy thought Roosevelt ought to step aside and let him be the nominee. But, Roosevelt had thwarted his chance a second time, and ran successfully for a fourth term. Still, even in this time of crisis, the ambassador had to vent his frustration.

"I see," replied Eden, "an obviously awkward situation facing you chaps. But now what do you propose to do General? I agree, this is a military decision."

After several hours, a course of action was developed. Since the advantage clearly laid with the Germans for the time being, the Allies would take advantage of the unofficial cease fire and replenish their supplies on the beaches of Normandy. But they would do so using only one or two ships at a time so as not to present a tempting target for another atomic attack. The remaining ships would also be dispersed for the same reason. The opinion was that the Germans probably had only a limited number of such weapons and would have to use them sparingly. The bombing attacks out of England would be placed on hold, but the struggle for Italy would continue although at a reduced level. The bombing raids out of Italy into the Balkans would continue. When the supplies in Normandy were again sufficient to support the one hundred and fifty thousand man force already ashore, the attack would be resumed, but with care so as not to present a worthwhile target for an atomic attack. This was passed back to Washington, where it was approved and forwarded to Moscow to reassure the Russians they were not being left alone in the struggle.

FOGGIA, ITALY

Staff Sergeant, Wayne Cooper, set in the side seat near his position as right waist gunner in *Big Stuff*, a Boeing B-17 bomber, waiting for the go ahead to take off. Across from him sat the left waist gunner, Kent Peterson, reading a book as usual. Looking across out Kent's gun port, Wayne could see the line up of the other bombers of the Fifteenth Air Force, pulling into their respective positions for takeoff.

This would be Cooper's thirty-fifth mission since arriving in Italy. The German airfield at Foggia on the East coast of Italy had been captured by the British the previous month and in three weeks had been made serviceable. The crew of *Big Stuff* had been assembled at Biggs Field in Northern Arizona. Two days later a flight of twelve new B-17s had been flown to Biggs Field straight from the Boeing assembly line in Seattle. They were now in the hands of the ten man crews assigned to heavy bombers. The first thing each crew did was to give their plane a name. *Big Stuff* was the name they selected for Cooper's plane. With a length of 67 feet, a wing span of 103 feet, a height of sixteen and a half feet and capable of carrying four tons of bombs seventeen hundred miles, the bomber was truly "big stuff."

The group of bombers left Biggs Field and flew to Florida where they refueled. They flew across the Gulf of Mexico to Venezuela and then to the east coast of Brazil. From there they flew across the South Atlantic to Africa and then on north to Libya and finally across the Mediterranean to Foggia. They soon became part of the newly-formed Fifteenth Air Force under the command of General Nathan Twining. The flight had been so long that the pilot and co-pilot were both agreeable to letting Cooper fly the plane at times after finding out he had been originally trained as a pilot.

Now on their thirty-fifth mission, the original crew was still together, although *Big Stuff* had suffered several minor damages to both anti-aircraft and fighter gun fire.

This morning *Big Stuff* was assigned to fly to the right of the lead aircraft in the very front of the fifty bomber squadron. "A dangerous position to be in," thought Cooper. But on this mission they were going to do something different. Instead of bombing the Ploesti oil fields and refineries and returning home, they would continue on east and land at a Russian airfield just east of the Romanian/Russian border, near Odessa. After an overnight stay, their bombers would be refueled and reloaded. On the way back home they would bomb some strong German and Romanian positions that were holding up the Russian advance across the Dniester River. In effect this would be two missions for the price of one. They were all looking to the fiftieth mission after which they would be sent home for a furlough. Of course, it was considered unlucky to keep score after the fortieth mission, as too many who did didn't make it to the big fifty.

Cooper could now see the lead bomber beginning to move down the runway next to theirs. Then the four twelve hundred horse power Wright Cyclone engines on *Big Stuff* began to wind up and they were moving down the runway. Shortly after take off, the squadron banked to the right and were soon over the crystal blue waters of the Adriatic Sea.

Cooper unbuckled himself from his seat and looked out of his gun port back toward the airfield. A long double line of bombers could be seen climbing up from the end of the runway. *Big Stuff's* pilot had throttled back the engines to allow the last ones off to catch up and form up into a close formation from which they could better protect each other from enemy fighters. Cooper shifted his gaze to another airfield a little farther north and saw what he was looking for. A squadron of twenty-five Lockheed Lightning P-38 fighters had also taken off to escort them. "Our little friends are joining us," he informed Peterson, who set his book aside and took his position at his station in anticipation of the pilot's orders to man their stations. Enemy aircraft could be expected as they approached the Yugoslavia coast which was now less than thirty minutes away.

By mid-morning of June seventh, in London and early morning in Washington, extras hit the news stands of both cities. News of the Normandy disaster and the death of Churchill and the King spread rapidly. The government, however, was successful in keeping the news of Roosevelt's stroke out of the papers.

Thousands of citizens in England had seen the flash of the blast, and within an hour, ships of all sizes were headed out to sea to rescue survivors. Soon they were pulling into port with thousands of wounded and burned troops aboard. As Eden had warned, the hospitals were quickly filling up and it became necessary to ship the less seriously burned victims to hospitals as far away as Scotland. Even Ireland, that was technically neutral, but highly pro-German, agreed to take some of the injured. The magnitude of the problems soon reached every corner of the

British Isles and the prewar pacifists began to take to the streets demanding an end to the fighting.

German agents in England were quick to report to Berlin what was happening in the streets.

BERLIN

Even before he had consolidated his power in Germany, Hitler had a strong admiration for the English and their management of the largest Empire in the history of the world. It was a fact that the sun never set on the English Empire. England controlled most of the choke points on the seas through their colonies at Gibraltar, the Suez Canal, South Africa, and Singapore. Even Cape Horn at the end of South America could be monitored from the Falkland Islands. Australia, New Zealand, Hong Kong, Burma, India, and Canada were so loyal to their motherland that they raised tens of thousands of troops to come to the aid of England in both World Wars. Hitler secretly admired the English ability to rule their Empire in such a manner that the ruled would always freely help their rulers. Hitler had a strong desire to form an alliance with England. He wanted each country to carve out their respective spheres of influence. Even after the English declared war on Germany, following the latter's invasion of Poland in 1939, Hitler tried to entice the British to join him and divide up Europe and Africa. In June of 1940, following the collapse of France, Hitler allowed the British to evacuate their forces from Dunkirk, when he could have annihilated them, hoping his benevolence would be recognized. But to Hitler's dismay, Churchill had managed to transform the defeat into a victory in the eyes of most Englishmen.

As Hitler contemplated his next move, his thoughts went back to May of 1941 when he had allowed his deputy, Rudolf Hess, to fly a secret mission to Scotland. Hess was to contact certain members of both the Houses of Lords and Commons who were against the war and who foresaw the possible end of the British Empire itself. Part of Rudolf Hess' mission to Scotland in April of 1941, had not only been an attempt to gather support from influential British politicians to force the government to seek a separate peace treaty with Germany, but also to advise these dissidents that the Germans had been in contact with the Duke of Windsor. The Duke had abdicated the throne in 1936 to enter an unacceptable marriage with the woman he loved. The Duke was now living with his Duchess in the Lisbon mansion of Ricardo de Espirito Santo Silva, one of Portugal's leading bankers.

In a secret meeting with the German Foreign Minister, Joachim von Ribbentrop, the Duke had stated that he was willing to accept a "high office" in Britain if an armistice could be reached. It was well known that the Duke was opposed to the war, describing the war "as a crime and the British hope for a revolution in Germany against Hitler as childish." The Duke's unconcealed loathing of Churchill's policies which he felt kept the war going was also well known. Unfortunately Hess had bungled his mission. But this time Hitler controlled the events personally. This time Hitler knew he was about to succeed in his lifetime ambition. With both Churchill and the King out of the way, Hitler saw his chance to reach an armistice with England and reinstate the sympathetic Duke of Windsor as King. He had all the bases covered, as the Americans would say.

WITH THE FIFTEENTH AIR FORCE

The bombers of the Fifteenth Air Force had cleared the coast of Yugoslavia and the B-17s each loaded with six thousand pounds of bombs were steadily moving in an almost easterly direction towards Ploesti. Their cruising speed was 315 miles per hour. So far there had been only light anti-aircraft fire, here and there, and no enemy fighters. Perhaps, Cooper hoped, the fighters of the German Luftwaffe One Unit, that were stationed to protect the oil fields, had been transferred to eastern Romania to help stop the Russian advance. This would leave only the Romanian fighters to contend with. Knowing that the defeat of their country was only a matter of time now, perhaps the Romanian pilots would not be eager to risk their lives attacking this formation, especially with its fighter support. Leaning over and looking up, Wayne could see several of the P-38s ready to pounce on any fighter coming at the bombers. It was a reassuring feeling.

As the bombers crossed into Romania, Major Anderson, the squadron leader, received a message from their base in Foggia. "On return trip after refueling in Russian occupied territory, you are not to return by way Ploesti for second raid as planned. Return by way of Southern Czechoslovakia to attack coal processing plants near Kosice and Nitra. Exact coordinates will be sent upon your arrival at Russian Base near Odessa."

"Major Anderson to navigator."

"Yes, Sir."

"There has been a change in our return trip. Please prepare a flight plan from Odessa to targets near Kosice and Nitra in Eastern Czechoslovakia."

"Yes Sir, ah, Major, since I see the two targets are about 160 miles apart, but in more or less a straight line on our way home, should I plot one run for the entire Squadron or plot two and divide the Squadron?"

"For our own protection, let's keep the squadron together and plan on each of us dropping half of our bombs on each target."

"Very good sir."

An hour later, the announcement came over the headset. "Prepare for bombing run."

The nose gunner in *Big Stuff* was the first to spot them. "Bogeys at one o'clock, low."

The twelve *Messerschmitt* ME-110s twin engine fighter-bombers were coming up and straight on at the three leading bombers. The low approach was an attempt to avoid the Lightnings which were flying high above the bomber formation. From his position, Sergeant Cooper could not see the enemy fighters, but saw the tracers passing by his side of the aircraft. "Coming your way, Coop!" yelled the co-pilot. Two of the ME-110s broke, and passed by the side of *Big Stuff*. As Cooper swung his fifty caliber Browning machine gun, he raked the side of the fighter and saw pieces flying off, as seven shells per second slammed into its tail section. Cooper noticed the Romanian insignia on the side of the aircraft and breathed a sigh of relief. Unlike their German Allies, the Romanians were usually only good for one or two passes. That would, hopefully, be the last they would see of them.

Cooper felt *Big Stuff* lurch ahead and upward as its 6000

pound bomb load fell away at the rate of one ton a second. Immediately afterwards there was a slight change in course as the squadron headed toward the eastern Romanian border, toward the Red Air Force base near Odessa. The flight was uneventful on the way but all gunners remained at their posts, scanning the sky for any signs of enemy fighters. The pilot came on the intercom. "Keep a sharp lookout men, our fighter escorts are pulling ahead of us so they can land first, as their fuel supply is getting low. Now the enemy has his chance while we are alone."

As expected the Romanian fighters did not reappear.

"Tighten up the formation," came the order from the squadron commander.

Fifty minutes later came the order, "Initiate descent for landing."

Ordinarily, the landing sequence was "first off, first down." However, three bombers had suffered some minor damage during the Romanian attack and were allowed to land first.

Big Stuff's wheels let out a screech as they hit the runway. The plane rolled to the end of the runway before being directed to a parking place. As they rolled by the P-38s, Cooper could see the pilots in groups surrounded by Russian ground crews. *Big Stuff* rolled to a stop, and the crew began to deplane. It was good to stretch and feel the solid ground under his feet again, thought Cooper. An English speaking Russian Officer greeted them and said that trucks were on the way to take them to their quarters and dinner. As a ten wheel Ford truck, part of the U. S. lend lease program to Russia, pulled up in front of the plane next to them, Cooper studied the face of the driver as the crew climbed in the back. "This is crazy, but I think I know the driver of the truck," he said to his gunner buddy, Peterson.

As the truck stopped, the driver's door flew open and out jumped a very familiar man. "Stu!" yelled Cooper as the two men rushed into each others arms. "I was afraid you had been killed when I heard you were missing in action!"

"Climb in the cab with me and I'll tell you all about it."

Cooper looked at his pilot who smiled and nodded his approval.

While Stewart picked up several more crews and then headed

for the barracks, he related how, on a mission out of England almost six months ago, they had been bombing German supply lines in western Poland when his B-17 had received a direct anti-aircraft hit on the tip of the right wing causing the wing to break off near the outboard engine. They jettisoned the bombs and the pilot thought they might be able to make it to the Russian lines, which were less then twenty five miles away. As they neared what they thought might be the front, they were so low that they began to take considerable rifle and light machine gun fire from German ground troops. Being the tail gunner, Stewart was the next-to-last to reach the exit and bail out. Everyone had jumped except the pilot, who was attempting to keep the plane level until he was positive everyone was safely out. As the pilot looked back and saw Stewart at the open hatch, Stewart gave the pilot the thumbs-up and dropped out of the B-17. By this time the bomber was so low Stewart wasn't sure his parachute would have time to fully open before he hit the ground, but it did and with in seconds he landed in a swamp which he soon discovered was controlled on the west by the Germans, and on the east edge by the Russians. Had his chute opened even fifteen seconds earlier he would have been an easy target for the Germans, who he later found had either shot his crew mates while they floated down helplessly in their parachutes or captured them as they landed. It appeared to Stewart that the pilot didn't get out of the bomber before it crashed. Both the Germans and Russians saw him land in the swamp and he could hear both German and Russian voices coming toward him through the tall cattails. After getting out of his parachute, he started toward the Russian voices, but, not knowing how close the Germans were behind him he moved as silently as possible to conceal his exact position. It was slow going through the thick cattails and water that in places was almost up to his waist. After about fifteen minutes, he could hear someone in front of him, and suddenly he was face to face with a Russian infantryman, who had his machine gun in his face. Stewart quickly pointed to the U.S. flag patch on his uniform. The Russian smiled, lowered his gun and extended his hand.

Stewart headed in the direction the Russian pointed, while the Russian followed covering their withdrawal. As the emerged from the swamp a group of Russians surrounded him, all wanting to shake his hand. In a few minutes an English speaking officer walked up. When Stewart asked about his fellow crew members, the officer explained what they had seen and he was probably the only one from the plane that hadn't either been killed or captured by the Germans. He then asked him if he could drive. When told all American soldiers could drive, the officer smiled and said, "Good we need all of the drivers we can find."

Stewart explained that since landing in the swamp he had remained with the Russian troops driving trucks back and forth from the railhead to the front lines. They carried supplies forward and the wounded back. Every time he brought up the subject of being sent back to England, he was informed that there was not yet a way to be transported. In time he resigned himself to the fact that he would probably spend the rest of the war where he was. Then a week ago, an English speaking officer at the railhead told him he was to get on the train which was going south and he would be delivered to a Russian airfield where some American bombers would arrive to take him home. Thankful for the good news, he boarded the train but felt sorry he had been unable to say goodbye to his friends who had rescued him at the front. Two days ago he arrived at this airfield and was put to work driving a gasoline truck to refuel the Russian fighters which operated out of the airfield.

"An extremely interesting story Stu," said Cooper. "You will have to tell everyone about the experience tonight."

"How soon will we leave for home? Do you know?" inquired Stewart.

"In the morning. On the way over, we received new orders to bomb some coal fields in southern Czechoslovakia on the way back." Cooper explained.

"That's none too soon for me. I haven't been able to even get a letter out of here since I was shot down."

The bomber and fighter crews were shown to their quarters and notified that dinner would be served in an hour.

"The food here is plentiful, but very plain and monotonous," explained Stewart. "If you have any rations with you, I am sure it would please our hosts if you gave what you could spare to them. Now, I must get back to work before I am fired." The two friends, who had gone to high school together in Salt Lake City, Utah, laughed and went their respective ways.

Later, Stewart ate with his fellow Americans and retold his story which everyone, including the Russian Officers that were present, enjoyed. The Russian Army female cooks did a good job in preparing a better than usual dinner for everyone, in spite of the fact that some of the American canned goods were unknown to them.

As they finished their dinner and the sun began to set, the air raid siren sounded.

"Air raid! To the bomb shelters quickly!" yelled an English speaking Russian Officer.

"Bomb shelters, my ass," exclaimed Major James Persons, the American fighter squadron leader. "Come on men, we are going to have some Krauts for dessert!"

"*Nyet! Nyet!*" shouted the Russian Officer. But it was too late, the P-38 pilots were already running out the door toward their parked aircraft.

"No time for parachutes. I can see them coming," yelled Persons, over his shoulder.

As they reached the line of P-38s, the pilots realized that in following the Russian's direction to park their planes wingtip to wingtip at the rear of the apron, they had been hemmed in as the B-17s subsequently pulled in front of them. With the exception of the last planes on each end of the line, there was no way to quickly get the around the B-17s. They would have to file out to the runway in two single lines.

Major Persons had been the last to land and as a result his aircraft was positioned at the far end of the line. He quickly climbed into the cockpit and in doing so, glanced at the approaching German aircraft, and recognized them as the bomber version of the Junkers JU-88. Although designed in the mid-30s it was still one of the leading German medium bombers, being similar in size to the North American B-25. The Germans were coming in side-by-side, in pairs. One row lined up with the row of bombers and the other row lined up with the P-38s, all of which were positioned like sitting ducks.

Flying from west to east, the first pair passed low over Persons' aircraft and dropped their string of ten, 100 kilogram bombs on the string of bombers and fighters at the far end of the ranks. Persons pulled out onto the runway. "No time to taxi to the end of the runway," he thought as the second pair of JU-88s streaked over his head and dropped their bombs closer to him.

"Smart move," thought Persons. Their attack pattern allowed each pair to have a clear view of the lineup without being hindered by smoke and flying debris from the previous bombs. As he turned the P-38 down the runway he realized he was already down one third of its length, but there still was sufficient distance for take off. As the twin Allison 1325 hp engines wound up, the P-38 shuddered as Persons put on the brakes to hold the plane back until the engines were at maximum power. As he released the brakes and the fighter lunged down the runway, Persons looked back and saw the P-38 from the other end of the line up also accelerating down the runway behind him.

The third pair of Junkers now swept overhead. As the P-38 lifted off, Persons could see there were three more pairs of them bearing down on the field for a total of twelve in the attack. Banking hard to the left to gain altitude before the next pair was over him, he looked at all of his instruments for the first time.

"Damn!" he exclaimed as he pounded on the fuel gage which was still hovering just above empty as it had been when he left it several hours before. Quickly he flipped over to the other pair of fuel tanks. They also were on empty. He had used all of the gasoline in the tanks on the first leg of the mission.

"Those lazy Russian bastards!" he cried out loud as he swung the P-38 back towards the incoming Ju-88s and lined himself up with the closest of the two of them. Fortunately, he had expended very few rounds of ammunition on the first leg of the mission and as the Ju-88 came into his sights he fired his 20 millimeter cannon and four 50 caliber machine guns simultaneously. One of the Junkers exploded forcing Persons to bank hard to the right to avoid the hurtling wreckage.

The pilot of the other Ju-88, seeing the new threats, aborted his bombing run and instead banked his aircraft hard to the left allowing both his top and bottom gunners to rake the second P-38, that had just lifted off, with their 7.92 millimeter machine guns. The P-38 faltered, and fell back flat onto the end of the runway and burst into flames.

"You bastards!" exclaimed Persons, as he swung in behind the German aircraft which only had half the speed of the Lightning. Again the P-38 shuddered as all of its weapons fired at once. The Ju-88 started to break up as the crew of four bailed out, much too low for their parachutes to be effective.

The other Ju-88s had now turned around and were headed back toward the airfield. Persons commenced firing at the same instant as the two leading Ju-88s. Although they each had only one forward firing 7.92 mm machine gun, a burst went through the right wing of the P-38 puncturing one of the two fuel tanks. The left engine on the closest Junker started smoking as the P-38 banked away, its left engine sputtering as it ran out of fuel. Persons continued to make a 180 degree turn to line up with the runway now about five miles in front of him. The Junkers made their last run over the airfield, strafing the planes and buildings with their nose guns as they approached, then banking so that both the top and bottom gunners could bring their guns to bear on the targets. As they cleared the far end of the runway they climbed and headed for home, their work well done.

Two miles out, Persons' other engine quit. Feathering the prop to cut down on the drag, he attempted to hold the Lightning in the shallowest glide possible without stalling. Realizing he was going to come in short of the runway but on a cleared approach, the squadron leader kept his landing gear up and pancaked onto the grass. By the time the plane came to a halt, a Russian fire truck was bearing down on the scene.

Back on the field, the Americans and Russians were examining the damage suffered from the German attack. Of the fifty B-17s, thirty two were completely destroyed. Eleven were very badly damaged, with little or no hope of being able to repair them at the site. The remaining seven, including *Big Stuff*, were slightly damaged but appeared to be flight worthy or could become so by cannibalizing parts from the more severely damaged planes. Only two of the twenty P-38s appeared to be salvageable.

The Russian base commander kept rubbing his hands together and repeating, "This is terrible! I am so sorry this happened."

"Colonel," asked the B-17 flight commander, "would you

please tell me where were your fighters that were assigned to protect this damn airfield?"

"This field was built as a forward base for our Stormovik tank busters which can defend themselves quite adequately against all German aircraft, except their top fighters. When we received notification that so large a number of you were coming the Stormoviks were temporarily transferred to another base to make room for your aircraft and crews."

"But I didn't see any Russian anti-aircraft fire to deter the attack either."

The Russian explained that, since it was a new base and they had never been attacked before, they assumed the Germans were unaware the base had been activated. Major Persons arrived just in time to hear the end of the story. "Tell me Colonel why the hell wasn't my aircraft refueled? The reason it is sitting out there in the field is because it ran out of gas! I was not only in danger from German guns, but from the incompetence of your ground crew as well."

"Rightly so," agreed the Russian. "But the fact is, all of your planes require far more gasoline than our normal complement of Stormoviks and so a special fuel convoy is on the way right now. But we didn't feel it prudent to bring all of the trucks here along the highway in broad daylight. They are due here in, ah, about two hours after dark."

"And there wasn't sufficient gasoline on this entire base to fill at least a couple of our fighters?" demanded the P-38 pilot.

"A gross oversight on our part, I must admit, and again I am so sorry this had to happen."

"That's the point! It didn't have to happen. What are our options now Colonel?" he asked, deferring to the bomber squadron leader's higher rank.

"Let's contact Foggia and see how soon they can get some transports over here to get us." Then turning to the Russian Officer, he asked. "In the meantime Colonel, could your ground crews start repairing the aircraft that can be salvaged? I'll have several of our men stay with them and answer any questions they can."

"Yes Colonel," he replied, "we'll get on it right away."

That evening the American officers spent several hours in

private discussing what had happened. Most were of the opinion that the Russians had actually expected the attack, and several went so far as saying they believed the Russians had actually leaked information to the Germans, letting them know when the Americans were scheduled to arrive.

Sergeants Cooper and Stewart, along with the other American airmen and most of the Russian troops, stood by the hangers watching twenty five P-38s coming in to land. Not willing to take another chance at the Russian airfield, Brigadier General "Tommy" Thompson the commander of the P-38 Wing at Foggia, had ordered a flight of fifty P-38s to escort the ten Douglas DC-4 Skymaster transports being ferried to the Russian base. Twenty five had flown ahead of the slower Skymasters and their twenty five fighter escort, to land, refuel and be back in the air flying cover for the transports and the other P-38s while they refueled and loaded up.

General Thompson flew his P-38 in first, and after taxiing to a stop, waited in his aircraft until the Russian ground crew had arrived and were making preparations to refuel the aircraft. After the General greeted his fellow Americans, he was introduced to the Russian Officers, whom he greeted rather coldly. It was obvious that Thompson thought the Russians were in on the German attack on the base earlier.

In thirty minutes the first of the Skymasters began to land. Each could carry forty of the flyers back, for a total of four hundred. The remaining forty-eight flyers would be divided up among the remaining seven bombers that had been made flight worthy. Included in the seven was *Big Stuff*.

Not wanting to be on the ground any longer than possible the newly arrived P-38 pilots began eating their K-rations. By the time the last Skymaster was safely down, they were ready to take off and provide cover while the other twenty five P-38s landed and were refueled.

"Men, this is a fast turnaround for you," said Thompson. "Those of you who desire to fly their own plane back home may do so. However, those who would like a break, may ride back in the Skymasters. There should be enough of the other pilots who have been setting around here that would like to fly back and see a little action on the way." Everyone laughed, and without exception, all of the men who had lost their own planes indicated their desire to pilot a P-38 back. Sensing their frustration, the newly arrived pilots consented to giving up their aircraft. This was an unusual situation, as most pilots felt very attached to their aircraft and were usually very possessive of them.

Turning to the two other flight commanders, General Thompson pointed out two P-38s that usually were used for reconnaissance purposes and therefore had two seats. Gentlemen, if a couple of you would like to fly back with us in one of these two aircraft you are welcome to do so. Major Anderson, who had always flown bombers and had never been in a fighter before, accepted the offer readily.

"On our way home we are going to give some air support to some of Tito's Yugoslavian partisans who have been boxed up in a canyon by some German tanks. It ought to provide some good hunting."

In less than forty-five minutes after the first P-38 had landed the fifty P-38s and seven flying fortresses were in the air on their way home. Riding with General Thompson was Major Anderson, the bomber group leader.

"As you my know Major," began General Thompson, after they had arrived at their cruising altitude, "the Yugo partisans have been fairly successful in keeping large areas of the country out of German hands. Unfortunately, the Communist faction under Tito is always quibbling with the other groups and so there has been no uniform and coordinated resistance against the Germans. This so annoyed Churchill that a while back he had a group of British advisors, under the direction of his son Randolph Churchill, parachuted in to get the Yugos to work together. So far it is working and now we can give air support when and where it is needed. Previously the partisans would report heavy German concentrations but wouldn't tell us the Germans were in combat with a rival partisan faction in the area and so we often ended up destroying both the Germans and partisans."

"Incredible," responded Anderson.

"I think we are going to have serious trouble with the Communists before this war is over Major," added the General.

"I agree sir."

In less than an hour the flight started passing over the Transylvanian Alps, from which the Buzau River emerged. Just up the mouth of the canyon, General Thompson, who was flying in the lead position, spotted what he was looking for. Banking the P-38 hard to the right he exclaimed, "There is a choice target for us Major. Can you see them? A column of German tanks retreating up the canyon."

"Yes, I see them. Looks like there are thirty or more doesn't it?"

"Attention all fighter aircraft," barked the General over the radio. "Enemy tanks off to the right. All forward escorts of the transports follow me in for one strafing run. Aft escorts divide in two to provide both forward and aft coverage. Continue on course. We will catch up with you after we have a little fun here."

With that, General Thompson peeled off from the formation, followed by the other twenty four Lightnings. Not being used to such a violent maneuver in a B-17, Anderson felt his stomach come up into his throat.

The P-38 vibrated as the General fired his four Browning fifty caliber machine guns and thirty millimeter cannon in one long burst, raking the entire line of tanks with withering fire. The following twenty-four Lightnings did the same. As they banked away Major Anderson looked back at the smoking line of tanks. Suddenly he yelled into the intercom, "General, call off the attack! Those are T-34 tanks. We are strafing a Russian column!"

"The hell you say."

"General I am sure of it. Believe me, I know tanks," stressed the Major.

"Well, you could be right Colonel. But it's too late now, we have completed our run. Accidents do happen you know, to tanks on the ground as well as to P-38s and B-17s on the ground. If the Russians report it, I'll probably have to prepare a formal apology, won't I?"

Anderson again looked back and wondered how many Russian tanks had been destroyed in the attack. But deep down he felt that the scored had been evened.

In another fifty minutes the formation was over Yugoslavian Territory where they attacked German positions around the town of Kragujevac, where the Germans had several hundred Partisans trapped in a canyon. As the Germans fled down the canyon to seek cover from the air attack, the Partisans could be seen climbing up and out of the canyon.

In another hour, the formation began their approach into their home bases. As Major Anderson and General Thompson climbed out of the P-38, they were greeted by Colonel John Smith, the deputy commander of the base.

"Welcome back General. Looks like you brought them all back."

"Yes, we did John."

"Ah... did you find any of the juicy targets you were looking for on the way back?"

"Sure did, didn't we Major?" the General asked, with a wink.

"Yes Sir, but now we have to organize another attack on those targets in Czechoslovakia we were supposed to hit on our return mission."

Two days later a flight of seventy five B-17s left Foggia for the area around Kosice in the Carpathian Mountains of Czechoslovakia. This time the crews had been briefed on the necessity of knocking out the mines that were producing pitchblende from which the Nazis were extracting the Uranium for their atomic devices. As fate would have it, *Big Stuff* developed engine problem as the plane crossed the Adriatic Sea and was forced to return to its home base. The spare plane which took *Big Stuff's* position in the squadron, took a direct hit from an eighty-eight millimeter anti-aircraft shell and exploded in mid air. There were no survivors. The mission was, however, a success and most of the Flying Fortresses hit their targets, destroying the above ground mining facilities and sealing off most of the mine shafts themselves. After this initial attack the mines were designated as primary targets and scheduled to be bombed on a weekly basis.

NORMANDY BEACHHEAD

By late afternoon on the tenth of June, five more American and British freighters had unloaded along the beaches of the

American and British sectors. From his still secure lookout point, Colonel Parduhn assessed the situation intently. The last of the smaller craft shuttling the supplies from the ships to the shore were, as evidenced by the slow down in activity on board the freighters, were about loaded. Only miscellaneous things were being swung over the side and loaded on them. The beaches were still loaded with new supplies although for the last several hours trucks had been pulling away from the beach and were headed inland. The beach was once again filled with men.

Oberst Parduhn picked up his phone and dialed his headquarters. "*Oberst* Parduhn reporting *Herr Feldmarschall*, with all the new activity going on here at the beach, I think this would be an opportune time to try out our V-1s."

"*Danke, Oberst*. I will pass on your recommendation."

General Roosevelt stood outside his command post, watching the sun sink slowly into the western sea. "Such a beautiful evening and so peaceful considering what happened here," he thought.

At first the faint buzz sounded like a flight of bees in the vicinity. But as it grew louder, the sound attracted Roosevelt's gaze to the east. Putting his field glasses to his eyes, he intently studied the eastern horizon. Suddenly, he saw the sun reflect off a metallic surface and then another and another as the objects climbed and caught the last rays of sunshine over head. Although both the sound and sight were foreign to him, Roosevelt ordered the warning of an imminent air attack to be sounded. As the line of strange aircraft approached, Roosevelt could see that they were in a single line flying over and parallel to the beach. It appeared there were several hundred them.

Within less than a minute the great buzz had ceased, and in horror Roosevelt watched as each of the V-1 flying bombs nose dived onto the crowded beach. Their loads of one thousand kilogram high-explosive warheads impacted the beach on the average of one every hundred feet. The cross range inaccuracy of the missiles caused some to hit just off shore while others hit up to fifty yards inland. One of the last incoming bombs nosed directly down towards Roosevelt's headquarters. Realizing this one had his name on it, and in a last act of defiance, Roosevelt pulled his sidearm and began firing at the incoming beast.

Within minutes, news of the new disaster was spreading throughout the invasion force, England, Germany, and even in the halls of the Kremlin.

MOSCOW

Marshall Semem Timoshenko hated these early morning meetings. "Just because Stalin has a difficult time sleeping, why does he have to punish the rest of us?" he thought to himself, as he walked down the great hall in the Kremlin to the office Stalin used when he was in the building. A guard gave Timoshenko a brisk salute and opened the large door for him. Stalin was already at his desk going over some documents with his Foreign Minister, Molotov, and Molotov's deputy, Andrei Vyshinsky. Marshall Kliment Voroshilov, Commander in Chief of the Stavka, The Red Army High Command, was also in attendance.

"Ah, good morning Comrade Marshall," said Stalin, looking up from the table, "and what are the reports this morning?"

"From what we can determine from Normandy, the Americans and British suffered another set back yesterday."

"How so?"

"It seems they had unloaded and stockpiled a large quantity of supplies on the beach, but before they could move them inland to their forces, they were obliterated."

"Another atomic device?"

"No, rather the Germans hit them with hundreds of flying bombs," explained the Marshall.

"What do you mean, flying bombs? I thought bombs were dropped from aircraft?" questioned Stalin.

"Usually they are dropped from aircraft. The Nazis have evidently developed a new type engine which is as near as we can tell, attached to a one thousand kilogram bomb. The device is then flown off of a portable ramp. The bomb can fly as fast, if not faster, than most fighters. At a preset distance it dives onto its target and explodes. It is an effective weapon for a crowded or compact target. Our sources have been reporting tests of this sort of aircraft over the Baltic Sea for several months now."

"We'll come back to this flying bomb business later," declared Stalin. "But for now, tell me about the attack we are experiencing on our central front, or is this a flying bomb attack as well?"

"It was a fairly large attack and the fascists managed to drive what forces we had on the west bank of the Bug River back across the Bug," reported Timoshenko. "Since the fascists were never able to take control of the large roadway and railroad bridges across the Bug and cross over themselves. As far as we know, no flying bombs were involved."

"What are their losses so far?" asked Stalin.

"Over three hundred tanks and armored vehicles and perhaps fifty thousand troops killed or wounded. Our commanders report that when the enemy pulled back out of range of our guns they left the battlefield littered with burning vehicles and dead and dying troops."

Stalin seldom inquired as to the losses suffered by his forces. To his thinking that did not matter, as long as Germans were being killed and driven back.

"Comrade Stalin, may I make a recommendation?" asked Timoshenko.

"*Da.*"

"I know we were not planning to launch our new offensive just yet, but under the circumstances I think we should begin as soon as possible."

"Why so soon?" Stalin inquired, raising a bushy eyebrow.

"Field Marshall Model's forces have just suffered a severe beating with heavy losses," explained Timoshenko. "Even though our forces are not yet up to full strength the over all balance of power is probably more in our favor right now than if we wait another week or ten days and allow the Germans to regroup and replenish their losses of this attack."

Turning to Molotov, Stalin asked, "And your opinion Comrade?"

"I think the Marshall has made a good point. Plus there is a political aspect to this as well."

"In what way?" inquired Stalin.

"The Little Allies have suffered two staggering losses in just a few days. With Churchill and the King dead, England is in turmoil. It is not inconceivable that under the right terms they may agree to a truce with Hitler."

"Bull shit! Hitler could never set the right terms for anything. And what about the Americans?"

"If England were to quit, the Americans would lose their 'Unsinkable Aircraft Carrier' as I believe they often refer to England. Under such a scenario, it is easy to see the Americans going home and concentrating on fighting the Japanese."

"And what effect would this have on us?" demanded Stalin. "Every day we are growing stronger, both in the number of troops, and in our own military productions. I just read a report this morning comparing our loss of tanks and aircraft to our own production rates. We are almost equal in both items."

"Those statistics are true, but there is another aspect on which we are still very dependant on our Little Allies, and that is food. We have recaptured much of the Ukraine which supplies most of our food. But the farm land is a wasteland. All of the equipment and even the draft animals are gone, to say nothing of the farmers themselves. All that is left is women, children, and few old men. Even now we are transporting tens of thousands of captured German troops to work the fields. But it is relatively late in the season to get much of a crop this year. Next year if all goes well, a fair crop, but this year - no. We are dependant on America to feed us for at least the next eighteen months." As he concluded, Molotov pointed to the piece of ham Stalin had left at his breakfast table. "Probably an Iowa porker."

Stalin set back in his chair and thought for a moment.

"I think Comrade Molotov is correct in his assessment," volunteered Voroshilov. "At this time we can not afford for the Little Allies to give up. A victory on our part would encourage them." "All right," conceded Stalin, "notify Zhukov to attack as soon as possible along his entire front."

Colonel Boris Yankovich had just given the order to a small platoon to cross back over the bridge to secure its west approaches. As the men cautiously started across on foot, Boris noticed a German staff car coming down the road towards the bridge. Scanning the vehicle with his field glasses, Yankovich could see that the only person in it other than the driver was a German officer standing up and holding a large white flag. "Hold your fire," he instructed the Captain leading the men across the bridge. "Meet him at the far end of the bridge and let me know what he wants. Perhaps this is my lucky day and he wants to surrender the rest of his troops that escaped yesterday."

The Russians ran across the one hundred meter wide bridge and were waiting when the Staff car drove up and stopped. Boris saw his captain salute first which told him the German officer was of higher rank. The Russian officer walked over to the staff car and Boris could see that they were discussing something. The German officer waved his arms out to both sides of the road. Then the Russian officer walked over to his radio man. "Colonel, the Germans wish permission to gather up their dead and wounded from the battle under a flag of truce," he reported.

"Oh, alright. Tell him we will give them two hours to do so."

"Yes, Sir."

The two enemy officers resumed their conversation and the Russian again picked up his phone. "As you can see Colonel, there are a number of disabled vehicles on the road. They would like to bring a tank out to push these vehicles off of the road so their trucks can get by to carry the wounded and dead back."

"This is stupid on their part. Don't they realize clearing the road will be a big help to us?" thought Boris. "Tell him to go ahead, but as the tank comes forward its turret must be pointed away from us at all times," he replied out loud.

The German could be seen nodding his head yes. The staff car then turned around and headed back down the road from whence it came.

In less than fifteen minutes a number of ambulances and four large ten wheeled covered trucks pulled out from the German lines and made their way slowly into the no-man's-land between the two large armies.

To the south of the two lane highway from a point near the bridge over the Bug River was a swamp which extended from the shoulder of the road south for about one kilometer and paralleled the highway almost six kilometers toward the German lines. In their attempt to capture and cross the bridge the day before, the Germans were forced to push their main forces down the highway and funnel their other forces down from the north. Thus, the bridge was a double choke point.

The German ambulances and heavy trucks began to fan out to the north of the highway, stopping to allow their crews to pick up the wounded and dead, which they loaded into the backs of the large trucks. One large truck continued toward the bridge picking up the dead by the side of the road, but less than a kilometer from the bridge, the driver stopped and started to turn around. The road was too narrow to make a U-turn and when the driver started to back up, he went too far and the rear wheels went off the road and down the bank. Frantically, the driver tried shifting the truck into low gear but was unable to do so while the truck was moving backwards. Since the grass was somewhat wet, the rear wheels slid as the driver locked the brakes. The truck, much to the amusement of the watching Russians, went into the water up to the tailgate, with the bodies spilling out like so much cordwood. Try as they could the driver and two other men in the cab were unable to get it unstuck. Finally, they started to walk back to their own lines. After going a few meters the three soldiers stopped and looked back at the truck, gesturing to it. The driver then returned to the truck where upon he drew his side arm and methodically shot and blew out each tire. He then lifted up the hood and emptied the Luger into the engine before returning to the others.

"I guess," laughed Yankovich, "they didn't want us to take it captive."

NUMBER 10 DOWNING STREET

Anthony Eden and several other leaders of the Conservative Party were just preparing to leave for Parliament. There was to be an open meeting with the loyal opposition where a recommendation for a new Prime Minister would be agreed upon. In the absence of a Royal sovereign, the Crown would not be in a position to formally accept the recommendation.

One of the staff members entered the room and walked over to Eden.

"Sir, the Swiss Ambassador is here and says he must see you immediately."

Looking at the others, Eden responded. "By all means show him in."

Meeting the Ambassador at the door, Eden took his hand. "It is good to see you Mr. Ambassador, even under these trying times. I assume you know everyone here?"

Looking quickly around the room, the Ambassador replied, "Yes, I think so."

Everyone nodded in agreement.

"Unfortunately Great Britain is, at the moment, not in a position to be of much assistance to any one," said Eden, "however, I will ask what can we do for you?"

The Ambassador chuckled at the little joke.

Opening his briefcase the Ambassador pulled out a large envelope. "This was just transmitted to me from Bern. It was delivered to our Foreign Office very early this morning by the German ambassador to our country. I will wait outside while you read it in case you wish me to take back a reply."

"Thank you, Mr. Ambassador."

Eden opened the envelope and quickly glanced at the contents. "Perhaps I had better read this out loud for all of you to hear."

"Gentlemen,

"Your actions of June sixth have forced me to demonstrate the power of the Third Reich through the use of our V-3 weapon and then our V-1s. It seriously grieved me personally, that I was forced to inflict such horrible punishment upon you, since as you are aware, I have always held Great Britain and her Empire in the highest regard. But my military advisors informed me we could simply not permit you and the Americans to establish a base on the European Continent. Hence our forceful response.

"I had hoped that after our first demonstration, you would have simply gone home like I allowed you to do at Dunkirk. But instead of sending transport ships to evacuate your brave soldiers you sent supply ships in an attempt to continue your folly. So naturally I was forced to put an end to the little game, but not as forceful as in our first response.

"Now I am informed, that even after suffering this second

debacle, you are, even as you read this, loading more vessels to sail for Normandy. I am going to give you one more chance to reconsider your actions by giving you a demonstration only this time. Tonight over each of your channel ports, Liverpool, and even London itself there will be a mighty display of our power precisely at 2300 hours. I am giving you ample warning just to demonstrate your inability to do anything about it.

"It is not my intent to make threats. I am a reasonable man, and now that the arch enemy of peace, Churchill, is not there to bully you into rash actions, why should we, the Great Nordic and Anglo-Saxon races be fighting among ourselves when the real threat to both of us is from the Bolsheviks and the Yellow Races of Asia. In order to rid the world of the Bolsheviks, we had to go through Poland because, as you know, we do not have a great navy such as yours to support amphibious invasions. But when we started on our long journey through Poland, you declared war on us. We are now fighting among ourselves while we are attempting to protect both our interests in Europe.

"The Bolshevik hordes are now approaching the heartland of Europe while we have to send a large number of our troops and sufficient equipment to oppose your thoughtless actions.

"Moreover, while we superior races are quibbling the Japanese are securing their positions throughout Asia, with their 'Asia for Asiatics' theme.

"It is not Germany's intent to deprive Great Britain of her rightful Colonies. But look what is happening in Asia since you are not there to protect your interests. The Crown Colony of Hong Kong is lost, as is Singapore, and large portions of Burma. The Dutch, French and even German holdings in Asia are now under the control of Japan.

"It may seem strange that we would talk about our Ally in this manner and you may be tempted to use this letter in an attempt to drive a wedge between Germany and Japan rather than heeding our heartfelt advice. Therefore, to alleviate any suspicions you may attempt to arouse in the Japanese, we have taken the precaution of sending one of our submarines to Japan, with copies of all the drawings and specifications for our V-1 and V-2 weapons. And in the case of our atomic V-3 weapon, we are shipping our Ally a completely assembled weapon."

"Good Lord!" exclaimed Eden.

Immediately there were several conversations going on simultaneously.

"Gentlemen, please let me continue reading this," requested Eden.

"Now Gentlemen our proposal is this:" continued the letter. "1. To avoid being annihilated, you are to begin an immediate withdrawal from Normandy and Italy. We will not hinder you in any way.

2. You will cease all hostilities against us and we will respond in kind.

3. You can devote your full attention to correcting the situation in Asia back to what it was before December 7, 1941.

4. You will cease supplying the Soviet war machine with supplies of any type.

5. We will continue the struggle with the Bolsheviks until they have been eliminated once and for all.

6. After we have established peace on the continent, we will grant the western European countries, (i.e., France, Holland, Belgium, Luxembourg, Denmark, and Norway) limited self rule. The Eastern European countries, with the exception of Russia, will become German colonies. Russia, after their capitulation, will have to be treated as an occupied country, probably for generations until Communism is no longer remembered there and ceases to be a threat to the world. Unlike you Englishmen, we Germans do not have the expertise in governing an Empire. In fact, I must confess that some of my subordinates have failed miserably in this respect. A point in case being Erich Koch, who I placed as governor over the Ukraine. Koch did the seemingly impossible by converting forty million Ukrainians, who had greeted our victorious army of liberators with garlands, into a seething people who became Partisans behind our lines. Since I cannot personally be everywhere at once, I would expect you to teach our governors how to successfully govern these countries, so that peace will reign in Europe for a thousand years.

7. In return, we will cease all hostilities toward you and begin to return your people who are our prisoners of war, as we expect you

to return our people. We will also recall our submarine, on the way to Japan, and explain to the Japanese when it does not arrive on schedule, that it must have been sunk.

"For obvious reasons we have not sent a copy of this proposal to the Americans, but will contact them later, in a separate note."

As he completed the letter, Eden looked around the room. "Well," he said, "this is an astounding proposal, with unprecedented international implications. Therefore, I believe we should invite the House of Lords to join us in our meeting with the House of Commons and in a closed session review and discuss this proposal."

"I agree," added the Secretary of the Exchequer. "We cannot just simply ignore this letter since we have enough opposition to continuing the war as it is. To ignore or quickly reject the proposal would add fuel to the peace-at-any-cost element's assertion that the government is inflexible in its policy of conducting the war."

"I believe the House of Lords is in session at the moment, is it not?" asked Eden.

"Yes it is," responded the Home Secretary. "Shall I request their Lordships to join us in our meeting?"

Eden glanced around the room, and saw that everyone was nodding in the affirmative. "If you would, please do. Oh, on your way out, Mr. Secretary, would you please ask the Swiss Ambassador to rejoin us?"

As the ambassador entered the room, Eden approached him with, "Mr. Ambassador, as you probably suspect, the letter you delivered was a proposal from Hitler for an armistice."

"I suspected as much, sir."

"Obviously it is beyond this group to make any decisions under the circumstances. But would you please notify the German representative that we are calling a joint session of the House of Lords and Commons to study their proposal. I need not remind you, Mr. Ambassador, that this conversation is extremely sensitive."

"I understand perfectly, Mr. Eden. May God bless you in your deliberations."

"Thank you sir. Some guidance from The Almighty would be very helpful, indeed."

Although Hitler had not sent a copy of the proposal to Washington, he had secretly through a German sympathizer, had a copy delivered to the United States Ambassador, Joseph Kennedy. Copies were also sent to members of both the House of Commons and the House of Lords who were anxious to terminate the hostilities. In addition, he informed the English politicians, that he was aware that the Duke and Duchess of Windsor were to arrive in England the next day from Lisbon where they had been living. Ostensibly the Duke would be there to attend his brother's memorial services. But in reality, he would discuss with the anti-war faction the possibility of his acceptance of a "high" government position should the offer be tendered.

After reading his letter from Hitler, The United States Ambassador, Joseph Kennedy, decided to sit tight and say nothing until he had heard from someone in the English Government. He had correctly assumed that if he had received a copy of Hitler's letter, so had someone in the English Government, who like himself, thought the war with Germany should be ended.

THE WHITE HOUSE

Miss Merryweather, the First Lady's personal secretary, entered Mrs. Roosevelt's office and quietly shut the door behind her. Eleanor looked up from the papers she was reading. She was quite possibly the most famous First Lady since the turn of the century, and certainly the most openly involved in the affairs of government in the country's history. Indeed, her hours in her office often rivaled the President's.

"Oh, it's good to see you, Miss Merryweather. How are things going this morning?"

"Not very well, I am afraid," responded Miss Merryweather, as she walked to the side of the First Lady. Hugging her she quietly said, "It's the President, Ma'am. Mr. Hopkins is in the outer office, he...he just informed me that the President passed away fifteen minutes ago."

The two friends held each other and gently cried.

"Was he alone when he died?" asked Eleanor.

"No."

"Oh, that's good, I think it is terribly sad when someone has to die alone."

"I agree."

"Was Lucy with him?"

"Ah."

"It's OK, I have known about Franklin and Lucy Mercer for years. She was once on my staff, you know, but when I found about their affair I let her go and Franklin promised me he would never see here again. He failed to keep his promise. But what hurt me even more was that one of my own children helped arrange their rendezvous."

"Oh...I, I wasn't aware," stammered Miss Merryweather. "But he was with his advisors, talking to Anthony Eden by telephone, when he had a stroke and was rushed to the hospital. Somebody must have notified Lucy as she arrived shortly after."

Eleanor cut her off with a slight wave of her hand.

"Franklin and I have been married almost thirty nine years now, you know. Of course, we have known each other all of our lives being distant cousins. When we married in 1905, my father had passed away, and so I asked my uncle Theodore Roosevelt to give me away and had his lovely daughter, Alice to be one of my bridesmaids."

"I imagine it must have been a wonderful wedding and reception," offered Miss Merryweather.

"Yes it was. Those were grand days."

Wiping her eyes Eleanor regained her composure and asked, "Did you say Harry Hopkins was in your office?"

"Yes."

"Do I look presentable?"

"Very much so, especially under these terrible circumstances."

"Well, show Harry in. Oh, and Miss Merryweather, thank you for breaking the news to me."

"I wanted to. I didn't think you could tell Harry what was in your heart."

Miss Merryweather opened the door. "Please come in Mr. Hopkins."

"Please stay with us, Miss Merryweather," requested Eleanor. "I may need some female advice as well as Mr. Hopkin's."

Walking over to her, the President's special advisor took Eleanor's hands in his. "I am so sorry for you, Mrs. Roosevelt."

"Thank you, Harry. But I know it is a blessing for my beloved Franklin. I prayed that when the end came he would not have to linger between life and death for long, and my prayers were answered."

"I think they were too, Mrs. Roosevelt. I know this is a terrible time for you, but we have notified Vice President Henry Wallace of the President's death. He and his wife are on their way here, where he will be sworn in as the new President. Supreme Court Chief Justice, Harlan Stone, is on his way to administer the oath. Since you have been so closely associated with your late husband's affairs, I thought it only proper for you to witness the event."

"Thank you for your thoughtfulness, Harry. I would like that very much. While we are waiting, Miss Merryweather, would you please place calls to my children for me. If they are not there please leave a message that I will be at Bethesda Hospital in an hour."

"Of course, I'll ring in on your phone when I reach each of your children, so you can talk to them."

Vice President Henry A. Wallace walked into the Oval Office and over to Eleanor. Taking her hand, he said, "Mrs. Roosevelt I offer you my deepest sympathy. Is there any thing I can do for you?"

"Thank you Mr....ah, let me be the first to say it...Mr. President. And the real question is what can we do for you in this dreadful hour?" she responded.

Following the swearing in ceremony, Eleanor and Miss Merryweather were driven to the hospital, while the Presidential staff and advisors began briefing the new President. Franklin D.

Roosevelt had never kept Wallace informed on the affairs of the country for the past three and a half years. As they broke for dinner, Harry Hopkins turned to the new President and asked ,"May we share a working dinner, Mr. President?"

"Of course, there is no time to waste on just eating. There must be a small dining room around here somewhere for the use of the President on short notice."

"Ah, yes this way Mr. President."

After the two men were served, Hopkins began. "I hope, sir, that you will take what I'm about to say in the manner in which it is intended."

"Go ahead, Harry, I am not oblivious to what most people around here think of me. Not knowing where this dining room was located should tell you how many times I have been invited here."

"A most unfortunate situation, Mr. President, but, if it is any consolation, Mr. Roosevelt treated your predecessor the same way. It so irritated Vice President Nance Garner that he once told me that in his opinion, 'The Vice Presidency wasn't worth a bucket of warm spit'."

The new President threw back his head and roared in laughter.

"As a matter of fact, Mr. President, that is what I want to talk to you about now," said Hopkins.   "The bucket of warm spit, or the Vice Presidency?"

"Well," laughed Hopkins. "Let's start with the Vice Presidency and see if we can put the bucket of warm spit to our use. Did you know that Mr. Roosevelt was going to run for a fourth term in November?"

"A fourth term? And in his condition! That would have been ridiculous, he has looked like the walking dead for almost a year now."

"Yes, but he insisted that he must see the war through to a victorious conclusion and get the post war relations with the Soviet Union going in the right direction. He thought of himself as a buffer between Churchill and Stalin."

"To hell with Stalin, I think he had even fooled Churchill," grumbled Wallace.

"I am in no position to judge that, Mr. President. But what we must discuss is your future. As the sitting President, it would be most natural for you to run for election in your own right this November."

"Well, I..."

"I am not pressing you for an answer, Mr. President," interrupted Hopkins. "But you would be one of the strongest contenders for the Democratic nomination."

"Oh, and who may I ask are the others? I am not aware of any of my colleagues in the Senate that were intending to run." responded Wallace.

"It is no elected official Mr. President. It is Joseph Kennedy."

"Good Lord, that, that traitor? Why F.D.R. appointed him Ambassador to England I'll never know. Churchill and England needed an Ambassador that could and would encourage and buoy them up during their dark days in 1940 and 41. And who did we send? Kennedy, who because of his Irish heritage felt that England was finally receiving what it had been dishing out to the Irish for years. Isn't that why F.D.R. had to send you over there so much, to do what our Ambassador should have been doing?"

"Well, quite possibly, yes. But in any event, Kennedy will be after the nomination. He has lots of friends and plenty of money behind him. I wouldn't bet on him losing the nomination....unless....."

"Unless what?"

"Unless you offer him the warm bucket of spit, and he accepts it."

"You are suggesting that I submit him, of all people, to the Senate to be ratified and appointed to the Vice Presidency?"

"That is correct, and the sooner the better. We will leak your announcement to the media. Within hours, Kennedy will be bombarded by phone calls and requests for interviews. Knowing how badly he wants a high political office I think he will probably be unable to think this through and will accept."

"I am beginning to see where you are heading," responded President Wallace. "Once I have given him the Vice Presidency on a silver platter, how could he run against his mentor in the primaries and seek the Presidential nomination for himself?"

"Exactly! and even if he did, the party leaders would be

obligated by tradition to reject his bid as unprecedented."

"What if the Senate would not ratify him?" asked the President.

"Leave that to me, Mr. President. The Republicans are so against Kennedy, that once I explain what we are doing to Senator Taft and several of the other leading Republican Senators, most of them will support us. The Democrats will be more divided, but there will be a sufficient number to join with the Republicans to get the confirmation."

"The only drawback is that I would be saddled with the man for four more years," lamented the President.

"True. But you could handle him like F.D.R. did you. Why, you couldn't even be accused of ignoring him. After all, you would be following the example of F.D.R.."

"And, in four more years, if we can bring this war to some sort of a successful conclusion, and that seems to be a big if from what you folks have been telling me, I'll be riding high on a wave of popularity and a shoo-in for the forty eight nomination. I like your plan Harry. Where is Kennedy now?"

"He was in his office a few hours ago when he was informed of the President's..., excuse me Mr. President, I should say, the former President's death. However, I suspect he is making arrangements right now to return to Washington."

"That plays right into our hand. Move right out on our little plan, Harry, so that when Kennedy steps off the aircraft or ship, the media is there to congratulate him."

"Very, very good, Mr. President. Now we had better get back to the Oval Office. Some military personnel and scientists from New Mexico are here to brief you on the status of something very important."

"What could be important out in New Mexico?"

"You have been kept in the dark, haven't you? Well what you are about to hear is very important to you," responded Hopkins.

"By the way, Harry, I would appreciate it if you would stay on as one of my advisors."

"Thank you, Mr. President, I was hoping you would ask."

PARLIAMENT, LONDON

Anthony Eden uncomfortably took the Prime Minister's chair on the front row in the House of Commons. After being recognized by the chair, Mr. Eden arose and addressed the crowded chambers. Gesturing to the chair he had just vacated he began, "How I wish our beloved Winston Spencer Churchill were addressing us today."

"Hear, hear!" roared the assembled bodies.

"But it has fallen upon my lot instead," continued Eden. "We have called this unique joint session for several reasons, but before we address the most difficult subject now before us, I would like the Home Secretary to review the plans for the memorial services for His Majesty and the Prime Minister. Mr. Secretary, if you would."

The Home Secretary took the better part of a half hour presenting the plans for the memorial services to be held for the King on the following day and for Churchill the day after that.

"Thank you Mr. Secretary," responded Eden. "This leads us into the second item of our agenda. With the death of His Majesty, I must bring up the subject of who we should recommend to become the new sovereign. The King's eldest daughter, Princess Elizabeth, is the next in line for the crown of course. However, she just turned eighteen in April, I believe. Quite young in the eyes of many to be given such a responsibility at such a critical time in our long history. Of course, one could argue that Victoria was younger yet, when she was made Queen. But back in 1837, things were much different. Great Britain was then the undisputed world leader, if we ignore the challenge coming from our American Colonies."

The hall was filled with chuckles.

"It is therefore proposed by this government, that we recommend to the Royal Family that Elizabeth's cousin, Admiral Louis Mountbatten, be appointed Regent for the duration of the war, or until Elizabeth reaches the age of twenty-one."

The stop-the-war element exchanged glances. They too had thought about an appointed Regent, but had the ex-king Edward the VIII, now the Duke of Windsor, in mind. Nevertheless they remained silent, thinking this was not yet the time to openly challenge the Government, especially when the proposal nominated one of the most highly respected personages in the extended Royal Family, and a brilliant military leader in his own right.

"Any debate or questions on Mr. Eden's proposal?" asked the chair. "It appears there is none, Mr. Eden. You may proceed with your agenda."

"Thank you. I added this next item to my agenda. Just hours ago the Swiss Ambassador personally handed me a letter from *Herr* Hitler." The Great Hall was immediately filled with murmuring.

"If I may, I would like to read the letter to this body." Eden began slowly reading the letter. When he finished the hall erupted into hundreds of small agitated conversations. Amid the clamor, a page walked up to Eden and handed him a message, which he quickly read. Seeing the shocked look on Eden's face, the Chair rapped for order and gave the floor back to the Foreign Secretary.

"Gentleman...Gentleman, If I may. I have just been given more dreadful information. President Roosevelt has just passed away."

A hush fell over the usually noisy chamber. The silence was broken by a question from the floor. "Mr. Secretary, it is somewhat embarrassing to have to ask this, but pray tell, who is the current American Vice-President?"

"Mr. Henry A. Wallace."

"Does anyone know anything about the man?"

"I have met him but twice," offered Eden. "He is a patriot of his country, almost to the extreme. We all remember what Churchill said from this very spot in defense of his decision to aid Russia after being such a staunch critic of Communism."

Everyone chuckled, remembering Churchill saying that if Hitler invaded hell he would feel obligated to say a few kind words in Parliament about the devil.

"Well," continued Eden, "I don't think Mr. Wallace even now thinks of the Russians as our Allies."

Sensing that now was the time to act, Lord Salisbury spoke up. "With this turn of events, it adds another reason why many in this body are of the opinion that we should seriously consider the proposal you received from Hitler."

Eden instantly shot back, "The only negotiations this government will make with the Hitler regime is their complete capitulation. We pledge to continue the policy of Winston, which was, 'Victory, victory at all costs. Victory in spite of all terrors, however long and hard the road may be. For without victory there is no survival. We shall go on to the end. We shall defend our island whatever the cost may be, we will fight on the beaches, we shall fight on the landing grounds, we shall fight in the fields and in the streets, we shall fight in the hills; WE SHALL NEVER SURRENDER!' What his Lordship has just suggested is nothing short of a cleverly disguised surrender."

The battle lines had now been drawn, and with that opening shot the entire stop-the war-contingent in both the House of Commons and Lords, lined up to deliver their support of an armistice. Not knowing that the opposition had received an advance copy of the Hitler letter, Eden and his supporters were taken back by the thoroughness and intensiveness of the attack on continuing the war.

All afternoon and into the evening the arguments raged.

THE UNITED STATES EMBASSY

Ambassador Kennedy had received notice of the President's death in his office in the United States Embassy and quickly recognized the power vacuum it created in the Democratic Party. "Rose, start getting our things together. We are going to catch the first available flight to Washington."

"Joe, do you think it is safe to fly at a time like this?" asked his wife, Rose. "I mean with all these new German weapons."

"I'm sure the Germans have more to do than attempt to track us and shoot us down."

"What about Edward?"

"Call him and see if he wants to go. It won't hurt if he misses a few days of school and he hasn't seen his aunts and uncles for some time."

Kennedy placed a call to Eisenhower's office and inquired as to the availability of space on the next flights back to the United States. He was informed by the flight scheduler that nothing was available for at least two days as every flight was loaded with the wounded and burned victims of the nuclear blast. However, the scheduler had heard there had been some cancellations on a British Sunderland seaplane that was leaving from Plymouth in the morning, bound for Nova Scotia.

"Would you have a phone number where I might pursue this lead?" inquired Kennedy, resisting the temptation not to demand space be made available for him and his family.

"If you will hold, Mr. Ambassador, I will attempt to ring them up for you. Three seats you say?"

"That's correct."

After several minutes, the scheduler came back on the line. "It's all arranged sir. Just be at pier twenty-three in Plymouth no later than 0700 tomorrow morning."

"Thank you, Lieutenant."

"Going to the President's funeral, sir?"

"Ah, well yes."

"Have a nice flight. Anything else I can do for you Mr. Ambassador?"

"No, thank you. Goodbye."

In his office in Southern England, General Eisenhower and his staff had been discussing the implications of the president's death among themselves.

"Gentlemen," continued Eisenhower, "we still have at least one hundred and fifty thousand men in Normandy who are fast running out of food. And we still don't know what the Germans are up to. But our men still need to be fed. Therefore, I have decided that we will attempt to supply them with food using just our landing craft shuttling back and forth across the channel. That way we will not present any more concentrated targets to the enemy, and secondly he can see we are not attempting to build up our military strength with the shipment of tanks and artillery. Any other ideas?"

"No," said General Bradley, "we must take some action while waiting for information on what is happening on the diplomatic side. By the way, General, are you going to go to the President's funeral?"

"I'll wait until I'm invited by the Secretary of War."

"Very good, Sir."

PARLIAMENT

"For hours the debate surrounding the German armistice proposal had been raging, but at the sound of Big Ben tolling the 9:00 o'clock hour, the Chair used the gavel for order. "Gentlemen, I am sorry to interrupt your lively debate, but by prearranged agreement with Mr. Eden I am going to terminate further discussion at this time. As you were informed in the German document, *Herr* Hitler promised us a little surprise at 11:00 P.M. Rather than remaining assembled here at the appointed hour, it would seem prudent for us to go our several ways rather then all be sitting here, to experience whatever Hitler has in store for us. We will reconvene at 10:00 A.M. tomorrow morning."

To a man, everyone thought it was a good suggestion.

"Before you leave, let me inform you," said Eden to the group, "we plan on having every available British and American fighter aircraft in the sky by 10:45 to repel any attack over our island. Also all bombers will be off and flying out of harm's way over the Irish Sea should the 'Demonstration' turn into anything sinister. We have also had all radio stations across the Island warning the populace what is happening and to take cover in our air raid shelters all across the country."

By 10:00 P.M. the bomb shelters across the islands began filling with mostly women and children. Many of the men decided to linger outside, to see what was going to happen, but close enough to be able to quickly duck inside should the need arise.

Eden, Eisenhower, and most of the British and American military staff were near the entrance to the British War Command Post which was deep underground near the end of Downing Street and St. James Park. Searchlights moved back and forth across the sky while the sound of dozens of fighter aircraft could be heard overhead. Nervously, everyone checked their watches as the appointed hour approached.

At the RAF radar site south of Ramsgate in the Kent countryside overlooking the English Channel, every radar screen was being monitored by two airman to detect any enemy activity approaching from occupied France or Belgium.

Group Captain William Williams walked around the room encouraging his men to report the moment anything at all was detected on the screens. At 10:50 Sergeants Turpin and Waters stiffened. "Captain, quick!" they both called.

Captain Williams looked at the screen in amazement; nine objects were seen to be rapidly rising simultaneously up over the horizon.

"Range?" inquired Williams.

"Seventy-two miles, Sir," replied Sergeant Turpin.

"Speed?"

"Eight hundred fifty three miles per hour, and rapidly increasing, Sir!"

"What?"

"Nine hundred and two miles per hour now and still increasing."

"Bearing?"

"Ah, can't tell, Sir. They appear to be going almost straight up."

"Any estimate of size?"

"From the strength of the signal, I would estimate them to be the size of a small fighter."

"Speed now twelve hundred and eighty seven miles per hour and still rising," interrupted Sergeant Waters, "and the altitude is now approaching sixty thousand feet. They are climbing above the reach of the antenna."

"Elevate antenna."

"It's no use, Sir. We can't track fast enough to keep up with whatever they are."

The three men watched, as one after another the three objects left the top of the screen, leaving it blank.

Captain Williams reached for the open line to Fighter Command.

"This is 'Bright Eyes' calling. We have detected nine unidentified flying objects taking off from south east of Antwerp, bearing not known, but speed approaching two thousand miles per hour when objects disappeared from the screen, evidently climbing faster than our tracking ability."

"Ah..'Bright Eyes', this is fighter command. Would you please repeat? We aren't sure we have your figures correct."

General Eisenhower stood studying the east when suddenly he saw what appeared to be a fast moving meteor streaking down on the city. "Look at that will you?" he called to the others.

The men stood in fascination watching the stellar show. Unbeknown to them they were actually watching the white hot jet vanes that extended into the exhaust plume of the V-2 rocket engine and by which the missiles were steered.

At fifty thousand feet a linear shaped explosive running down the side of the rockets warhead exploded, ripping open a tank containing two thousand pounds of high octane aviation gasoline, spewing it into an ellipsoidal mist over one hundred feet across and nearly five hundred feet long before it exploded into a large fireball. The missiles all exploded within three seconds of each other in a triangular pattern over the city. The loud whoosh of the fuel detonating was mixed with the sharp cracks of the sonic booms reaching the ground at the same time.

Eisenhower and the others rushed down the stairs to the war room where the report from Captain Williams was being reviewed along with reports coming in from the fighter pilots circling the city. No one reported seeing anything out of the ordinary, except for several sightings of meteors over the city, prior to the fireballs.

"It must have been some sort of rocket propelled bomb capable of very high speeds," ventured one staff member.

A shudder ran down Eisenhower's spine as he thought of the ramifications if Hitler's demonstration had been a rocket carrying the atomic device they had experienced just days before. "The entire city along with its several million inhabitants would have been wiped out in seconds," he thought. Eisenhower caught Eden's eye. Both men were having the same terrible thoughts.

Within minutes calls from Liverpool and Manchester were pouring in. Each city had experienced a similar set of fireworks.

RUSSIAN FRONT

From a line fifty kilometers south of Brest and its key bridge across the River Bug to the eastern outskirts of Konsingberg, the capital of East Prussia on the Baltic coast, the Red Army stood posed to launch its largest offensive of the war. Spread along the almost 300 mile long front were 126 infantry divisions, 6 cavalry divisions and 45 tank brigades. A total of over two and a half million men were backed by 2200 tanks.

At precisely 0330 just as the first hint of dawn was breaking, some 10,000 artillery pieces interspersed with almost 5,000 multi-rocket launchers spaced less than 40 meters apart, open fired on the German positions. For an hour the shelling continued unabated. At 0430, Marshall Zhukov ordered his troops and tanks to advance. As they did, ten search lights to the mile lit up and began playing back and forth across the German positions. Any member of the *Wehrmacht* unfortunate enough to be looking into the glare of a beam was temporarily, or in some cases, permanently blinded. The Russians had used this trick very effectively on previous occasions.

Colonel Yankovich stood up in his American made Jeep on the west side of the bridge crossing the Bug, watching the T-34 Tanks pour across and begin to fan out to the north of the highway. Above the roar he reached down and tapped his driver's shoulder and motioned for him to start down the highway along the south shoulder of the highway, allowing room for his tank column to roar past. Knowing the Russian counter attack was imminent, Yankovich could not keep but wondering why the Germans had made no serious attempts to destroy the bridge after retreating across the Bug.

As they drove by the stuck German truck, Yankovich thought he heard a small diesel engine running, with the sound coming from the direction of the stuck truck. Curious, he motioned to his driver to stop and turn off the engine. In between the roar of tanks rushing by the men could hear the other engine running. Yankovich ordered his driver to investigate the truck. The driver slipped out of the jeep and slid down the bank and then waded out into the water. Once in back of the truck he motioned to Yankovich that the noise was definitely coming from the back of the covered truck. Yankovich nodded and grabbed the mounted 7.62 MM machine gun, trained it on the back of the truck and signaled for his driver to open the tailgate. As he did so German corpses fell out into the water. But there standing beside a large machine that almost entirely filled the back of the truck stood two technicians in white coveralls. The driver motioned with his side arm for the men to come out. The first man carefully climbed down out of the truck into the water and began working his way along the side of the truck and up the bank. As the second man started down he reached over and grabbed a handle as if to steady himself.

The resulting fireball consumed the truck and the nearby bridge, as well as vaporizing almost the entire lake along the south side of the highway, lifting some 50,000 tons of water and mud vapor into the morning sky.

At his command post at Biala Podlaska six kilometers back down the highway, *Feldmarschall* Model saw the flash and immediately placed a call to Berchtesgaden. "*Mein Führer*, everything went as planned. All troops were pulled back six kilometers one hour before the artillery barrage began and when the Bolshevik hordes started pouring down the highway the device was detonated. I could see the flash from here."

"*Wunderbar*," answered Hitler gleefully. "Phase two will begin in less than ten minutes." Continuing to hold the handset near his mouth to allow Model to hear, Hitler looked across the table at the head of the *Vergeltongswaffe* and exclaimed, "Order your men to launch the V-2s, General Dornberger."

Dornberger picked up his phone and barked, "*Achtung*, all units fire in three minutes."

On milk stool like launch pads, over 2,000 V-2 rockets had been secretly set up around the wood lakes near Olsztyn. All were launched within a two minute interval, but giving each sufficient time so as not to interfere with the launch of its nearby neighbor. The rockets arched gracefully high into the sky and out of sight as they raced toward their respective targets. Within ten minutes the first missiles began their impact into the long line of heavy Russian artillery. One missile with its thousand kilogram war head impacted every 750 feet along the entire front.

To the northeast at Narva, the seven submarines of the Russian Baltic Fleet slipped out of their protective pens to attack any German boats sent along the coast to evacuate troops cut off by the Red Army now advancing along the Baltic coast. At that moment, out of the cloudy skies, twenty German AR-234 jet bombers swept in toward the subs that were still on the surface. Coming in low and at top speed the bombers were upon the submarines before they were even heard. Five submarines were sunk outright, while the last two, that were just emerging from the protective pens were damaged but able to reverse and back into the pens before the bombers had time to attack again. However, on their second run, the bombers managed to seal off the entrances. It would take days to reopen them.

Under the cover of darkness and the remains of the storm that had swept across Normandy just before D-day, the German Battle Cruisers, *Scharnhorst, Gneisenau* and *Prinz Eugen*, and the pocket battleship *Admiral Scheer*, along with their escorts of destroyers and E-boats, managed to slip undetected into the Gulf of Danzig. Still under the cover of the morning fog they laid in wait for the Russian tank forces that were sweeping down the coast, bypassing the German garrison at Konsingberg. By 0700, the tanks were within range of the warship's twelve inch guns. From on the ground spotters, the ships received their coordinates and began firing with devastating results.

Several Russian tank commanders immediately called for air strikes against their still unknown attackers. Within fifteen minutes 50 Stormovik fighter bombers and 75 American built Bell P-39 Airacobra fighters, which the Russians found very effective against enemy tanks, were on their way from forward bases. As they flew out over the Baltic in search of the now identified German ships, they were attacked by 35 ME-262 Jet fighters. After losing 15 of the much slower Stormoviks in the first five minutes the Stormoviks headed for home at their top speed of 275 miles per hour, leaving the fight to the 375 mile per hour Airacobras, which were still vastly outclassed. In the 30 minute melee that followed the Russians were able to down five of the ME-262s but at a cost of 27 of their aircraft. Thus ended the Russians first air-to-air combat with the new Nazi jet fighters.

Left with no air support, the Russian advance down the coast had halted under the withering fire of the German naval forces all of which had now moved to within range of the coastal roads.

By 0800, a black dirty rain started falling out of the large mushroom cloud, as it slowly drifted to the northeast. As it fell on vehicles the Russian drivers were forced to stop and clean the mud off the windshields. As the Russian ground troops advanced through the muddy rain it made black streaks down the faces of the Russian troops who joked at each others appearances.

With little, if any German ground resistance, in the northern sector, but south of the fierce battle raging along the Baltic Coast, the Russians Field Commanders requested permission to stop at 1100 to allow their men time to eat and rest and for supplies to catch up with them. Zhukov granted the request, but was still trying to get through to Moscow to report the detonation of a large bomb, the results of which were still unknown.

As the Russian troops began eating their rations, waves of intense nausea began to sweep through their ranks and they began retching, and soiling themselves from uncontrollable diarrhea. The officers, who were to be the last to eat, ran through their troops. "Its the food, don't eat the food, the Americans have sent us poisoned K-rations."

By noon, word of the disaster on the front had been reported to the Kremlin, where Stalin hastily called a meeting of his military and scientific advisors.

As the reports came in, many of the Senior Officers wondered if their government had been warned by their English and American Allies of what to expect. The rumor was that a new German weapon had been used on the Allied invasion force on the sixth. However, none dared to ask the question.

"What about the reports of the poisoned American food?" asked Marshall Klifment Voroshilov, the Commissar for Defense.

"There is no poisoned food, Comrade," replied Andrei Sakharov, the head of the Russian nuclear development program. "The men are suffering from radiation sickness."

"Radiation sickness?" asked Molotov. "What the hell is radiation sickness?"

"As near as we can tell," explained Sakharov, "during the instant the nuclear weapon is detonated, billions of subatomic particles are released. These particles apparently hit other atoms and thereby slightly alter them. These altered atoms can in turn combine with still other atoms they come in contact with and change them as well. When enough atoms in one's body are altered, you get sick and in some cases may actually die from it, as did Marie Curie the famous French woman scientist in 1935."

"How can that be, Sakharov?" asked a skeptical Stalin. " The French have never worked on an atom weapon."

"That of course is true, Comrade Stalin, but there are natural radioactive elements, that give off these particles on their own, such as radium. Curie had been unknowingly exposing herself to these particles during her experimentation with radium."

"Well, if you know that much about it, Sakharov, get to the front with our doctors and start curing our troops so we can get on winning this war!" ordered Stalin.

"I would welcome the chance to see first hand where the device went off, but I am afraid there is no cure for this affliction. It is not a sickness in the usual sense, where your body is invaded by foreign living cells that infect our own body cells. In that case, all we have to do is find a way of helping our body kill off the invaders, Comrades. Think of this as more of a...a...perhaps a mechanical problem, where the foreign subatomic particles actually change each type of cell in our body to a slightly different type of cell. It is like the alchemist's dream of changing one material, such as lead into another, like gold. But, once the cells have been changed, they cannot be changed back, and they may no longer perform their natural functions. It seems the cells in our digestive system are most susceptible to the alteration, hence the nausea."

"Well then, how long will the troops be sick?" inquired Stalin.

"Again, I can't tell you exactly. But it will probably be for at least several months, and many, perhaps most, will die."

"Several months? That is out of the question!" roared Stalin. "Do you think the Fascists are going to quit fighting while our troops take a dump? A lot of our glorious troops have fought before while sick or injured. Notify Zhukov that he is to reorganize his troops and resume the offensive in forty eight hours. Everyone knows that if you don't eat, your system will purge itself within forty eight hours."

Sakharov was about to inform Stalin that such was not the case here, but Molotov caught his eye and shook his head ever so slightly in warning. "I'll arrange a flight for you to get to the scene as soon as possible, Comrade Sakharov," he added.

OVER THE MID ATLANTIC

As the Sunderland flying boat plodded along at its cruising speed of two hundred and ten miles per hour, Ambassador Kennedy, his wife Rose, and youngest son Edward sat around their table looking out the forward window, watching the sea slowly move by. From its altitude of fourteen thousand feet it was difficult to discern the movement of the aircraft.

One of the stewards walked up to the table. "Ready for lunch, Mr. Ambassador?"

Kennedy deferred to his wife who was quick to respond, "Yes, please."

"I'm sorry we don't have a real selection of food, only some cold cuts, bread and cheese and some fruit. Tea or coffee?"

As the Kennedys were eating their lunch, the steward approached them again. "Mr. Ambassador, the pilot wishes to inform you that your new president is about to have his first news conference. If you would like to listen to it just put on these headphones."

The family all slipped on headphones and adjusted the individual volume controls to their liking.

"Good afternoon, Mr. and Mrs. America and all the ships at sea," began Walter Winchell, with his usual opening remark. "I am here now in the Oval Office to bring you the first radio interview with our new President, Henry A. Wallace."

"Mr. President, thank you for giving us a few minutes of your time. We all realize how busy you must be at a time like this. But there are several questions that perhaps you could answer to alleviate the worries and fears that seem to be sweeping the country. The death of President Roosevelt has been a shock to millions of individuals who have looked upon him as the father of us all; one who saved us from the devastation of the Great Depression and one who we felt would also save us from our enemies. What would you like to say about these concerns?" inquired Winchell.

Slowly and gravely, the new President began speaking. "First of all it is with mixed emotions that I address the nation as its chief executive officer, an office that I never expected to hold. I, too, have prayed that the Almighty would spare Mr. Roosevelt's life until this war was brought to a successful conclusion. But I want to assure the American people, and in fact, all of the freedom loving peoples of the world, that my administration will continue to pursue the polices that the late President had laid out over the past twelve years."

"Mr. President, there are reports that the Nazis detonated another atomic device on the Russian northern front. Can you confirm that, sir?"

"At the moment we have no official confirmation on that from either the Germans or from the Russians. However, we have had numerous reports from the Polish underground that an explosion of unprecedented size has occurred just behind the Russian lines somewhere west of Brest. Also there are reports from southern Sweden of a brilliant flash in the southeastern sky, which would be some three hundred and fifty miles away. So, all in all, I am inclined to believe that there is some basis to the rumor. We are, of course, trying to confirm this."

"Mr. President, it looks like these new German weapons are tipping the balance of the war back to the Nazis. What protection, if any, do we have against these weapons and are we here in America vulnerable to such an attack? One of these devices exploded in New York harbor would kill millions."

"Such an attack would indeed cause death and destruction on an unprecedented scale," responded the President, his anger showing in his voice. "However, from what my scientific advisors tell me, it appears that the atomic device is very large. Too large, in fact, to be carried by any known existing German aircraft. In addition, since the Nazis only set off one device along the entire, over one thousand mile long Russian front, seems to indicate they have a very limited number of these weapons in stock, and may even be using them as fast as they are built. Therefore, I want to assure the American people that first of all, due to the size of the weapon it would have to be shipped, not flown, across a very large ocean that is teeming with Allied warships and patrol aircraft. The number of warships and aircraft are being beefed up for additional security even as we speak. Secondly, although we cannot guarantee our European Allies the same degree of security, I want it to be known to the whole world and the Axis powers in particular, that any future atomic attack anywhere upon ourselves or any of our Allies, will be repaid ten fold as soon as our own atomic weapon is perfected."

"Mr. President, are you saying that we also have such a weapon?" interrupted a surprised Winchell.

"Yes indeed. It has been developed under the tightest of security. In fact, I was only made aware of it myself after being sworn in as President. I am only breaking that secrecy now to warn the Axis powers not to underestimate the technological ability of this nation. We, too, have mastered the secret of the atom. Also, the industrial might of this nation is unsurpassed. In fact at Henry Ford's Willow Run Plant in Michigan they are producing one Consolidated B-24 Liberator heavy bomber every hour, twenty-four hours a day, seven days a week. Thus, this one American plant is probably out producing the entire Germany industrial complex in the output of bombers."

"Now, as one of my first official acts as President, I have directed the Secretary of War to rush the completion and expand the production capability of our first atomic bomb factory. And note, I said bomb output not device output. In weeks now we will be producing atom bombs like Willow Run is producing bombers," the President exaggerated.

"That sounds very encouraging Mr. President," said Winchell. "Now if you have time for just one more question, I would like to ask you about your plans for your cabinet and also have you considered submitting a name to the Senate for approval for appointment to the Vice Presidency?"

"Two good questions, Mr. Winchell. President Roosevelt surrounded himself with very experienced and capable men, both as advisors and members of his cabinet. I have asked everyone, with no exception, to remain with me until at least the end of my term next year. Then, if any desire to leave, they may do so. But I need all of the experienced help that is now available. In answer to your second question, I have sent feelers to the Senate and have received a favorable response to my proposal to nominate our Ambassador to Great Britain, Mr. Joseph Kennedy, as my Vice President."

"Ah, well, that is quite a surprise, if I may say so Mr. President," responded Winchell. "Especially in light of the well known fact that the two of you are opposite sides of the spectrum when it comes to the purpose and conduct of our war with Nazi Germany."

"I thought it would raise a few eyebrows," laughed the President. "But the fact is Mr. Kennedy is a highly respected man in his own right and he has had first hand experience in Europe as to what is actually going on there. Something in which I am lacking. It is true we have our differences, but I prefer not to be surrounded by 'Yes Men'."

"Has Mr. Kennedy officially accepted your offer, Mr. President?"

"No, and in fact," laughed the President, "he is probably unaware of it unless he is listening to this broadcast. We have tried to reach him in London, but he is evidently on his way back to America right now to attend the funeral services for President Roosevelt."

"Well, he probably will be surprised. Thank you for your time Mr. President."

"Thank you, Mr. Winchell."

The President's proposed nomination for the Vice Presidency caught Kennedy by complete surprise. Rose looked at her husband and exclaimed, "Now I know why you wanted to get to Washington so quickly! You had a hunch this was happening, didn't you?"

Edward joined in, "This is just the opportunity you have been waiting for, isn't it Dad?"

Others aboard the Sunderland gathered around Kennedy to

offer their congratulations. In a few minutes the pilot's voice came over the intercom. "Mr. Kennedy, I have just been informed that the President's personal plane will be waiting at Halifax when we arrive to transport you to Washington. My personal congratulations Mr. Ambassador."

Kennedy's mind was in a whirl. Things were happening too fast and he suddenly felt out of control. He could hardly refuse the nomination, and yet it would put him in a position where he wouldn't, or couldn't, be as effective in ending the war in Europe as he could be as the Ambassador to England with his contacts with the end-the-war movement there. He also pondered what to do with the copy of Hitler's proposal that was in his briefcase. He obviously would soon have to disclose it. If it become known he had not passed it on for review by the U.S. government he would be getting off to a very bad start as a member of the administration. But he really wasn't the Vice President just yet and there was an outside chance that his nomination might be rejected by the Senate, in spite of the fact that the Republicans had become very accommodating in an effort to enhance the war effort. Being rejected would be a terribly blow to his image and family name. He decided to sit tight and see what was going to happen.

RUSSIAN FRONT

The co-pilot of the Russian TB-7, four engine bomber gently tapped Sakharov on the shoulder. "Sorry to disturb you doctor, but we will be landing in Brest in about twenty minutes."

"Oh, yes, thank you."

The co-pilot continued working his way down the aisle waking up the other physicists and medical doctors that made up the investigation committee along with the two political commissars assigned as security agents.

After the aircraft had landed and rolled to a halt, a truck was waiting to take them to breakfast. During breakfast, they had an opportunity to hear first hand eyewitness reports of the atomic explosion from some others in the dining hall. As they boarded the truck for the blast site, Sakharov, asked, "How long will it take to get there?"

"Less than an hour, Doctor," replied the driver.

As they approached the River Bug, Sakharov, who was riding with the driver could see down the road to the river. From there on, there was little sign of where the bridge had been or the road continuing on the other side of the river. The truck stopped and the men got out and walked to the end of the road. All that remained of the bridge was a couple of broken off reinforced concrete pilings and curiously what appeared to be the shadow of the bridge burned into the sand beneath where the bridge had once been. Scanning across the river with field glasses, they saw a crater over a half kilometer in diameter and the bed of an almost empty lake where there should have been a lake running along the south side of the roadway, according to the map.

"My God!" exclaimed the atheist, Sakharov. "Can we get across the river?" he asked the general who was escorting them."

"We had better not," cautioned the general. "Although it has been peaceful since the explosions, the Germans are still entrenched just down the road, and as you can see we no longer have any troops on that side of the river."

"Any idea how the Nazis delivered the weapon to this site?"

"No sir, all of the witnesses are--are just gone. We were in constant radio contact with our forces from the time they advanced across the river until the explosion. Nothing out of the ordinary was reported back to us."

"I understand some new type of jet powered aircraft attacked right after the blast, is that correct?" speculated Sakharov.

"Yes, but they were all reported up north along the coast providing air cover for the Nazi warships that were shelling our coastal positions."

One of the scientists in the group who was monitoring a crude scintillator, spoke up. "We had better get out of this area as quickly as possible. My equipment shows that we are in a dangerously high radiation area, right now."

"You're correct, I am sure we are at risk here," agreed Sakharov. "Let's be on our way before we become radiated ourselves."

As they got back into the bus, one of the medical doctors spoke up, "Where are our sick troops?"

"Yes," chimed in Nikita Khrushchev, one of the political commissars. "Where are these so called sick solders? We have orders to get them on their feet and advancing once again."

"The first field hospital is down the river about twelve kilometers. Everyone between here and over half of the way there was killed outright in the blast."

As they proceeded down the river levee, the scene was one of utter desolation. Sakharov had seen battlefields before, but there was always something left if just a broken off tree stump or the remains of a farm house and outbuildings. But here there was nothing, absolutely nothing.

The field hospital was nothing more than a few tents. Thousands of Russian troops lay about on the ground, some writhing in agony. The stench of burned flesh permeated the air, forcing several of the visitors to cover their noses and mouths with their handkerchiefs.

The medical men immediately stopped to examine the burned men, but the sight was too sickening for Sakharov and he had to turn away, tears running down his face.

Meanwhile, along the Baltic Coast, the German warships continued to pound the Russian forces within a thirty five kilometer arc. However, the battle cruiser, *Gneisenau*, having taken several hits from Russian bombers was forced to withdraw from the action. By now, little was left of the advance Russian army which was continually being raked with gun fire from the German jet aircraft. Farther east along the coast the black rain continued to take its toll. All infantry caught in the rain in the open were deathly sick, and even those in tanks were beginning to feel the effect. Overhead, wave after wave of Russian fighters and bombers swept in from the east in an attempt to beat off the German attack. It was a typical Russian attack against an extremely fortified position; overwhelm the enemy by sheer numbers. But the German jets were holding their own, although vastly outnumbered. As one group of jets had to break off to return for refueling, another group flew in to take its place. Several times throughout the day, however, the sheer number of aircraft the Russians were throwing into the melee forced the German command to call for assistance from the AR-234 jet bombers to assist the ME-262s in repulsing the Russians. Although designed as a light bomber, the AR-234, or *Blitz* as the Germans referred to it were still more than a match for the Russian fighters and light fighter bombers which they concentrated on.

The air battles of April 1944 over the southern coast of the Baltic Sea exceeded the numbers of sorties flown over England during the height of the blitz. This would go down as the greatest air battle in history.

WOLF'S LAIR

West of the battle lines at Gastenburg in East Prussia, Hitler and his staff were in his headquarters for the eastern front. Hitler had given the headquarters the name of "*Wolf's Lair*." It was located in a thick dense forest, and actually consisted of two compounds, approximately one kilometer apart and separated by a road. Each half was secured by a high barbed-wire fence. Because of the dense forest surrounding the compounds they were not only invisible from the air, but from the road as well. Hitler's own personal residence and bunker were at the northern-most end of the northern compound. All of the windows in his facility faced north, as Hitler believed that Nordic races, if continually exposed to the sun, would eventually become a darkened and inferior race.

With Hitler were *Feldmarschalls* Wilhelm Keitel and Alfred Jodl, *Reichsmarschall* Herman Goering, *General* Rudolf Schmundt, Hitler's personal military aide as well as his newly appointed historian, *General* Walter Scherff. Sitting in an easy chair in the corner of the room was Eva Braun, Hitler's mistress.

As the men received reports of the events of the last forty-eight hours, they were euphoric. Goering was in ecstasy as he saw the former days of glory returning to his beloved Luftwaffe.

"How soon can our troops safely enter the contaminated areas?" Hitler asked Keitel.

"The rain has stopped, *Mein Führer*," he replied, "and as soon as the ground dries out so the mud will not stick to the men and their equipment, it should be safe to dash across the contaminated area, which is only about thirty kilometers wide. Since we expect little, if any, Bolshevik resistance in that area now, we should be able to cross it in less than two hours. So the risk to our men should be minimal. I would expect we could begin the offensive tomorrow morning."

"Perfect! perfect!" responded Hitler. "Did you hear that my love?" he asked Eva. "The turning point of the war will begin tomorrow."

"That's nice, Adolf," Eva responded in her soft voice, as she continued to knit.

"Frauen," mumbled Hitler over the table to his officers. "They never realize when they are living in a momentous time, let alone understand it."

The officers smiled and nodded.

RUSSIAN FRONT

As Sakharov, Khrushchev, and the other members of the team continued moving down the front, they soon left the bank of the Bug as it swung westward into the German lines.

Everywhere they stopped, hundreds, and in some instances thousands, of Russian troops lay on the ground, many in their own vomit and feces, uncontrollably produced as a result of their intense radiation sickness. Others with horrible burns were screaming in pain. "Get me some morphine for these men," one of the medical doctors with Sakharov ordered a nurse who was moving among the injured.

"I am sorry comrade Doctor," she replied, with tears running down her cheeks. "It is all gone. There is nothing we can do. This is a hopeless situation." And with that, she completely broke down into uncontrollable sobs. Sakharov grabbed the young woman and held her to his chest to comfort her.

"What can be done?" he asked the medical doctors that were examining several of the burn victims.

"Nothing, I am afraid, absolutely nothing," answered one.

The pitiful scene, along with the screams of the burned and the moans of the sick, was too much even for the hardened Political Commissars.

"Well, if you can do nothing, I will," declared Khrushchev decisively, as he unbuckled his side arm. Kneeling by one of the burn victims, he asked, "Comrade, would you like to end your suffering?"

With pleading eyes the man nodded his head affirmatively. There was no mouth through which he could speak; only a hole where his nose and mouth had once been. Khrushchev handed the man his pistol, and stood back. With blackened hands the soldier placed the pistol to his head and pulled the trigger.

"Oh, no!" cried the nurse.

"Under the circumstances, it is the only human thing to do," declared Sakharov as he escorted the nurse from the area. "The only human thing to do."

The medical doctors reluctantly nodded their agreement. "I had better find an officer around here and have him bring more firearms," said one. "The Commissars' arms are totally inadequate for the size of this job."

It was plain to all, including the Commissars, that Stalin's order to regroup and continue the attack was completely out of the question. The only problem was how he could be told, and who would tell him?

INDIAN OCEAN

The German raider, *Atlantis*, lay almost dead in the water. Her twin screws turned just enough to keep the vessel headed into the wind which was gently blowing from the west at five knots. The *Atlantis* had been in the Indian Ocean for ten months, praying on unsuspecting Allied tankers and freighters running across the Indian Ocean. The *Atlantis* was a ship of many disguises. A single-stacked freighter of 7,860 tons displacement, she had been commissioned on December 19, 1939 and now roamed the Indian Ocean seeking targets of opportunity. She was diesel-powered which gave her a great radius of action compared to the majority of freighters which were still steam-powered. Her cargo holds were packed with supplies of every kind including three thousand tons of diesel fuel, twelve hundred tons of fresh water, and four hundred tons of food. On her forward deck were four large weatherproof cargo containers arranged in a diamond pattern. On the shorter aft deck, two similar containers were stowed in tandem. In reality the containers were dummies. The two on the forward deck each contained two torpedo tubes which could be uncovered by rolling up the side panels like a roll-top desk. The other two each contained two anti-aircraft guns. One container on the aft deck, contained a total of ninety-two mines. In the other was the fuselage and detached wings of a single engine Heinkel 114 seaplane. The detached wings could quickly be attached to the fuselage and the seaplane in a matter of minutes. The aircraft could then be lowered over the side for takeoff. The Heinkel was essentially the eyes of the *Atlantis* ranging out and around her until a target was found.

Through the use of false smoke stacks and bridges, and by flying flags of various neutral countries, the *Atlantis* could often unobtrusively get within range of unsuspecting Allied ships. Concealed behind collapsible bulkheads, which looked like her sides, were six one hundred-fifty millimeter guns, and two seventy-five millimeter guns. While passing an Allied ship the bulkheads could quickly be rolled up and the enemy ship shelled or torpedoed. Often the hapless victim would sink before even being able to send off a description of its attacker. If the Allied ship, which was usually very lightly armed, if at all, was only initially disabled, the *Atlantis* would usually pull along side, board the victim and transfer all it's food supplies to the *Atlantis* and transfer sufficient bunker oil to top off its own tanks. Any other valuables aboard were not overlooked either. Thus the raiders were often looked upon as nothing more than modern pirates. After the crew was taken prisoner and transferred to the *Atlantis*, the disabled ship would be scuttled or sunk by gunfire. The forward hold of the *Atlantis* had been modified into cells, wherein a large number of prisoners could be safely incarcerated. Unlike in submarine warfare, where the crew of a sunken vessel was left in the sea, the raiders always attempted to rescue as many of the crews as possible. Since most of the time the crews were civilians, the next time the raider put into a friendly or neutral port for supplies and fuel, the prisoners were put ashore.

In command of the *Atlantis* was forty-five year old *Kapitän* Bernhard Rogge who entered the German Navy in 1915. Surviving under his command were nineteen officers and 128 petty officers and crew.

Ten days ago, Rogge had received orders to cease hostilities and to avoid contact with any other ships. He was also directed to proceed to a ninety degrees east twenty degrees south position, where on the late afternoon of the nineteenth, or early morning of the twentieth, they would rendezvous with the U-168. The Captain of the submarine would give Rogge additional orders. However, just the day before the order was received, while patrolling in the south of the Bay of Bengal, the *Atlantis* intercepted and captured an empty Shell Oil Company tanker returning to Iran for another load of fuel oil for the British forces fighting the Japanese in Burma. While his men stripped the tanker of its valuables, *Kapitän* Rogge informed the Dutch skipper, *Kapitän* Hans DeVere that his officers and crew were to be taken aboard the *Atlantis* and the tanker would be scuttled. As the Dutch crewmen were being loaded into a longboat to take them to the raider, an animated discussion broke out between DeVere and his First Officer. Although they were talking in Dutch, *Kapitän* Rogge caught enough of the conversation to realize that there were others beside the crew still aboard the tanker.

Instead of getting into the longboat, DeVere motioned for *Kapitän* Rogge to follow him below deck. At the hatch of a large storage room, DeVere gently knocked on the door and then slowly opened it. With his hand on his side arm in case it was an ambush, *Kapitän* Rogge looked into the room, where he saw a group of very frightened English military nurses. Seeing the German officer, all of the nurses, who were officers themselves, stood at attention and saluted the German Captain. Rogge returned the salute and made a slight bow. One of the nurses, who was a Captain herself, stepped forward.

"I am Captain Ruth Lewis, Captain. We were at Singapore until it was about to be overrun by the Japanese, but were fortunate enough to be evacuated to Burma before the city fell. For over two years now we have been working in field hospitals with our Army fighting in Burma. Last week, we were informed that we were going to be returned to England for a furlough. And, well you know the rest."

"I am happy to meet you *Kapitän*," said Rogge in his rough, but best English. "I am *Kapitän* Bernhard Rogge. But unfortunately, I must inform you that we have captured this vessel and are about to sink it."

A gasp escaped from several of the nurses.

"Oh, I'm sorry, *Fraüleins*, I didn't intend to alarm you. We will transfer all of you along with the crew of the tanker to our ship first. Now if you will get your personal gear together and follow me please."

The nurses all began to frantically stuff their belongings into their duffle bags.

"No need to rush, *Fraüleins*," assured Rogge. "Please take your time and make sure you have everything you need."

As Rogge walked out on to the deck of the tanker with the nurses in tow, a murmur ran through his men, as he had expected.

"*Achtung!*" he ordered. Instantly, all of his men, and the nurses snapped to attention. Turning to the Dutch *Kapitän*, Rogge continued, "What I am about to say applies to your men as well." Turning back to the rest of the group he ordered, "Now hear this. These *Fraüleins*...ah...please, everyone be at ease, are going to be our guests for some unknown time. They are not only *Fraüleins* but officers in the British Army. Therefore, if there are any reports from any of these officers of unsolicited offensive behavior on your part, the perpetrator of the offense will be dealt in accordance with military code." Turning to his first officer the *Kapitän* went on, "*Kapitän-leutnant*, please see that these instructions are given to the men back on the *Atlantis*, as well."

"*Jawohl, Herr Kapitän,*" came the reply.

Again directing his attention to the Dutch *Kapitän*, Rogge went on, "Since we have no provisions to accommodate our *Fraüen* guests, I will have the ship's carpenter furnish your crew with materials to partition off your quarters in the forward hold as soon as possible to provide private quarters for them. Fortunately at the present time we have no other captives aboard."

"Very good, *Kapitän*," nodded DeVere.

"One other thing," Rogge continued, "our vessel is a German

warship, in spite of its outward appearances. But since you and your crew are civilians, albeit our enemy, during the day you will be free to walk the deck of the ship, but only the main deck. Each night you will be locked in your living quarters. Now, I know it is the fear of seaman everywhere to be locked up tight on any ship, let alone a warship. But, I want to assure you that when you are locked up there will be a guard with a key stationed outside the door, so that in the event of any life threatening situation you can be released."

"Thank you *Kapitän*," replied DeVere.

"Yes," echoed Captain Lewis. "Thank you very much."

"Now," went on Rogge, "in return for this liberty, I am asking each one of you to promise not to hinder or interfere with our operations in any way. Those of you who can live with, and obey these stipulations, please raise your hands."

All of the Dutch crew and the nurses quickly raised their hands.

"*Danke. Ach*, in the event we enter into a combat situation, you must all return to your quarters as quickly as possible. This is for your own safety as well as our security. Now *Kapitän-leutnant*, please escort our guests to the *Atlantis* and prepare to scuttle this ship."

Back on board the *Atlantis*, Kapitän Rogge returned to the bridge. From the hold in front of him was heard the sound of saws and hammers as the Dutch crew immediately began working on building suitable quarters for the nurses in the aft end of the forward hold. The Dutchmen had decided to quarter in the foremost section of the hold, which was more subject to the pitching of the vessel in rough seas.

The next morning, *Kapitän* Rogge noticed Captain Lewis emerge from the forward hold and walk around the forward deck, ending up directly in front of the bridge. Glancing up, she saw Rogge looking at her. She motioned that she would like to come up to the bridge. Hating to set a precedent, Rogge was at first hesitant, but finally waved for her to come up.

Entering the bridge, Captain Lewis looked around briefly, and then got to the purpose of her visit.

"Captain, I want to thank you for the kindness and

consideration you have extended to us. It isn't what...what we had expected and feared at all."

"Why, thank you *Kapitän*. I am pleased you have found out we Germans are not the barbaric Huns you may have supposed. But I suspect war brings out the worst in all of us at times."

"Yes, I suppose so," responded Lewis. "But in any event, Captain, it looks as if we will have plenty of free time on our hands for some time to come."

"Very likely."

"Well, we have discussed this and all agree that to repay you and your men for your kind consideration, and to keep busy ourselves, we would like to offer our services to help your cooks prepare the meals. It would give them a rest and perhaps we could offer a change to the menu. It would also provide us with something useful to do."

Kapitän Rogge looked at the seaman on watch, the radar and sonar operators, and the helmsman. Although he did not ask for their opinions of the proposal, the looks of approval on their faces required no words.

"I think that is a splendid idea *Kapitän* Lewis. When would you like to start?"

"What about tomorrow morning? We'll have a surprise breakfast for your men as well as the Dutch crew, if that is alright."

"*Gut*. Let's go down to the galley and I will introduce you to the *Kochen* and they can show you around."

Following the next day's meals, it was the first time in *Kapitän* Rogge's career that he had not heard any of the real or joking complaints about the ship's meals from anyone aboard his vessel. His cooks had agreed that if the nurses would prepare the meals, they would clean up and do the dishes. But, to their satisfaction, the cooks found that they didn't even have much of that to do, as there were plenty of volunteers from among the crew to assist the ladies. In fact, there were so many, a sign up sheet was prepared to allow everyone an opportunity to serve as a *Galeerensklave*.

At 6 bells on the morning of the 20th, the *Atlantis* was scheduled to meet with the U-boat. *Kapitän* Rogge double-checked his charts to insure he was on station. They arrived early, and had been holding position for almost four hours.

Kapitän Rogge and the lookouts were scanning the horizon to ensure they were not being observed, when the sonar operator suddenly spoke out.

"*Herr Kapitän*! I think the U-boat is approaching!" he exclaimed, as he began to adjust the hydrophones. "I can hear the faint sound of a boat coming almost directly toward us!"

Kapitän Rogge and the lookouts automatically swung their field glasses to the west, the direction from which the U-boat would most likely be coming.

"You won't see anything *Herr Kapitän*, I am sure it is submerged, and from the sound of its motors and screws, I am sure it is one of ours, running on its batteries."

"What do you estimate its range to be?"

"Twenty five thousand meters and closing dead on."

"Inform me when they are at twenty thousand meters."

"*Jawohl, Kapitän.*"

Rogge placed a call for all officers to report to the bridge where upon he informed them they had probably detected the U-168 and would verify it in a few minutes.

"Twenty thousand meters and still closing, *Kapitän.*"

"Very well, send out one sonar pulse."

Aboard the U-168, Commander Pitch was standing behind his sonar operator, who suddenly raised his hand to his ear piece. "We have received one sonar pulse *Kapitän*, from almost dead ahead."

"You are positive?"

"*Absolut, Mein Kapitän.*"

"Very well then, respond with two pulses when at fifteen thousand meters."

When the returned double pulse was received aboard the *Atlantis, Kapitän* Rogge ordered, "Ahead one quarter, hard right rudder, bring her about to new heading of one eight oh."

"*Jawohl, Herr Kapitän.*"

Aboard the U-168, Commander Pitch was listening on one of the hydrophones and heard the *Atlantis'* screws increase in speed. A smile crossed his face. "It is responding according to plan, it must be the *Atlantis*. Up to periscope level."

As the boat leveled off, Pitch ordered, "Up periscope!"

Pitch quickly swung the periscope around to look at the ship and observed, "Still too far to absolutely identify, but it is turning and has now presented its side to us. Hardly the thing an enemy would do to a boat."

"Surface."

As the U-168 breached the surface, Pitch ordered, "Open all vents, start diesels and shut off electric motors. All ahead one quarter."

Aboard the *Atlantis,* everyone except those who were actually running the vessel were at the starboard rail, waiting to be the first to spot the submarine. The U-boat broke the surface at such a sharp angle and speed, the bow actually leaped spectacularly into the air. For the British nurses it was the first time any of them had ever seen a submarine, let alone witnessed a spectacular surfacing. Even the crew of the freighter, for whom the submarine was regarded as the scourge of the sea, were awed by the sight.

In a half hour, U-168 was moving at a matched speed, along side of the *Atlantis* and at a distance of fifteen meters off its port side.

A bosun's chair was quickly rigged between the two vessels and within minutes the officers of the U-168, followed by several of the enlisted men were transferred aboard the *Atlantis*. After the officers of the two vessels had introduced themselves, Commander Pitch announced that they had brought mail to the crew of the *Atlantis* from home. A roar of approval swelled from the crew. Even its officers could not disguise their excitement.

Leaving the enlisted men to visit on deck, Kapitän Rogge invited the officers of the U-boat to join him and his officers in the officers' mess hall for refreshments. Then turning to his senior enlisted man, he announced, "Beer rations for all."

Once seated in the officers' mess hall, *Kapitän* Rogge eagerly turned to Commander Pitch "Now *Kapitän*, please bring us up to date as to what is happening back home. As you know on this type of duty we are essentially entirely cut off from Germany."

As Pitch was reviewing the significant change of events in the war, the door to the galley opened and to the surprise of the officers of the U-boat, in walked several of the British nurses in their crisp white uniforms, carrying refreshments. Instantly, all of the officers stood up and Pitch looked to Rogge for an explanation.

"*Ach, Kapitän*, let me introduce you to several of our special quests and fellow officers.

"*Kapitän* Pitch, may I introduce *Kapitän* Lewis of the English Army's nurses *Korps*? *Kapitän*, Lewis, this is *Kapitän* Pitch, of the U-168." The two officers exchanged salutes and smiles.

"Before we received the message to rendezvous with you," continued Rogge, "we intercepted and captured a Dutch tanker. Upon boarding her we found *Kapitän* Lewis and several of her fellow, ah is that the correct term?...officers aboard. It seems they were headed back to England for a well deserved rest, after being in the thick of things in Southeast Asia. I regret that we have somewhat delayed their furlough, but we are trying to make up for our inconsideration by letting the *Frauen* enjoy a free sea cruise aboard the *Atlantis*. Since the *Kapitän* and her associates have found time on their hands, they have most graciously volunteered to give us the benefit of their culinary skills, which, I might add, we have enjoyed immensely."

"I see." responded Commander Pitch. "It seems that their misfortune has been greatly to your advantage."

After the women had left, Rogge asked. "Now *Kapitän*, what is our meeting here all about and what are our new orders? The high command did not give us any information other than when to meet you here."

"That was because our mission is of the utmost secrecy," explained Pitch. "As I have already mentioned, our scientists have developed this most extraordinary high powered bomb, which derives its power from the atom itself."

"The atom?" questioned Rogge, "I thought atoms were the smallest parts anything could be broken down to. How could you get much power out of such small things?"

"You had physics, did you not, in college?"

"Well...*ja*."

"Do you remember that Jew, Einstein, and his $E=MC^2$ equation?"

"Vaguely."

"Well, it seems the Jew was correct. A small bit of matter can be turned into a large amount of energy. We are talking here of a few kilograms of some rare material that when set off will produce an explosion equal to hundreds of thousands of kilograms of dynamite."

"*Mein Gott!*" responded Rogge.

"In addition," went on Pitch, "the Luftwaffe is now flying high speed aircraft that are propelled by jet engines. They are decimating the enemy's best fighters."

"I have heard of this type of aircraft," responded Rogge.

"All this brings us to the purpose of our meeting," continued Pitch. "Since our Japanese Allies have not fielded a new improved fighter since the start of the war, they are suffering extreme losses of aircraft to the newer and faster American fighters, which are being developed. What we have aboard the U-168 is a complete set of drawings and specifications for our new ME-262 jet fighter V-1, flying bomb and V-2 Rocket. Once the Japanese have these weapons in production they will be able to regain control of the skies, not only over their homeland, which is being bombed every day, but also over all of the many fronts on which they are fighting."

"This all sounds very good," responded Rogge. "The more pressure the Japanese can exert against the Americans, the less the Americans will be able to oppose us."

"Exactly. However," went on Pitch, "the transfer of the plans are not the only purpose of our mission. For within the forward compartments of U-168 we have a fully assembled ready-to-fire atomic device, which we are going to give to the Japanese. It, of course, would take them too long to build one on their own, even if we supplied them all of the drawings and specifications."

"But," objected Rogge, "such a device must be a very large piece of equipment? How could you possibly get such a large device through the small hatches on the boat?"

"We didn't go through the hatches," explained Pitch. "The dock workers actually removed some of the deck forward of the conning tower and removed all of the bulkheads and rearranged the equipment. All of our torpedoes, and everything else that wasn't absolutely essential were removed. The device was then lowered into the hold and the deck reinstalled. Of course this has greatly compromised the strength of the boat and as a result we are limited to a submerged depth of only fifteen meters. This is why we dare not enter the Pacific war areas."

"I assume this is where we come into the picture?"

"*Ja.*"

SOUTHERN ENGLAND

Two hours prior to the scheduled arrival of the Duke of Windsor's chartered plane from Lisbon, the crowd around Plymouth's aerodrome on the southern coast of England had grown to almost fifteen hundred people in spite of the government's attempt to keep the time and place of his arrival hidden from the public. The roads leading into the city were packed with supporters walking or riding bicycles. A surprising number were even driving their automobiles burning what precious few liters of petrol they were allotted through the rationing system.

Turning to the Commander of the local Home Guard, Constable Taylor expressed his concern. "I don't know sir. I have only thirty five available officers and with a crowd like this, well if it should turn ugly, it could quickly get out of hand. I think it would be well if you had a few of the regular home guards on hand, just in case."

"Quite right, my friend. Better to be safe than sorry. In fact I'll have them line up as if they are an honor guard of sorts. No need to antagonize all of the Duke's supporters."

"Very good, Sir."

An hour and a half later the crowd had swelled to what Constable Taylor estimated to be close to twenty thousand persons.

"I think I had better notify London what is happening here," ventured Constable Taylor.

"Right, home guards should be arriving at any time now,"

responded the Home Guard Commander.

Half an hour later, the drone of the DC-3's engines could be heard in the overcast sky above the aerodrome. A sudden hush fell over the throng as everyone strained their eyes to be the first to see the approach of the aircraft bringing the Duke and Duchess of Windsor home to England and to what the crowd hoped would be the first step to ending the war. As the plane rolled to a stop the crowd rushed forward and surrounded the plane. Steps were rolled into place and as the door opened and the Duke and his wife appeared in the doorway the crowd spontaneously broke into "God Save The King."

Obviously moved, the Duke stood at attention with tears rolling down his cheeks. As the last strain of the national anthem faded away the crowd began to chant, "Hip, hip, hurray. Long live the King."

Somewhat embarrassed by the greeting, the Duke raised his hand for silence. A portable microphone was handed to him and he addressed his large following.

"My loyal friends, the purpose of my visit is to attend the memorial services for my brother, George the VI and Prime Minister Churchill." At the mention of Churchill, many in the crowd booed. Raising his hand, the Duke continued. "Many of us, myself included, did not approve of Mr. Churchill's war-like policies, nor this unfortunate war which has brought our country so much sorrow and misery. Nevertheless, he was the elected leader of our government, and deserves the respect appropriate to that honorable position."

Sensing the mood of his followers, the Duke continued. "As many of you are aware, representatives of the German Government have contacted me and asked...no, begged me, to use my influence to bring about an end to the existing hostilities between ourselves and the German people and thereby allow Germany to concentrate on its primary purpose of exterminating the threat of Communism once and for all."

The crowd immediately broke into cheers and applause.

When the Duke was finally able to quiet the crowd, he continued. "It is my intent, with the help of all of you, to address the House of Lords and Commons in a joint session in an attempt to end this madness which threatens our very existence. Thank you for your support."

Following his short remarks, the Duke and Duchess slowly made their way through the throng, shaking as many of their well-wishers hands as time would permit.

Anthony Eden and the other leaders of Churchill's government were shocked as they listened to the Duke over they radio and heard his open support for ending the war. Lord Beaverbrook was the first to speak. "I believe our best course of action would be to call for a vote of confidence as soon as possible."

"It would be under normal circumstances," replied Eden, "but you must remember that technically with Winston gone, it could be argued that there is no government. I think we will have to schedule a general election as soon as possible. Then with the vote of the people behind us we can effectively deal with re-establishing the monarchy."

Glancing around the room, Eden acknowledged the agreement of all of his associates.

"Yes then, let's move out on it. I'll notify our Allies what we are going to do."

BERLIN

Hitler was ecstatic as he listened to the speech of the Duke over the BBC, and the roar of approval from those in attendance.

"It looks like our plan is working, Eva"

"*Ja*, it does, *meine Liebe*. What are your plans now?"

"I must show the British people my sincerity."

"Speaking as a *Frau*," responded Eva, "what would be a better way than to immediately return all of the Englander prisoners we are holding in Normandy? That would certainly go a long way in winning over the *Mütters* and *Frauen* of the men involved."

Hitler thought for a moment, and then said, "An excellent idea! Such an act would also have an effect on the *Mütters* and *Fraus* of the other Allied troops facing us in Normandy. They will greatly influence public reaction. I'll see that it is done right away."

WASHINGTON

Joseph Kennedy walked down the hall of the White House escorted by a presidential aide. As they approached the Oval Office the aide opened the door.

"Go right in Mr. Ambassador, the President is waiting for you," instructed the aide.

"Mr. Ambassador, it is good to see you again," said President Wallace, as he arose from his chair and walked over to meet Joseph Kennedy as he entered the Oval Office. "I appreciate your meeting with me on such short notice."

"I am aware that these are not normal times. You are carrying an enormous burden, Mr. President."

"Yes, and that is, of course, why you are here. I need you, Joe, to help me and our country at these perilous times. I must apologize for the way you were made aware of my decision to select you for the Vice Presidency. We had a call into your office in England but you had evidently already left for the States. My aides continued to try and locate you and I thought they had done so by the time I went on the air with Walter Winchell," he lied.

"No harm done, Mr. President. You know I would never turn down an important calling from my country, regardless of the circumstances."

Kennedy's brain raced as he tired to figure out just what was really going on.

"Good," continued the President. "Now if you will, the cabinet is waiting for us and that is as good a place as any for you to get your feet wet. Also you will be sworn in as Vice President there." That evening in the Blair House when they were alone in their bedroom, Kennedy went over the day with his wife, Rose.

"I just can't believe this is happening, Rose. For years the vice presidency has been a dead-end road for any politician."

"Except for those who were presiding over the Senate when the President died," Rose interjected.

"True, my dear, but the President and I are both the same age and he appears to be in good health."

"Just the same dear, I think this is one more step toward your ultimate goal."

"Perhaps you are right. In any event, I am going to give it my best."

NORMANDY

The field phone jumped as it rang in the Field Marshall Montgomery's headquarters.

"Yes," answered the radio man, "This is Field Marshal Montgomery's office. What road did you say? And just where are they now? Yes, I'll see that he gets the message immediately."

Montgomery looked up from his map. "Yes, what is it?"

"Sir," replied the radio man. "We just received a message from one of our forward field commanders, who is right here." He said, pointing to the map. "It appears that some of our missing men are coming toward our lines unescorted by the Germans."

"What the bloody hell is going on now?" questioned Montgomery, as he placed his helmet on his head and headed out the door toward his jeep.

As they traveled toward the front lines, another call came in and then another. "Sir, we are getting calls from all over our front lines. It appears that the Germans are letting all of our prisoners go. That is, all of their English prisoners. No American or other Allied prisoners have yet been released."

RUSSIAN FRONT

Along the entire front, Field Marshall Model attacked the Russian lines with everything he had. Nothing was held in reserve. It was a dangerous gamble but they had to get across the forty kilometer contaminated front line as quickly as possible if the troops were not to become victims of the new strange radiation sickness. The contaminated zone was no place to become bogged down.

From the Baltic Coast on the north, to Brest on the south, the troops under Model's command rolled forward almost unopposed. Dead and dying Russian troops lay everywhere. In less than two hours, the front line combat troops had crossed the contaminated zone. As evening fell, the advance was halted in order for the supply convoys to speed across the zone and resupply the assault force.

As first light advanced towards the front, the air was filled with the scream of the pulsejet engines of the hundreds of V1 Buzz bombs that rained down on the Russian lines. As the Russian built Stormovik and American built Bell P-39 Airacobra tank busters raced toward the front to make short work of the Panzers, they were intercepted again by dozens of ME-262 jet powered interceptors. Their only salvation came from the fact that the ME-262s had a short range and were not able to pursue the Russians, as the ME-262s soon had to turn and headed for home to refuel. Nevertheless, over half of the Russian planes never made it back to their bases. The planes could be replaced, but the Red Air Force was now running low on experienced pilots.

NUMBER 10, DOWNING STREET

Anthony Eden, Lord Beaverbrook, and their wives sat silently listening to the radio, as the results of the hastily scheduled election came in. From the very first returns, it was all too evident that the Tories were going down to defeat by a wide margin as the Labor Party and the newly formed Peace and Prosperity Party candidates took an early lead.

"Do you think that Mr. Attlee would actually form a coalition government with the Peace Party and negotiate a truce with the Germans if Labor wins?" Lady Beaverbrook asked.

"He may not have any choice," ventured Eden. "Even though the reports from the cities, which are always the first to come in, show strong support for our opposition, when the rural votes start coming in, I am confident we will do better. Without a decisive majority in parliament, Attlee will be forced to form a coalition with the new party, if he expects to be able to get any legislation passed."

"Dinner is ready", announced Mrs. Eden. "Maybe after a good meal things won't look so bad after all."

But by ten P.M. it was obvious that the Labor Party was going to take at least forty percent of the seats in the House of Commons, followed by the Tories with less than thirty percent, and the Peace and Prosperity party taking at least twenty-five percent. The remaining five percent of the seats were too close to call.

Getting up and walking toward the phone, Anthony Eden said, "I think it is time to call Mr. Attlee and offer my congratulations on his victory."

"May I suggest that you call General Eisenhower first, and let him know what you are going to do?" ventured Lord Beaverbrook.

"Quite right my friend. I do need to assure our American cousins that we will do all that we can to prevent this struggle from falling entirely on their shoulders."

Two days later, all of the members of both the House of Commons and the House of Lords assembled in Westminister Abbey. The Parliament buildings were still too badly damaged to be of any use. Seated beside Clement Attlee on the front row was the mathematician and pacifist philosopher, Bertrand Russell, now a member of Parliament and the leader of the new Peace and Prosperity Party.

Clement Attlee slowly rose from his chair amidst thunderous cheers and applause from both sides of the aisle, much to the surprise and dismay of Eden and his loyal, but now much smaller, following. Raising his arms for silence, the Labor Party leader made no mention of the election which had given Labor forty-eight percent of the vote. The Torries came in second place with thirty-two percent, and the Peace and Prosperity Party was third with twenty percent. Instead he went directly to the heart of his policy.

"As we are all aware, the Germans have beat us in the race to control the awesome power of the atom. As a result, we, and our Allies, including the Soviet Union, have suffered enormous casualties. This, together with the advance the Germans have made in the development of jet propulsion aircraft and unmanned missiles, and in their actual deployment, has unfortunately, but dramatically, shifted the balance of power out of our hands and into theirs."

Not a sound arose from the usually noisy gathering.

"As most of you know the Germans have, through diplomatic channels, offered us, Great Britain, an armistice proposal, which my colleagues and I feel is not totally unreasonable. I have asked Lord Russell to again read the proposal in its entirety to this body for the benefit of the new members. After which I propose that a committee comprised of members of the three parties represented by their percentage of seats in Commons review the German proposal in depth and work out a fair and honorable compromise."

This statement did get a noisy response from the loyal conservatives, with cat calls such as "no more appeasement." "We will not be a party to another Munich. This will not bring another 'peace in our time.'"

When the uproar died down, Attlee continued, "It is not with joy that I make this proposal. But, the fact remains, we are in dire straits. What if the missiles that the Germans recently exploded over several of our cities, in fact had been carrying atomic devices? In a matter of a few short minutes, we would have suffered more deaths than in all of our previous wars combined. Our medical facilities, which now have been stretched to the limit caring for the injured from the Normandy disaster, would be completely overwhelmed. Moreover, I have been advised by several of our most prestigious physicians that they have no effective treatment for the terrible sickness that the radiation victims suffer. Most of them will die a horrible, slow, lingering death. In fact, reports we are receiving from the Eastern front tell of the shooting, or assisted suicide, of thousands of Russian troops to end their terrible suffering."

"Now, if you please, Lord Russell, would you please read the German proposal?"

With all of the dramatics the great orator could bring to bear, Russell eloquently began to read the German proposal.

When the popular pacifist had finished, Attlee again stood up and the Chair banged the gavel for silence.

"There is one more item of business that we must address before the House breaks up for detailed review of the proposal, a copy of which is available at the door for each of you. That item of business deals with the loss of our King. Princess Elizabeth is, of course, the rightful heir to the throne. However, in light of her youth and these trying times, it is our proposal that the Duke of Windsor be appointed Regent until these perilous times have passed, or until her Royal Highness reaches her majority, whichever occurs first."

With that, the Prime Minister motioned to the audience in the balcony where the Duke was sitting with his wife. The Duke acknowledged the applause by standing and waving to the assembled body.

WASHINGTON D.C., THE OVAL OFFICE

"Good Lord," sighed the President, as General Eisenhower finished briefing him, over the phone, on what had he had just witnessed in the House of Commons. "General, what would you recommend that we do on this end, to head off this possible calamity of the British pulling out of the war? Should I arrange a meeting with the new Prime Minister as soon as possible?"

"I think that would be the best possible course of action, Mr. President," agreed Eisenhower.

"I will move right out on it, General, and thank you for the information. Please keep us informed on what is going on over there."

"I will Mr. President. Goodbye."

Vice President Kennedy had been invited to listen to the conversation on another phone. As he set the phone down, he had mixed emotions. He was happy that the English were taking steps to end the bloodshed, but, on the other hand, he knew what a dilemma it placed the United States in.

"What do you think, Mr. Vice President?" asked President Wallace. "You probably know the new Prime Minister better than anyone else. Do you think he will actually settle with the Germans? And if he does, where will that leave us?"

"I am sure he means what he says, Mr. President. And when it happens I think we will lose our bases not only in England, but in some other English protectorates as well. Of course, Canada, Australia and New Zealand will probably stick with us."

"You are probably correct. Now, will you please work with the War Department and see how soon we can have a contingency plan put together in case England actually pulls out of the struggle. In the meantime I will try and get in touch with the Prime

Minister, and arrange for a private meeting."

"Yes sir," responded the Vice President, as he arose and walked out of the office.

After the door had closed, Cordell Hull, the Secretary of State, spoke up. "It seems like you are giving more to the Vice President to do than I thought you would, Mr. President."

"Well...yes. I guess I am, but there seems plenty to do around here and he does follow through on the tasks I have asked him to do. He just may turn into a valuable member of our team after all."

"That is possible," responded Hull.

THE KREMLIN

"I knew the Little Allies would stab us in the back as soon as they got the chance!" raged an infuriated Stalin, after hearing about Attlee's speech.

"Perhaps the Americans can talk some sense into the English," ventured Molotov. "As soon as I heard what had happened, I requested the American Ambassador, Averell Harriman, to come to my office and we discussed the situation. The Americans are as upset and concerned about this turnabout by the English as we are. Harriman reassured me that regardless of the consequences of the British action, the United States will stay in the war. He also stated that they felt that Canada and most of the small Allies will also continue the struggle."

"Do you really believe that, Comrade? Don't you see what is really happening? It is a conspiracy, carefully orchestrated by all of the Little Allies to throw the entire burden of the struggle against fascism on our shoulders! But, if that be the case, so be it. We will carry on by ourselves and still be the victors. In fact, I have decided that if the Little Allies pull out, the Red Army will not stop after we have conquered Germany. We will sweep to the North Sea and have control of all of Europe as well!"

None of the men in attendance dared to bring up the fact that the mighty Red Army was being driven back all along the northern front following the atomic attack, and was barely holding the line along the southern front under the relentless attack of the German jet aircraft which were proving to be almost invincible. Moreover, with the threat of more atomic attacks, the Red Army's policy of massing tens of thousands of men and thousands of tanks to overcome their enemy, was no longer feasible.

BERLIN

"It's working, *Mein Führer*, the English are going to work an armistice with us!" responded Goering to the news coming out of London.

"So it appears. But we must keep the bait in front of them."

Picking up the phone, Hitler ordered, "*Achtung*, notify all of our prison camps holding any Englander prisoners that they are all to be shipped to the English lines in Normandy and released. This is a priority order and is to be accomplished as quickly as possible."

"*Mein Führer*," asked von Ribbentrop, the German Foreign Minister, "what about the prisoners we are holding from Canada, Australia and the other English Commonwealth Nations?"

"I want to continue to hold them until those countries also agree to cease hostilities," responded Hitler.

"*Sehr gut, Mein Führer*," responded von Ribbentrop.

INDIAN OCEAN

The *Atlantis* leisurely made its way eastward across a very calm and beautiful sea. Captain Rogge and Captain Lewis stood on the bridge, having a cup of coffee while enjoying the view.

"What a perfect morning," ventured Lewis.

"*Jawohl*, it is. Makes it difficult to believe there are such terrible things going on in the world, doesn't it?"

"It certainly does. By the way, Captain do you have a family?"

"Yes, my *Frau*, Eva, and I have three *Tochters*. The oldest is married and has two little boys. My youngest grandson was born after I left on this mission so I haven't seen him."

"Are they all right? I mean, from the bombings and all?"

"So far, they are all right, according to a letter I received from Eva which was delivered to me when we met with the U-Boat.

You see, we live on a small farm along the Danube River south of Ulm. The farm has been in my family for over two hundred years. It is fairly isolated, and with no military targets anywhere around, my *Frau* and two youngest *Tochters* are as safe as can be expected in these times. My oldest *Tochter* and her *Mann* also live in a nearby small town. Eva says they have taken in twelve children of friends and relations that are living in target areas. And your family?"

"My parents live in the small village of Godmanchester, which is about eighty miles north of London, and they are doing the same thing with a number of children that were evacuated from London during the blitz. But what about your son-in-law? He must be of military age."

"*Ja*, he is. But he is an engineer and is working for Messerschmitt on new advanced aircraft and so he is fortunately deferred from serving in the military. But what about you? I notice you are not wearing a wedding ring."

"No. With the war and all I haven't met Mr. Right yet. I was getting serious with a young man at the beginning of the war but he didn't come back from Dunkirk."

"I'm sorry to hear that."

"Now I am concerned about my brother. He is an Ensign aboard a destroyer named *Swift*. The last time I heard, he was going to be involved in the invasion at Normandy."

"Do you know if he survived the atomic attack?"

"I haven't heard."

"By the way Captain, I want to thank you for not sending us back to Europe on that submarine. We would have all been terrified to be cooped up in that thing under the water."

"So would have I," laughed Rogge. "That is the reason all submariners are volunteers and carefully screened to ensure they can handle the confinement of a boat."

"Boat?"

"Yes, submarines are usually referred to as boats."

"I wasn't aware of that."

"I believe the term is quite universal."

"May I ask Captain, where we are headed with the supplies or whatever you took off of the ah, boat?"

"Singapore."

"But, that is controlled by the Japanese!" exclaimed an alarmed Lewis.

"That is correct. But remember, the Japanese are our Allies. However, you needn't be alarmed. If we don't meet a neutral ship headed west that we can transfer you to before we reach Singapore, we will just keep you out of sight until we have completed our business in port and are on our way again. I have no intention of turning you *Fraülein's* over to the Japanese."

"Thank you Captain. For a minute there, a ride on the boat didn't seem so bad after all."

Rogge laughed, but added, "However, I must warn you *Kapitän* that you all may be in for a long cruise before this is over."

"Well it certainly hasn't been too bad so far. But, we may have some problems coming up."

"How's that?" inquired Rogge.

Lewis nodded towards the bow of the *Atlantis* below them. Several of the British nurses and young German officers were lying on the deck, enjoying the sun and obviously each other.

"You are correct *Kapitän*. I'll have a talk with my officers during our evening meal."

"I'll do the same. Now if you will excuse me Captain, I am sure you have more important matters to attend to than talking to me."

"It has been my pleasure," responded Rogge as he watched her walk away.

HYANNIS PORT, MASSACHUSETTS

Edward Kennedy stood by the big bay window in the Kennedy home, looking out across Nantucket Sound.

"What a beautiful clear day it is. After living in England so long I had almost forgotten that there are actually days like this."

"Yes, Edward," responded Rose. "It is good to be back home. But come and help me unpack. I think all of our things have now arrived from England."

"When will father be back?"

"Well, if the Rolls was on the ship that docked in Boston yesterday, he should be able to drive our car down here in less than three hours even with the thirty-five mile-per-hour national speed limit."

As Rose walked by the phone, it rang suddenly causing her to jump. "Oh, that startled me. I wasn't expecting anyone to find out we were here yet," she said to her son Edward, as she picked up the phone.

"Yes? Oh, it is good to hear your voice Joe. How are things going in Washington?"

Rose Kennedy let out a gasp and put her free hand up to her face.

"When did it happen, and how? Yes dear, we will leave right away and meet you at the White House as soon as possible. I'll say a prayer for you. Yes, you're right, it needs to be for both of us."

As Rose Kennedy slowly hung up the phone she turned to her youngest son, "Edward, that was your father. President Wallace has just been shot and killed. Your father is being sworn in as President in a few hours. Get your things together quickly. We are going to be flown down to Washington with him in a special airplane that is being sent up for us. Quickly now. We'll talk more about it on our way to the airport."

WASHINGTON D.C.

"How could you have let this happen!" an irate J. Edger Hoover asked the Presidential Staff, Secret Service and FBI members that had assembled in the Oval Office. "I warned you to be extra careful. There are thousands of Nazi sympathizers in the country, and probably dozens that would do everything in their power to add to the confusion at this time."

"Mr. Director. If I may," ventured Secretary of State, Cordell Hull. "The President was shot on the front porch of the White House as he was about to get into his limousine. The gun was one of our own fifty caliber sniper rifles equipped with a telescope sight and was found on the roof of the Mayflower Hotel almost a half of a mile down Connecticut Avenue. There was no way to prevent what happened. It would be impossible to cover all of the windows and roofs of buildings that look down on the steps of the White House."

An unimpressed Hoover pressed on. "How did you locate the rifle so quickly then?"

One of the Secret Service Officers spoke up. "Sir, the sniper rifle fires a regular fifty caliber machine-gun round and makes a very loud report. Several residents from the hotel immediately called the police to report a gunshot."

"But no one saw anyone, is that correct?"

"We are questioning everyone that was in or around the hotel at the time, right now," replied the officer. "We have recovered fragments of the bullet that hit the president. It is not the standard solid bullet normally used by the military, but was a hollow point that caused extreme damage when it hit the President in the chest. It would be impossible for a man to survive a hit with a bullet like that regardless of where he was hit, either in the head or torso as the President was. I'm sure you know that hollow point ammunition has been outlawed by the Geneva Convention as being inhumane."

"Of course," responded Hoover. "But keep me informed and send any evidence over to our lab for analysis, immediately."

"Certainly," responded Hull. "Now, we must get the cabinet members, Secretaries of War, Navy, Army and Air Force all over here so that when the Vice President arrives we can brief him on what is happening."

At 8:15 P.M. on November 26, Joseph P. Kennedy was sworn in as president. As he was being briefed on the status of the war in general, President Kennedy pondered his position. He truly wanted the war in western Europe to end and allow the Nazis and Communists to fight it out until they were both exhausted. Then he would step in and orchestrate a possible settlement. But he realized that there would be much opposition to this course of action, unless it became obvious that it really was the only option under the circumstances. His first executive order was to call a meeting of all the leaders of government, the military and scientific fields to review the world situation. They would lay out a course of action to be taken if Great Britain actually pulled out of the war.

INVERNESS, SCOTLAND

The JU-88 emerged from the low clouds and gently touched down on the runway. The two Spitfires that had been its escort ever since the JU-88 left the coast of Denmark, made one low level pass over the airfield to ensure the German aircraft was safely down, and then turned and made their own landings. As the JU-88 rolled to a stop, it was met by a Rolls Royce. Three men quickly exited the plane, and climbed into the back seat of the automobile. As they drove away, the JU-88 was quickly rolled into a secure hanger which was guarded by a detachment of Royal Marines who surrounded the hanger.

The Rolls Royce entered Inverness and after traveling several blocks turned into the parking lot of the Inverness Inn. The passengers were met by several armed military policemen who escorted the three Germans to the top floor of the Inn, which had been cordoned off from the rest of the building. Upon entering one of the large suites the Germans were met by Clement Attlee, the new Prime Minister, and Bertrand Russell, leader of the newly formed Peace and Prosperity Party.

"*Herr* Minister," acknowledged Attlee, as he extended his hand.

"Mr. Prime Minister, may I offer my congratulations on your recent election," said von Ribbentrop, "and thank you for inviting us to talk to you about our Government's proposal."

After mutual introductions of von Ribbentrop's and Attlee's associates, Attlee nodded to one of his men, who walked over to and opened the door to an adjacent room. He beckoned to someone waiting inside.

To the surprise of the Germans, in walked Rudolph Hess who had flown to England in 1941 in an attempt to reach his own accommodation with Great Britain at that time. His attempts were rejected, and he had been held a prisoner. There had never been an acknowledgment from the Germans that he was actually working in an official capacity for the government.

"Rudolph!" exclaimed von Ribbentrop as he rushed over and embraced his old friend. "You are looking well my friend. The English food must agree with you."

"I thought you might enjoy seeing one another again," offered Attlee.

"*Ja, Danke.* It is good to see someone from home," said a visibly moved Hess.

"Hopefully we are here to finish what you started," offered Von Ribbentrop.

"Ah, well, yes. Please sit down anywhere," said Attlee. " I didn't want to make this a formal meeting. Perhaps in an arm chair atmosphere we may be able to reach an agreement easier than glaring at each other across a table."

"I agree," acknowledged Von Ribbentrop as he sat down in an easy chair, and motioned for his two aides to follow suit.

"Now where would you like to begin Mr. Prime Minister?"

SHANGRI-LA, CATOCTIN MOUNTAINS, MARYLAND

Not since the signing of the Declaration of Independence had such an August assembly of prominent men gathered in one body to decide the future course of action for the United States. Sitting around the large table at the presidential retreat with the new President were: Cordell Hull, the Secretary of State; Henry Morgenthau Jr., Secretary of the Treasury; Henry L. Stimson, Secretary of War; James V. Forrestal, Secretary of the Navy; Harold L. Ickes, Secretary of the Interior; Sam Rayburn, Speaker of the House; Presidential Advisors Bernard Baruch and Vannevar Bush. Joining them were Generals Eisenhower, Douglas MacArthur, Mark Clark, George Marshall, Henry (Hap) Arnold and Leslie Groves; and Admirals Earnest King, Chester Nimitz and William Leahy. From the scientific fields were Drs. J. Robert Oppenheimer, Edward Teller, and even Albert Einstein. The gathered men along with their respective aides totaled seventy three individuals.

"Gentlemen," began President Kennedy. "I have called this unprecedented meeting to seek your advice concerning the future conduct of the United States in the war against the Axis powers. As you are all aware, the Germans have mastered the development of atomic weapons before we have with disastrous consequences. Furthermore, with the recent results of the elections in Great Britain, it is very possible that the English may drop out of the struggle, if not altogether, at least in Europe."

With this announcement, murmurings started throughout the assembled body.

"Gentlemen, please," continued Kennedy. "If I may continue. I plan to meet with the new British Prime Minister as soon as possible, hopefully no later than next week, and learn what their plans are first hand. In the meantime we--those of us here--must come up with a contingency plan in case the English do drop out. I realize that many of you have traveled a great distance to be here today and are very tired from your long journey. Therefore we will reconvene tomorrow after you have had time to rest and gather your ideas. At that time we will put together our most promising options. Thank you all for your support."

The next morning the President greeted the group and said, "Hopefully you have had some time to rest up since our short meeting yesterday. To start the meeting, I would like Doctor Vannevar Bush as Director of our Office of Scientific Research and Development, to brief us in regard to where we stand on catching up with the Germans in atomic research, missiles, and jet aircraft. Once we know where we stand, and how soon we can catch up, we will have established some time lines upon which we can plan our actions. Vannevar, if you will."

The fifty-four year old former Dean of Engineering and Vice President of the Massachusetts Institute of Technology took his place by a screen.

"First," he began, "let me address the jet-powered aircraft situation. We have both Lockheed and Bell Aircraft Companies working on the development of such an aircraft. This leaves our other aircraft companies free to continue to produce propeller driven aircraft which we will still need in large numbers for some time to come. Bell has all ready flown a P-39 Airacobra modified with a General Electric jet engine. Within the next sixty days, Lockheed should be able to fly a jet entirely designed and manufactured from scratch. It is currently being identified as the X-80. With Lockheed's industrial capacity, with help from a number of major sub-contractors, we believe we will be able to out-produce the Germans to the extent that within six to eight months we will equal their jet aircraft in total number.

"In the meantime, through our war efforts, if we continue to destroy German aircraft when we can on the ground and when lucky, once in a while in the air our numbers will soon equal theirs. The Russians have suffered an overall loss of twelve-to-one when engaging the German jets in the air. But, we have reason to believe that by using our latest models of the North American P-51 Mustang, we can reduce that ratio to a tolerable level until our own jets are available. Also the British have began to produce a jet-powered fighter of their own which they call the Meteor. We are in the process of getting the drawings and specifications on the Meteor from the British so we can start producing them here at Grumman Aircraft's facility on Long Island.

"With regards to the rockets, I am afraid we have nothing comparable to the V-2s raining down on us, even in the early design stage. However, Northrop Aircraft has developed a pilotless flying bomb similar in size to the V-1. It is a simple aircraft and we can produce them by the thousands. So what we lack in design sophistication, as compared to the V-2, we can make up in quantity through the use of thousands of the simpler Northrop craft. Now, to where we stand in our efforts to develop an atomic device, I will turn the time over to General Groves and his associates. General."

"Thank you," responded Groves. "We have been working around the clock the last few months, not only in the development of our own atomic device, but in the last week, analyzing the data coming in from the German explosions. We are still six months away from having our own device ready, I am afraid. However, we do have some very good news."

"Well," interrupted President Kennedy, "the six months is very bad news. So what is the good news?"

"Dr. Oppenheimer," asked Groves, "will you please explain what you have found?"

"Yes, thank you. The principle of the atomic explosions is through the fission, or splitting, of an atom of uranium. When the uranium atom is split it breaks up into two smaller atoms, and also releases two or three neutrons from the core of the atom. The combined weight of the two smaller atoms plus the two or three free neutrons are not as heavy as the original uranium atom. As early as 1905, Doctor Einstein, predicted that the lost matter would be transferred into energy, and the resulting energy would be equal to the lost matter multiplied by the square of the speed of light. Thus, a very small amount of matter turns into a very large amount of energy."

"Now," Oppenheimer continued, "the two or three freed neutrons hit other uranium atoms and split them. This process is repeated so rapidly that it is almost instantaneous. The first problem we have had is that although uranium is fairly common in nature it is comprised of 99.3 per cent of the isotope with the atomic mass of 238. The remaining .7 per cent is made up of isotopes with the atomic weights of 234 and 235. Trying to split the common uranium 238 is impossible with our current technology. We need the other two, preferably the 235. We are presently getting our 235 through a process we call gaseous diffusion, which is sort of like screening out the lighter 235 atoms from the heavier 238. It is a very slow process. Presently, we almost have a sufficient quantity to assemble our first device. The second problem is how to hold the uranium together long enough for all of the atoms to finish splitting before the energy given off by the first split blows the hunk of uranium apart. We are still working on this problem."

"The good news is that after analyzing the data from the German explosion at Normandy. From the findings of the explosion on the Russian Eastern Front, we have confirmed that both of the German devices were powered by uranium 235 fission. And they must be having the same problems we are in getting the U-235 in sufficient quantities."

"A week ago, I talked to Doctor Einstein and asked him if he had any ideas on how we could speed up the process. Doctor, would you please tell us what you have found."

Einstein got up and walked over to a black board. "You must excuse me, gentlemen, for I cannot talk without scribbling on a board."

A ripple of laughter filled the room.

"Four years ago, four of our scientists discovered a new element that has been named plutonium. It has an atomic mass of 239 and like U-235, it is fissionable. Unfortunately, like U-235 it is extremely rare in nature. After pondering this question, I have come to the conclusion that if we take some common U-238..." Einstein began writing equations on the board and drawing figures as he spoke. "And we place the U-238 in the atomic pile of the U-235 that we now have, neutrons emitted from the radioactive U-235 will hit the U-238 atoms. However, they will not be hit with sufficient energy to split them, but rather cause them to capture the neutron and turn the U-238 in to Pu-239, which as you can see from my equations should be relatively easy to split like U-235."

Again, a chuckle arose from the group as only one or two of his rapt audience could follow Einstein's equations.

Somewhat embarrassed, Einstein started to apologize, but Openheimer stood up and said. "Our group in New Mexico has studied these equations, and believe your calculations are correct Albert. We are pursuing this idea right now. Unfortunately, your calculations only tell us what to do, but not how to do it," joked Oppenheimer.

"Details," responded Einstein, winking at the audience.

After the laughter had died down, Oppenheimer continued, "Gentlemen, the bottom line, is that the Germans may produce enough U-235 for maybe one or two devices per month, but when we get Albert's 'details' worked out, we will be in a position to produce one a day."

The room burst into applause.

As Einstein was about to leave the blackboard, Oppenheimer walked up to his side and said, "Just a minute, Albert. Gentlemen, see these marvelous equations? Let me tell you about some other equations of Doctor Einstein. This is a story that Albert may not even know himself. In the 1920s, one of the big questions had to do with the size of the universe. Finally, in 1929, the great astronomer, Edwin Hubble, discovered through observations that the universe was actually expanding. He contacted Doctor Einstein and invited him to California to see for himself, as both of them were working on the same question. Albert took his good wife with him and traveled to California. While Albert and Edwin were busy one of the other astronomers took Mrs. Einstein on a tour of the great Hale Observatory and explained to her that thanks to its magnificent telescope the mysteries of the universe were being solved. In all innocence, Mrs. Einstein looked up at the large one hundred inch telescope and replied, 'You know, my husband does the same thing using just a pencil and the backs of old envelopes.'"

Again the room filled with laughter.

"Well," said the President after the laughter had died down. "Doctor Einstein's equations may be our salvation yet. But how are we to get through the next six months?"

James Forrestal, the Secretary of War, stood up and suggested to the President that it would be a good time to review the Allies present military positions around the world.

"Yes. Please proceed."

"General Marshall will be our speaker," responded Forrestal.

As General Marshall walked to the wall and pulled down a large map of Europe, an aide walked over to the President and whispered in his ear.

"General would you please excuse me? Lord Halifax, the English Ambassador, is on the phone and says he must talk to me right away. Let's all take a fifteen minute break."

Walking into an adjoining office, Kennedy picked up the phone.

"Yes, Mr. Ambassador, what can I do for you?"

"Mr. President, I apologize for interrupting you, but I have received some disturbing information through unofficial channels. This is a difficult thing for me to do. But I believe you should know what is happening before you get official notice from my government."

"Notice? About what?" queried Kennedy.

"Mr. President, the leaders of His Majesty's Government have been in secret meetings with representatives from Germany. They evidently have now completed their talks. Within the last couple of hours the Germans have left for home, and since they were allowed to take Rudolph Hess with them, it can mean only one thing."

"My God!" exclaimed the President. "They must have come to some sort of an agreement."

"I think so too, Mr. President," replied Halifax. "That's why I called as soon as I heard what was going on. Obviously, I am not happy to hear this either. That is why I am acting on my own, and informing you of what is happening."

"Mr. Ambassador, I greatly appreciate your call. Right now, I am being briefed on the status of the war and taking recommendations on how we should proceed in light of recent military developments. Since you have compromised your own position to inform me of these new political developments, I would be pleased if you could join us in our deliberations. That is if you would feel comfortable doing so?"

"If you think I could be of any assistance, I will be happy to join you. In any event, I'll be turning in my resignation as ambassador as soon as I officially receive notification of the agreement, to show my opposition to the policy."

"Please, Mr. Ambassador, don't act too hastily. We may need you now more than ever," responded the President. "My office staff will make arrangements for your travel to where we are meeting. How soon could you leave?"

"Within the hour."

"Fine, we will be looking forward to seeing you in the morning, if not before."

Upon returning to the meeting, the President informed the group of what the English Ambassador had told him. Feelings in the room ran from disbelief that Britain would pull out of the struggle, to rage that Britain, after doing everything in her power to get the United States involved in two European Wars in twenty five years, would now desert the U.S.

"Gentlemen, I propose that we adjourn for the day and reconvene tomorrow morning at 0800, when the English Ambassador will be with us. In the meantime, please put together some proposals as to what we should now do, based on the assumption that Great Britain is now a non-combatant. We will probably lose the use of her facilities."

The following morning, as the leaders reassembled at the mountain retreat, along with Lord Halifax, there was an overall feeling of apprehension in the air. At the beginning of June, the feeling had been that the invasion of France was the beginning of the end of the war. Now, in just a few short weeks, the victorious end appeared to be farther away than at any other time since 1939.

"General Marshall, what are your findings?" asked the President as he slid into his chair.

"Well sir," the General began, "It is our opinion that we will lose our bases in England. Is that a correct assessment in your opinion Mr. Ambassador?"

"I think you are correct, General," responded the Ambassador, "and if I may add, you will probably lose access to all of our British bases in the Mediterranean area and Near East as well."

"That being the case," continued Marshall, "we will be faced with an almost impossible situation of supplying our troops now occupying the beaches of Normandy with the necessary supplies to continue the war. Moreover, once the British troops pull out of Normandy, our entire left flank will be exposed with little chance of bringing in sufficient reinforcements to replace the British. Needless to say, if we had not had the English Islands as a staging point we would have never considered the invasion in the first place, but would have had to continued to slug our way up the Italian peninsula or invade Greece."

"Where do we stand in Italy at the present time?" asked the President.

"General Clark, would you like to address that subject?" asked Marshall.

General Mark Clark, commander of the fifth Army, stood up and walked to the maps. "At the present time, our front stretches across Italy from here on the west to Ancona here on the Adriatic. We are steadily pushing back Field Marshall Albert Kesselring's Army Group C, but the fighting has been severe. Without the pressure the fighting in Normandy was putting on the Germans, they could greatly reinforce Kesselring. Our only hope would be to greatly increase our troops as well, which we could do from Africa. But, if we had sufficient troops to push back the Germans our forces would be so concentrated they would be a prime target for an atomic attack as the Russians found out. Also, we have the problem of the loss of the English army which has been holding almost half of the front."

"This brings us back to the question of how many nuclear devices the Germans have, and what their actual production rate is, doesn't it?" asked the President.

Everyone nodded in agreement.

"Even if the Germans did not use their new weapons and we continued to advance, I'm afraid that we would eventually be stalled once we reached the Alps," continued Clark.

"Hannibal fought his way through, although from the opposite direction," suggested the President.

"That's true, Mr. President," interjected General Marshall, "but remember he had the secret weapon of the day, the elephant."

Everyone, including the President laughed.

"Yes, I had forgotten about the elephants," noted the President, as he continued. "Do we know where the Germans are building their atomic devices, and if so, can't we destroy them by bombing the hell out of them?"

"We have a good idea where they are getting their Uranium ore and have bombed the mines," offered Marshall. "However, just where the devices are being assembled is still unknown. We have reason to believe it is in, or around, the German town of Haigerloch. Otto Hahn, the German physicist, who was awarded the Nobel Prize for work he did on nuclear fission, has been reported to be living in Haigerloch. He would surely be involved in the development of their atomic weapons. However, we have the problem of bombing the area as our bombers are sitting ducks for the new German jet-powered fighters. Still, we could probably overwhelm their defenses by sheer numbers if we were willing to pay the price."

"Probably a very costly option," ventured the President.

"Very much so, Mr. President. But one we may have to pay."

"I'll have to think about that. Can you give me some estimation as to what our losses would be?"

"Well," responded General Arnold of the Army Air Corps, "in some raids even before the Germans had jets, we lost close to forty percent of the attack force."

"I can see that our losses now would be prohibitive," responded the President. "Now, if I may, let me change the subject. Is there any good news about the struggle with the Japanese?"

"Yes and no," continued Marshall. "General Stillwell and the Chinese are still making little progress on the Chinese front. But the British and Indians are slowly pushing the Japanese back in the Burma campaign. Of course, if the British pull out of the fight there, the Indian troops could not possibly hold back the Japanese by themselves. What is your opinion Mr. Ambassador, regarding your government's position on the war in Asia?"

"Correction, if I may, General. I no longer consider it to be my government," responded Halifax.

"I'm sorry...I...we all, understand your feelings," responded Marshall.

"Thank you. But now, in response to your question about Asia. It is my opinion that Great Britain will continue to wage war on the Japanese. Failure to do so would not only result in the loss of the Crown colonies of Hong Kong and Singapore, but also in Australia and New Zealand pulling out of the Commonwealth. Of course, we really won't know until we find out what the terms of the German agreement are."

"If we don't hear from Attlee by tomorrow I will call him myself," said an angry President. "Please go on General Marshall."

"Two days ago we broke the back of the Japanese Naval Air Power in the Philippine Sea, and badly crippled their naval forces in general. At the present time the second and fourth Marine Divisions are winning the struggle on Saipan in the Marianas. From Saipan, the Japanese home islands will be within reach of our B-29 long range bombers."

"Where do we stand on the problem of the Germans giving the Japanese their latest atomic and jet-power technology?" asked the President.

"The German note to the British said they were shipping that technology to Japan unless the British agreed to their demands. Again, until the British inform us of the agreement, we don't know what is happening. We, along with the Australians, are doing everything possible to intercept any sub or ship crossing the Indian Ocean. But our chances are slim, I am afraid, in intercepting any one particular vessel."

"What then do you recommend we do?" asked a very serious President.

"It is the military's recommendation," went on General Marshall, " that if the British pull out and deny us the use of their island, we evacuate Normandy. This will, of course, outrage the

Russians and we must keep them in the struggle or possibly have to come to terms with the Germans ourselves. But, if we keep pressure on the Germans in Italy and perhaps even transfer some of our troops to the Russian front, we probably can reassure the Russians that regardless of what England did, we are in this struggle to the end. As soon as we are in full production of our own atomic weapons and jet aircraft we will eventually be in a position to order the Germans to either surrender or face mass destruction like the world has never seen!"

The room broke into applause.

"However," went on Marshall, "since we don't know the status of the transfer of technology to Japan, and cannot trust the Germans to stop the transfer, we recommend an invasion of the Japanese home islands as soon as possible. Otherwise, an invasion could result in another Normandy-type disaster."

"What if the German device has already arrived in Japan?" asked the President.

"That is a chance we will have to take. General MacArthur, would you please explain how you propose to minimize the risk?"

"Yes, thank you General."

Pulling down a large map of Japan, MacArthur began. "Our plan is to first gain control of these two small islands, Yaku and Tanega, located here off the southern coast of Kyushu, the southernmost main island. This will be accomplished by the Fourth Infantry Division under the command of General Donald Myer. We estimate their operations can be completed within ninety six hours, unless the Japanese have the German atomic device and use it. These two islands will give us control of the sea lanes to the landing beaches on Kyushu itself.

"On the third day, the Eighth Army comprised of six infantry and two armored divisions will initiate Operation Coronet by landing here at Tateyame which controls the entrance to Tokyo Bay. This is a well fortified area, so immediately following the landing, the First Army comprised of three Marine and three infantry divisions, will land farther North near Mobara and cut off the peninsula, isolating the defenders facing the Eighth Army.

"On the fifth day, Operation Olympic will commence with the Sixth Army landing the Fifth Amphibian Corps here on

Kyushu just south of Kushikino. At the same time the Eleventh Corps will land here on the southern tip of Kyushu, the First Corps will go ashore at Miyazaki. The Ninth Corps will be held in reserve to go ashore where needed as will the Fortieth Division that took Yaku and Tanega. The Eleventh Airborne Division will also be held in reserve for quick deployment as needed. A total of fourteen divisions and two regimental combat teams will be involved.

"The Sixth Army will work its way up Kyushu and cross over to the main island of Honshu here at Kitakyushu, while the Eighth and First Army sweep around towards Tokyo.

"All of the time the entire Pacific Fleet will be bombarding the coastal defenses with gunfire, while carrier aircraft will control the air over the beach heads."

"What do you estimate our casualties will be General?" asked the President.

"Very high, I am afraid, sir. Of the eight hundred thousand troops involved, we can expect to suffer more than twenty-five percent casualties, and if Japan should fight to the very end, and in all likelihood they will, we may have close to one million casualties. That is more than we have suffered so far to date in both the European and Pacific Theaters. And that's based on the assumption that the Japanese do not have the German atomic device."

The President said nothing, but placed a hand over his eyes.

In a moment he looked up and quietly said, "Now I have some understanding of how Lincoln felt when the casualties during the Civil War were coming in."

"It is not a pleasant thought," offered Secretary Hull. "But even these losses compared to our present population are not as great as the Civil War losses when compared to the country's population in the 1860's."

"If I may," continued MacArthur, "with regards to the Japanese having a German atomic device, we have three things going for us. First, perhaps the British as part of their deal with Germany may have had the delivery canceled. Secondly, our Navy, together with the Australians, has a chance of sinking the ship delivering the weapon before it reaches Japan. Third, as has been pointed out, the devices used so far have probably been planted in advance because they are so large it would have been difficult, if not impossible, to deliver them like regular munitions. That, in fact, is why we have planned the invasion like we have. The invasion of the small southern islands first will be thought to be a diversion and not worth the use of the device, if they have it. When the First and Eighth Army go ashore east of Tokyo and Yokohama, we will do so when there is the usual morning easterly wind blowing toward their most populated area. They are sure to have heard of the radiation sickness that follows the debris cloud, and will think twice about using the device when the cloud would drift over Tokyo. Of course, that may not deter them, in which case they could have more casualties than ourselves.

"How soon could you be ready to invade, General?"

MacArthur looked towards Marshall, who stood up and walked over and stood by MacArthur. "We have been planning for our big invasion of the Philippines, which is scheduled for early January. If we were to put all other operations against the Japanese on hold and just concentrate on the invasion of the mainland, we could probably do it by mid January."

"General," interrupted General Groves, "I feel that we would be taking an unacceptable risk by waiting that long."

"How so?" asked Marshall.

"Well, to begin with, I don't think the Germans will call off the delivery of their atomic device to the Japanese. They realize that we are probably not about to cave in to their demands like the British. Therefore, it follows that by keeping the Japanese as a major threat, we will have to devote a large portion of our war effort against the Japanese, thereby taking some of the pressure off of themselves. Also, as I recall, the Germans want a settlement with the west so they can concentrate on the Russians. As long as Japan is a threat to Siberia, Russia has to maintain a large army in the east, which otherwise could be used on their Western Front. So it follows that by furnishing the Japanese with atomic weapons on a continuous basis they will be a formidable enemy for some time to come. In fact, if I was in Tojo's shoes, I would put the second device I had in a submarine and detonate it off the coast of Los Angeles as soon as I could. Such an explosion would greatly reduce our aircraft and oil production."

A murmur ran through the group.

"Well, wouldn't you?" Groves asked no one in particular.

"You have made a good point, General," acknowledged the President. "A very good point indeed."

Everyone agreed that it was a very likely possibility if the Japanese had such a weapon.

"I agree with General Groves," stated the President. "We must knock Japan out of the war as soon as possible."

LONDON

"When and what are you going to tell the Americans?" pressed Bertrand Russell.

"Well, I had better do it right away, before the Germans say anything," responded a somewhat downtrodden Attlee.

"The Americans can't blame you. You are only responding to the will of the people who have spoken through the election."

"I suppose that's true, but, it is a difficult thing to do after the Americans have come to our rescue twice in the last quarter of a century," responded Attlee.

"How many atomic devices would you have let explode over our country before you would have been forced to surrender? Surely you and the Americans see that this armistice you signed is far better than that. And believe me, it would have come to that," stressed Russell.

"That is true. I couldn't sit here and see our country totally destroyed."

"Of course not. No one could. There are times when we have to do what we have to do, regardless of the consequences,"

Picking up the telephone, the Prime Minister said, "Please put me through to the President of the United States as quickly as possible. Yes. Thank you."

WASHINGTON

Putting the phone down in his private quarters, President Kennedy turned to his wife and said, "Well Rose, the British did it. They actually came to terms with the Germans and signed an armistice."

"Did they tell you what the terms were?"

"Yes, I think they told me everything and were not holding anything back. Let's see, where did I put my copy of the German proposal?" as he rummaged through his brief case. "Ah, here it is. Now, let's see what the Germans had proposed, as compared to what Attlee said they agreed to."

"Well, they agreed to cease all hostilities and exchange prisoners. The English will also cease supplying the Russians with war material. And, lastly, we are to remove all of our troops from English soil as well as from all of their African and Middle East territories, within thirty days. The British will continue in the struggle against the Japanese, but the Germans will also continue to supply the Japanese with their latest technology, which I can only assume, includes atomic weapons."

"But, I thought in their original agreement, they said they wouldn't assist the Japanese?"

"They did. But they originally had included that we, America, would cease all war-like activities against them as well as the British. Obviously, the Germans knew the British couldn't speak for us, so it gave them a way out to continue to assist their Allies, which of course is to their advantage."

"What else did they agree to?"

"Well the British held their ground and refused to be of any assistance in teaching the Germans how to control their newly acquired conquests."

"Is that good? Perhaps the British could have convinced the Germans to be more benevolent masters and make it easier for the conquered peoples of Europe."

"That may be so," said Kennedy as he turned and walked out of the residential section of the White House and headed for the Oval Office.

For almost three years, Kennedy had been trying to get the United States out of the war with Germany. Now, as he walked down the hall, he knew he had his chance. But he also realized he would have to play his cards right to get the rest of the leadership of the country to agree with him. Slowly, a plan came to mind.

The East Room of the White House was again full of governmental leaders of both parties as well as the nation's military leaders and leading scientists. After reviewing the British and German agreement, the President got right to the point. "Gentlemen, after careful consideration of the status of the war, our own technology status, and the fact that the British are essentially out of the war, I would like to propose, for your consideration, the following: One: We withdraw our troops and aircraft out of all British territory, as they requested, and out of Normandy as well. Without a base in England, our troops, if left in Normandy, would be without an adequate supply base for arms and food to sustain them."

"Hell! Excuse me, Mr. President," interrupted General George Patton. "With the forces we still have on and around the British Isles, we could tell the British to go to hell with their request and take them over in less than sixty days."

"General Patton!" exclaimed an irate President. "We are trying to end a war, not expand it into another. Is that clear!"

"Yes sir!" responded Patton.

"Now if I may continue," went on the President. "Two: We withdraw from Italy, as well, providing the Germans do likewise. Three: We will exchange prisoners of war. Four: Since Germany insists on continuing to give aid to the Japanese, we will also continue to give aid to the Russians. Five: We proceed with the invasion against the Japanese home islands as soon as possible. Lastly, General Groves, we must have an atomic device. No, not a big device; we need an atomic bomb that will fit into one of our B-29 bombers as soon as possible. Whatever resources you and your people require to accomplish this are yours for the asking."

"Thank you sir," responded Groves. "We will do what we can."

"Mr. President," asked General Marshall. "Are you proposing to enter into a formal signed agreement with the Nazis like the British?"

Kennedy realized that such an agreement was out of the question, although he would like to have reached one, so he explained. "No. No formal agreement. However through diplomatic channels we will inform Germany of what we are going to do, and what we expect of them in return."

"Then, technically, a state of war with Germany will continue to exist. Is that correct?"

"That is correct. Still at war, but not warring. That should give us more flexibility in our future course of action, should it not?"

Everyone nodded in agreement.

"After we finish off the Japanese, will we turn our attention back to ridding Europe of Nazi domination?" asked MacArthur.

Kennedy really wanted to sit back and let the Russians and Germans slug it out, but again he realized this was not the time to propose such a course of action. "Yes, if possible," he replied. "But that, of course, must not get out of this room."

"Mr. President," asked Admiral Nimitz. "With regard to your proposal to withdraw from Italy."

"Yes, what about it?" replied the President.

"Two things, Sir. If we pull off of the European mainland now, we would have a very difficult, if not impossible, task of ever conducting another invasion later on. In light of what happened at Normandy, I am afraid large invasions, with the necessary mass of ships and men, may be a thing of the past in a day of atomic weapons. Secondly, if we are not tying down a significant number of German forces somewhere, the Germans could bring their entire military might to bear on the Russians. In such an event, the Russians could collapse like they did in 1917. If that happened, heaven forbid, later on we may find ourselves all alone in defeating Nazism or else be forced to live with the Nazi domination of western Europe, for who knows how long. Hitler's boast of a thousand-year Reich might become a reality."

Kennedy looked around the room and saw that to a man, everyone was nodding in agreement to Nimitz's assessment of the situation.

"You may be correct, Admiral," conceded Kennedy. "General Marshall, would you and your associates put together a plan on how we could conduct some sort of holding action in Italy?"

"Yes Sir."

"Any other questions or comments at this time?"

"Mr. President," offered Presidential advisor, Bernard Baruch. "Speaking not only as an American, but also as a Jew, I would like to bring up one serious item of business you have not discussed here."

Einstein, Oppenheimer, and the other Jews in attendance all nodded their heads.

"Oh? what is that, Bernard?"

"It is the Jewish question, Sir. It is a well known fact that the Nazis are systematically rounding up the entire Jewish population of conquered Europe and sending them to various death camps. Is this going to be allowed to continue? Or will it be 'unofficially' addressed along with our withdrawal from mainland Europe?"

The question caught all of the others in attendance off guard. For several years now, Jewish leaders had been pressing both the United States and England to bomb the death camps, since the inmates were about to be killed anyway, or at least continuously bomb the railways and highways leading to the camps. But the leaders of both countries had adapted the philosophy that the destruction of more strategic targets would end the war more quickly and put an end to the extermination going on more quickly. However, in some circles it was felt that the number of German troops involved in the rounding up of the Jews together with utilizing so many trains in their transportation was actually saving many Allied lives by tieing up so many men and resources. Thus the philosophy of "better them than us" held sway.

"Ah, well, Bernard why don't you prepare a proposal for me to review and we will see what can be done," stammered the President.

"It will be on your desk in the morning, Mr. President."

"Now gentlemen," went on the President. "Let's get down to planning the invasion of Japan."

MOSCOW

Stalin was busy reading reports from the front as Molotov entered the room and quietly took a chair across from him.

"You have heard the latest?" asked Stalin.

"About the English coming to terms with the Nazis?" inquired Molotov.

"Of course."

"Well, we half expected it. Didn't we?"

"Yes, I knew they couldn't be counted on."

"I think we should call in the American ambassador and find out how the Americans plan on handling this turnabout."

Looking up, Stalin asked, "Do you really think he would tell us the truth?"

"I don't know. But it couldn't help but give us some insight into what is going on."

"You are probably correct. See how soon he can meet with us."

Molotov reached for the phone and asked Stalin's private telephone operator to put him in touch with the American Ambassador.

In a few moments, one of the Ambassador's Russian speaking aides came on the line.

"I am sorry, Mr. Molotov, the Ambassador is not here at the present time. He was suddenly called back to Washington for an important meeting. Can I help you?"

Through the interpreter, Molotov explained that the Russian Government needed to know as soon as possible what America was going to do in light of the English/German agreement.

"I think that is what the Ambassador was called home for. I'll pass on anything we hear as soon as possible."

"Please do," responded Molotov as he hung up.

"Well?" inquired Stalin.

"The Ambassador is in Washington right now."

"Probably plotting how to stab us in the back." ventured Stalin. "Maybe it is time we had a meeting with our military and scientific experts and do a little plotting ourselves. Set it up as soon as possible."

"Yes, Comrade Stalin. I'll get right on it."

NORMANDY

Lt. General George Patton, commander of the US Third Army stood in the turret of his lead tank at the top of a small hill that fell off in front of him. He watched as his tanks and armored vehicles rolled up to the edge of the hill on both sides of him, and spaced themselves about fifty yards apart. When all were in position, the line stretched for almost a mile. Behind him, lined up facing almost due east and toward the German lines, now some three miles away, were the balance of the Third Army's tanks, backed up by heavy infantry. The new line of tanks were forming a line to protect the Americans' left flank that had previously been covered by the British Eighth Army, but which was now withdrawing. Running along the base of the hill was a major highway leading to Caen. The highway was filled with British vehicles of all descriptions, each loaded with British troops, all headed toward the coast where the British Navy stood ready to evacuate them from France for the second time in four years. By the time Patton received word that all of his armor was in position he could see the end of the British column, which was made up of Scottish troops. Bringing up the rear were the Royal Highlander Pipes and Drums playing *"Scotland the Brave."* In front of the pipers were the regimental colors and a staff car. In the staff car was Brigadier General Alexander McDonald, commander of the Scottish troops. Seeing Patton's pennant flying on his tank, McDonald ordered his driver to drive to the base of the hill, which the General then climbed. As he approached Patton's tank, he stopped and saluted.

"Come on up," yelled Patton over the engine noise, as he returned the salute.

"General, this is a very sad day for me," ventured McDonald. "It is with a very heavy heart that I am leaving you here."

"It is a sad day for me as well, General," replied Patton. "And I am worried that we may be following you shortly, unless my leaders in Washington get some courage."

"It makes me wonder where this will all end."

"Where were the Germans when you last saw them?" asked Patton.

"Right behind us, General. They have been tailing us by about two miles ever since we pulled out of our forward positions."

"The bastards."

"No hostilities. They are just following us. As a matter of fact I can see the dust of their advance column now."

Patton raised his field glasses and scanned the road. "Yes, I see them. Just infantry, and light armor, but I sure in hell don't like this. I don't want one of them on this side of the Orne."

At this time, the Royal Highlanders were passing below Patton when the pipes squeaked to a stop. They began to play *"The Battle Hymn of the Republic."*

Upon hearing the familiar strains, tears welled up in Patton's eyes.

"Damn it, General. A lot of your brave men died for that road down there and I am not about to just hand it over to those Nazi bastards." Turning to his radioman, he ordered, "Shut off the radio!"

"Sir?"

"I said shut off the damn radio!"

"Yes, Sir!"

"Watch yourself General," said Patton as he personally started to swing his turret and gun towards the oncoming German column.

"We're with you, General." exclaimed McDonald as he realized what was going to happen and he jumped from the tank and ran back down the hill toward his column.

Patton glanced at his flanking tanks. Both Commanders were standing in their turrets looking his way and obviously trying to reach him on their head sets.

"Damn it, just do it," thought Patton, as he glared at the tank commander on his left. The commander raised his hands in exasperation but began to swing his turret toward the Germans.

"Attaboy," mumbled Patton. "No orders. Just do what we have to do."

One by one all of the tanks on both his flanks began swinging their guns to bear on the Germans.

"Gunner, give me a star shell!"

"Sir?"

"Soldier, if you don't want to load tell me, and I'll come down and I'll do it myself."

"No sir, that won't be necessary," he said as he ran a shell into the gun and closed the breach with a clang.

"Give me maximum elevation."

"Maximum elevation."

"Left five degrees."

"Left five degrees."

"Fire!"

"Fire, sir?"

"Fire!"

The tank arched back from the recoil as the shell left the barrel.

The German commander saw the puff of smoke from Patton's tank, and before he heard the report he was reaching for his phone.

The star shell exploded high above the lead German column causing the ranks of infantry to break as they sought cover by the roadside.

General McDonald had reached his troops, whereupon the Highlander Pipers did an about face and formed up their ranks, while the Scottish infantry formed up on both sides of them.

Within two minutes phones were ringing in the offices of Field Marshall Rommel, Field Marshall Montgomery and General Eisenhower.

General Patton saw the tank commander next to him climb out of his tank and started running toward him.

"Didn't take them long," muttered Patton.

"Sir?" questioned his gunner.

"I said it didn't take them long to figure out what we have done here."

As the Major from the next tank reached Patton's, he stopped and saluted.

"Sir. General Bradley is on my radio. He said to tell you to get on your radio right now. He wants to have a few words with you."

"I bet he does at that. Thank you Major."

"Ah, is your radio out of service, Sir? If it is, I'll bring my tank over closer so you can use mine."

"No, that won't be necessary Major. I'm sure my radioman will have the problem corrected in short order."

As the Major ran back to his tank, Patton squared his shoulders and scanned the view below him. The Germans were still hunkered down.

"OK, Sparks, turn the radio back on. All good things must come to an end, sooner or later."

"Patton here," he said into the microphone.

"George, just what in the hell are you doing up there?" demanded a very upset General Bradley.

"Now Brad, I just wanted those Nazi bastards to know who still had control of this area. No one got hurt."

"Damn it, George, you know perfectly well what your orders are. No hostilities of any kind. Now, you and your corps turn around and head back to the coast right now. We are evacuating Normandy per a Presidential Order!"

"A what?"

"You heard me George. Now, do it. That's an order. And no questions. I want a report from you every hour on the hour of just where you are. Is that clear, General?"

"Yes, sir," responded Patton.

"Good. Now I'll expect to hear from you in your new position in another thirty five minutes."

As the connection went dead, Patton thought. "I'll be damned if I'll just turn tail and run. Follow me!" he barked into his radio to his corps commanders. "Driver, back away from this position. Slowly, very slowly."

"Very slowly it is, General."

Seeing the American tanks withdrawing, the Scottish regiment reformed and resumed their reluctant march toward the sea.

ATLANTIS, EAST INDIAN OCEAN

The gentle knock on her cabin door woke Captain Lewis from a shallow sleep. She had still not gotten used to the rolling and pitching of the ship, even when it was fairly light. She looked at her watch on the night stand--2:20. As she reached for her robe the knock was repeated. Lewis opened the door just a crack and saw Lieutenant Debbie Johnson standing there.

"Yes, Lieutenant, what is it?"

"Captain, I ... that is, we are sorry to disturb you at this hour. But we must talk."

"We? Who is with you?"

A German Ensign stepped from the shadows into the light from the open door.

"Captain this is Fritz ... I mean Ensign Stuben. May we please come in?"

As she stepped aside, Captain Lewis responded, "Yes, I know the Ensign. Come in."

Captain Lewis sat down on her bed and motioned Lieutenant Johnson to join her while offering the only chair to Ensign Stuben.

"I am almost afraid to ask, but what is this all about?"

"Captain, Ensign Stuben and I have been secretly seeing each other and we have grown very fond of one another."

"You are both officers in your respective country's military," interrupted Lewis, "and you both know what fraternizing with the enemy can mean to each of you."

"Yes, we know," responded Johnson.

"*Ja,*" agreed the Ensign.

"Please," went on Johnson, "tonight Fritz told me something which we decided you should know. Please tell her Fritz, as I still don't understand everything you told me."

Captain Lewis looked at the blond-haired young man and could understand how easy it would be for Johnson to become attracted to him.

"Go ahead, Ensign. What is it that I should know?"

"It's about the cargo we took off the U-boat a few days ago, *Kapitän.*"

"What about it?"

"As you are aware, the Allied invasion of Normandy was brought to a halt by a large explosion, as was a large Communist offensive in Poland a few days later."

"Yes, your Captain has let me listen to some of the short wave radio reports we have picked up." Captain Lewis put her hand over her mouth.

"Oh, no! Are you telling me we now have one of these, these, atomic devices on board?"

"Yes, we do. We are to deliver it to the Japanese in Singapore."

"But, why are you telling me, an enemy officer, this?"

"As an officer myself, I have no feelings against the use of these weapons as they have been used. But the rumor is, that the Japanese will take the device and set it off near Los Angeles, where most of the American aircraft factories are located. That will result in an enormous number of civilian casualties. I was educated in America and have a degree in physics from MIT. I know the technical capabilities of the Americans, and realize they will soon have atomic devices of their own. If the Japanese destroy an American city with the device we are carrying, the Americans will know where they got it, and in retaliation, will utterly destroy not only Japan but my country as well."

"I would hope so," thought Lewis to herself. "But why are you telling me this?" she asked out loud. "What can I possibly do about it? After all, I am your prisoner and under your control."

"I will help you notify your people of the peril."

"This is where I come in," responded Johnson, as she smiled at the Ensign. "I know the radioman that is now on duty has taken a shine to me. What Fritz and I suggest is that I go down to the radio room and entice the radioman to join me for a little while on the aft deck. As soon as he leaves with me, the two of you will slip into the radio room."

"And I will attempt to contact any Allied ship in the area," picked up the Ensign. " After we have made contact, it will be up to you *Kapitän*, to convince whoever picks up our message that this is genuine."

"And what are we going to tell them? Sink this ship with us on it?"

"We will be in Singapore in three days. After the Allies know that you are prisoners on-board and where we are, I hope they will track us and determine what Japanese ship we put our cargo aboard and then sink it. The Allies must have numerous spies and informants in Singapore, so we will be easily identified as will the Japanese ship."

"And when do you propose doing this?"

"Right now *Kapitän*. Only a few men are on watch and your forces can use all of the time we can give them to get ready. As I said, we will be making the transfer in about seventy-two hours."

"Also," added Lieutenant Johnson, "if we don't do it now I may not have the courage later to do what I may have to do."

"Are you sure you want to go through with this Debbie?" asked a sympathetic Lewis.

"Yes, if it will save thousands of lives."

"*Ja*, believe me, it will," responded the German officer.

"Very well," sighed Lewis, "let's do it."

"Ah, Captain may I use some of your make up?" asked Debbie, "I need to be at my best for this."

"Help yourself," said Lewis as she gave the younger woman a hug.

USS SWORDFISH, EAST INDIAN OCEAN

Captain Gordon Underwood stood in the conning tower scanning the faint horizon with his field glasses. The submarine was almost dead in the water, but Underwood could feel the throbbing of the diesel engines as they recharged the batteries needed for underwater running. He yawned and looked at his watch. His two-hour watch would be over in less than an hour and he could get back to bed.

First Officer Max Larsen climbed up the ladder.

"Captain, you had better go to the radio room. A curious message is coming through. It could be related to the U-Boat we are looking for."

"Thank you. We could use a break in this search."

As the Captain entered the small radio room, the radioman handed him a head set and explained. "About ten minutes ago, a very faint message came through. It was too faint to make out. But when it was repeated, I was able to make some sense of it. At first I thought the message was weak because it was coming from a great distance. But the second message though still weak, was somewhat stronger than the first. The signal strength couldn't be attributed to the change in distance in only a couple of minutes. I think whoever it is, is gradually increasing their transmission strength until they have contacted someone. It is like they want to be heard, but by as few as possible."

"That is interesting."

"If they follow the same pattern we should pick them up again at any time now."

The third transmission though still weak, but a little stronger still, came through in less than a minute.

"This is the *Atlantis*. Please acknowledge."

"That is the name of a German raider operating in the area. Go ahead Sparks, acknowledge the message and identify ourselves."

"It could be some sort of a trap, Captain."

"Yes, but it is not an imminent one."

"This is the USS *Swordfish*. We hear you. Go ahead."

"This is Captain Ruth Lewis, formerly with British forces in Burma. A number of us nurses are being held prisoners aboard the German raider, *Atlantis*, bound for Singapore. Also aboard is an atomic device that has been transferred from a German U-boat. Our present position is approximately eighty-seven degrees thirty minutes East, and five degrees two minutes South, on a direct course to the Strait of Malacca at a speed of approximately twelve knots. Must end transmission, due to danger. Please intercept us."

"Quickly, acknowledge we understand, Sparks."

"Aye, Aye, Captain. It's done. They have signed off, Captain."

"Sparks, did it sound like to you that someone was coaching this Captain Lewis on their location and course?"

"Yes, at times I thought I could hear someone with a German accent in the background."

"I did too. All the more suspicious. But it is doubtful that an English nurse could get access to the radio room and send such a message with location and all without help. Please put a call out to all of the officers to meet me in the chart room as soon as possible."

By the time the sleepy officers began to arrive, Captain Underwood had worked out a course for intercept. After going over the message he asked for his officers' opinions. To a man, they all agreed that although it could be a trap of some sorts, they needed to intercept the *Atlantis*.

"According to my calculations, we can intercept the *Atlantis* about right here," as Underwood pointed to a chart. "That's based on our position here, and the reported position of the *Atlantis* being about here. Mr. Larsen, please set us on a new course to intercept the *Atlantis*. We will run on the surface for maximum speed."

I'll plan an intercept a little farther east in case the position of the *Atlantis* given us was not quite correct. Better to arrive a little early than a little too late."

"Good idea. Also check on what the estimated maximum speed of the raider is. The closer they get to their destination, the more temptation there will be to speed up and get there before they are detected."

"I'll plan the intercept on all contingencies. But, off hand, I would guess we could make contact as early as 0100 tomorrow."

"Captain," asked the second officer, "when we make contact what are your plans? Sink her outright? Disable her? Or capture her?"

"Good questions. Obviously, we will have to handle this mission by ourselves. If we try to contact others for help, the *Atlantis* may find out and take evasive actions, or the Japanese may find out and send out help. Let's just hope we are the only ones that picked up the message and Captain Lewis got away with it without being detected. As to what we will do if and when we find the *Atlantis*, I have yet to decide. To sink her outright would be the prudent thing to do. Otherwise she could get away and deliver her deadly cargo. However, there are possibly very brave British female officers aboard who are placing their lives on the line knowing we just may sink them without warning."

With that the Captain dismissed the officers and walked to his room.

"We did it *Kapitän*," whispered Ensign Stuben, "now let's get out of here before we are discovered."

"Right!"

Turning off the light, the German cracked open the door and listened. There was no sound other than the water lapping against the side of the *Atlantis*.

"Quickly now, *Kapitän*. Follow closely behind me to your quarters."

As she quietly opened the door, Captain Lewis turned to the German Officer. "Thank you very much, Ensign. What you have done took a lot of courage. If we get out of this alive, I will see that you get the credit for saving countless lives."

"You can do that, but only if the Allies win."

"Ah, right you are. Only if we win and you lose."

The German smiled, saluted, and slipped down the passageway and was gone.

As Captain Lewis lay back on her cot, she suddenly realized

she was trembling. Was it from the danger of what she had done or the unknown of how the Americans would respond? The natural thing she reminded herself would be for them just to sink the *Atlantis*.

A few minutes later, she heard the next door where Debbie and several other of the nurses shared quarters, open and close.

WASHINGTON, D.C.

"There you have it, Mr. President," said General Marshal. "Per your executive order, all of our troops in Normandy are being evacuated even as we speak."

"Where is General Patton's Third Army?"

"Ah, well, most of it is at Normandy awaiting evacuation."

"And just where is the General?"

"His last report placed him within four miles of the beach. He is in his words, 'bringing up the rear'. In fact, from our aerial reconnaissance report, he is actually in the last tank in the last column and he is flying his pennants."

"What is he trying to do? Get some trigger happy German to take a shot at him?"

"I would like to think he wants the German High Command to know that he is still there in case they try to pull a fast one."

"Do you think they will, General?"

"No, Mr. President, I don't think so. There are reports from the underground in Holland, Belgium, and Denmark that the German combat units are already pulling out and heading into Germany, leaving behind what can best be described as a light occupational force in the cities."

"Well, that was in their terms to the British. Germany will give the western occupied countries some degree of independence in running their own internal affairs. I know, General, that my order to withdraw from France was not completely supported by the Joint Chiefs of Staff and War Department, but until we have our own atomic devices it was the best course of action I think we could take."

General Marshall did not answer. To break the embarrassing silence, the President went on. "By the way, what are the British doing?"

"All of their troops are off the continent and they are returning the German POWs under their control. The Royal Navy, or what is left of it, is still in battle formation off the coast of Normandy, presumably providing additional coverage for our own evacuation. As you know, we are now in a very vulnerable position with so few troops left on shore. Should the Germans attack now, most of our men on shore would be killed or captured."

"Yes, I realize that. But I also remember that when they had the British trapped at Dunkirk they let them go. In fact, if Churchill had accepted that generous act and come to terms with Hitler, then all of this could have been avoided."

"Ah, that may be so," replied Marshall. "Now if I may Sir, I need to check on the situation in the Indian Ocean."

"Yes, of course, General. Keep me informed of what transpires there. We must prevent that cargo from getting into the hands of the Japanese."

"I will, Sir. Good day."

Kennedy wondered if there ever would be any more good days.

BERLIN

Hitler and the General Staff stood looking at the large map of Europe.

"Now," asked Hitler, "since it appears the Americans are withdrawing from France, how many troops will that free up for use on the Eastern Front?"

"At least 300,000 immediately," responded *Feldmarschall* Keitel," and if we do not have too much disturbance from the underground in France, another 100,000 or more."

"*Wunderbar*," responded Hitler rubbing his hands together happily. "Now, what exactly is happening on the Eastern Front?"

Feldmarschall Model stepped over to the large map of the Baltic regions. "As you remember, *Mein Führer*, when we started our offensive in the northern region here, our line ran roughly from Brest down here to the outskirts of Konigsberg up to here in East Prussia."

"Certainly I remember," interrupted Hitler.

"Well," continued Model, "after we decimated the massed

Bolshevik offensive force with our nuclear device, our troops pushed them back to just beyond Bobrujsk in the south, with our line running up east of Minsk, which we have by-passed to save time, to the outskirts of Vilnius, the capital of Lithuania. From Vilnius the line continues north to Riga, the capital of Latvia, which we took just yesterday."

"Of course," interjected Goering, "our jet aircraft made this swift advance possible."

"*Ja*," agreed Model. "Having air superiority made our advance much easier. However, *Mein Führer*, I must admit that I am concerned about advancing any farther until the southern front can be moved forward. I feel uncomfortable having my army so far in advance of the others. An unexpected Bolshevik thrust to our exposed southern flank could cut us off."

All of the other staff members nodded their head in agreement.

"What is happening on the front south of our offensive?" asked Hitler.

"The front has more or less stabilized. The Bolsheviks are fearful of massing troops for an offensive and we are taking advantage of the lull to reinforce and resupply our forces. We are now awaiting your instructions, *Mein Führer*." responded Keitel.

"This is where the troops from the west will come in," stated Hitler. "I want them rushed to the front and used to push back the Bolsheviks in the south sector to Rostov-on-Don. This will win back the Balkans and Ukraine. Then I have two main objectives left. But wait, I forgot to tell you. Don't worry about the large Bolshevik forces facing us in these areas. At best, some of them will be pulled back, or at worst they will certainly not be reinforced."

As the officers looked at one another in bewilderment, Hitler smiled.

"Even now, I have ordered the transfer of the nuclear device crossing the Indian Ocean to proceed. That, together with the promise of a second device as soon as we have another one available, was sufficient to get the Japanese to agree to attacking the Bolsheviks at Vladivostok, Chabarovsk, and Blagovescensk in Siberia. When Stalin has to make the choice of defending the

Balkans or mother Russia, he will choose mother Russia."

"That is good news indeed," stated *Feldmarschall* Rommel. "But, you said before that you had two objectives left in the east, *Mein Führer*. May I ask what they are?"

"Of course, of course. First, after we stabilize the center of the front, we will drive east from Rostov-on-Don to Astrachan here at the mouth of the Volga river on the Caspian Sea. We will then drive south to the Turkish and Persian borders, giving us control of the vast oil fields in the area. This will ensure our oil needs for the foreseeable future. Secondly, it will cut off the Bolshevik's access to the Black Sea. My second objective is to drive along the Baltic Sea, take Leningrad, and push to the Finnish border, cutting off the Bolsheviks access to the Baltic. With the Japanese taking the Russian ports on the Pacific the Bolsheviks will be completely landlocked and more agreeable to our terms."

Feldmarschall Model, who was in charge of the northern sector, was the first to speak.

"*Mein Führer*, we spent one thousand days besieging Leningrad to no avail. How do you propose we take it this time?"

"This time there will be no Leningrad to take."

"But, you just said?"

"A slip of the tongue on my part. I meant to say, push past where Leningrad was, and on to the Finnish border."

"Was?"

"*Ja*, was. Leningrad will be obliterated by another atomic device!"

Everyone present was taken completely off-guard by this revelation, and began talking to his neighbor as Hitler stood smiling, with his arms folded.

Feldmarschall Rommel was the first to speak up.

"*Mein Führer*, if I may? It is one thing to destroy an invasion force or break up a large offensive with our new super weapon, but quite another to destroy an entire city full of helpless civilians."

"Helpless!" screamed Hitler. "If they were so helpless, how did they manage to hold one entire army of the *Third Reich* at bay for one thousand days, my dear *Feldmarschall*?"

Rommel realized it was impossible to reason with the man.

Fortunately, *Feldmarschall* Model came to Rommel's rescue. "*Mein Führer*, I think the point Erwin was trying to make was, if we do this it will be classified as...ah, how did the American President, Roosevelt, put it? *Ja*, it will become a day that will live in infamy."

"Then so be it," responded Hitler. "Those so called helpless civilians had their great day of glory when they saw our troops withdrawing. Now the whole world will see how short their 'victory' really was, when they end up paying the ultimate price for it. Their destruction will be an example to whoever else stands in our way of total victory. Now, have your plans ready for me to review the day after tomorrow. You are all dismissed."

As Rommel and Model walked out of the room together, Model whispered, "This is madness Erwin. Can you imagine completely destroying the Paris of the East?"

"*Nein*, I can't. We must do something before it is too late."

EAST INDIAN OCEAN

Captain Underwood awoke with a start as the diesel engines shut down and the boat began to sink beneath the surface. At the same time, his phone rang.

"Captain, I think you should come to the SONAR room. We have some company," reported the First Officer.

"I'll be right there."

As Underwood entered the room he was handed a pair of headphones.

Placing one headphone to an ear, he could hear the unmistakable sound of several screws turning at such a rate they were causing cavitation bubbles to form and collapse.

"We picked these up about ten minutes ago, while we were still on the surface. Although they are close enough that we could have seen them if it was daylight, we didn't, so they must be running without lights."

"What do you think it is, seaman?" asked the Captain.

"From all of the noise, I would say they are Japanese. One ship has twin screws and the other two each have one. Probably a heavy cruiser and two small destroyers. And from what I can determine I would say they are on the exact opposite course as the *Atlantis*."

"They must be going to rendezvous with her," ventured Underwood.

"In all probability."

The USS *Swordfish* wasn't the only one to detect the noise from the Japanese warships. Just before dawn, Captain Rogge and his officers aboard the *Atlantis* also were listening to the warships as they bore down on them.

"Any idea who they are?" asked Rogge.

"*Nein, Mein Kapitän*. But from all of the noise they are generating, they are not any of the newer class American ships, which are much quieter."

"What is their course?"

"Unless they change course, I think they will pass ten or twelve thousand meters to our port, *Mein Kapitän*."

Turning to his First Officer, Rogge ordered, "Hold our present course and speed. If they are hostile, be prepared to respond to any contact with our planned disguise."

"*Aye, Aye*, Mein Kapitän."

"*Kapitän*, they are changing their course, so they must have detected us. They are swinging toward us!"

In thirty-five minutes, through the dim morning light, the warships were close enough for Rogge to identify the Rising Sun flying from the Japanese Cruiser.

"It appears our Allies are eager to get our little present and can't wait until we get to Singapore," ventured Rogge.

"Either that, or they want to get it before the *Führer* changes his mind," someone added.

"What about our prisoners?" asked an alarmed Ensign Fritz Stuben, thinking about Debbie and the other English nurses. "We can't turn them over to the Japanese."

"You're correct Ensign," replied Rogge. "And since you brought it up, it will be your task to get all evidence of their presence, as well as the *Fraüleins* themselves, out of sight until we have made the transfer and are on our way home. In fact, I suggest you get started right away."

Stuben slipped out of the door amidst several good natured

jokes and kidding about his *Kindergarten* job.

Within another twenty minutes, the Japanese warships were close enough that the *Atlantis* was able to make contact through its semaphore. The lead destroyer acknowledged the signal, and within the hour the *Atlantis* and Japanese cruiser were side by side, with the two destroyers on their flanks. The cruiser let down a longboat and Captain Rogge could see a Japanese Admiral, a Captain, and several men in civilian clothes lowered down in it. The *Atlantis* let down a ladder as the longboat came alongside. Captain Rogge and his officers saluted the Admiral as he came aboard. In perfect German, the Admiral introduced himself as Rear Admiral Yamashita. The Captain of the Cruiser was named Togo. The two civilians were from the physics department of the University of Yokohama.

"Glad to have you aboard," said Rogge. "I am *Kapitän* Rogge, *Kommandant* of the *Atlantis*."

"Thank you, *Kapitän*," responded one of the civilians, also in perfect German. " I am Professor Numora from the University of Yokohama. This is my associate, Professor Matsumora."

After exchanging introductions, Captain Rogge went on. "You gave us a little concern when our SONAR first detected you. We were not expecting you, having been informed that the transfer was to take place in Singapore."

"Originally it was," stated the Admiral. "But the city has come under some air attacks within the last couple of weeks and so it was decided to meet you here, where we have less chance of being attacked."

"Probably a good idea under the circumstances, Admiral. But how did you know where to meet us?"

"Ah, we had been informed of where your rendezvous with the U-boat was to take place, so we took the liberty of having you, shall we say, trailed? Just to ensure nothing happened to you, of course."

"Of course."

"There are a number of British and American submarines in this part of the ocean. In fact, just last night one of our boats picked up what may have been an American boat headed toward this general area."

Instinctively, the Germans all made quick scans of the water around them.

"Probably just a coincidence," ventured the Admiral. "There have been no further reports. Nevertheless, I believe it would be prudent to make the actual transfer as soon as possible. Could we now please see this device, and have your people go over its operation with our scientists?"

"Of course. Please follow me. I presume everything is ready, Ensign Stuben?"

"*Ja, Herr Kapitän.*"

"*Gut.*"

Captain Underwood stood looking through the periscope at the Japanese warships as they met the German Raider. Every few minutes he scanned the sky around his position keeping track of the position of the two seaplanes the cruiser had launched. Fortunately, the *Swordfish* had gotten within the radius the planes were patrolling, and with the boat stopped, there was no tattle-tale wake from the periscope. Unfortunately, the *Atlantis* was between him and the Japanese Cruiser. This left him with the choice of sinking the *Atlantis* with the British nurses aboard, or waiting until the transfer of the weapon was completed and then try and get a shot at the cruiser. Underwood decided to wait for a clear shot at the cruiser.

In less than two hours the transfer had been completed and Underwood saw the longboat pull away from the *Atlantis*, and head back to the Japanese Cruiser. The Cruiser was facing west while the *Swordfish* was facing south. Underwood realized that the Cruiser would require a large turning radius to turn around and head back towards Singapore, so all he had to do was wait and see which way the Cruiser turned. If it was toward its port side, all he had to do was slowly move forward, get in position and wait for the Cruiser to cross his path. If it turned to the starboard he could just hold his position, and fire from his rear torpedo tubes as the cruiser crossed his stern. Underwood watched intently as the cruiser slowly pulled away, and then the raider slowly picked up speed and began to turn around.

Underwood turned to his first officer. "Let me know the course of the *Atlantis* as soon as it can be determined. I would like to be able to follow it, if possible, as soon as we have taken care of the cruiser."

"Aye, aye, Sir."

As Underwood swung the periscope back toward the cruiser he froze in horror. Bearing down on him were the two Aichi Tokei Type 92 seaplanes that had been launched from the cruiser.

"Down periscope and crash dive! The patrols evidently spotted us!" screamed Underwood.

The boat pitched down at a steep angle as it sought refuge in the murky depths. But within thirty seconds, it was violently rocked as two, one-hundred kilogram bombs exploded off to his starboard. Five seconds later, two more bombs exploded even closer.

"Damage report!" barked Underwood who was interrupted from the SONAR room.

"Captain, this is damage control. We have some serious bulkhead leaks in the forward torpedo room. I suggest we not descend any farther, if possible."

"Dump 500 gallons of fuel oil, and fire out all garbage and extra clothing from both forward and aft tubes. Shut down all engines, and attempt to hold depth. Maybe we can make them believe we have been hit and are sinking."

Realizing their chance of escaping was nil, Underwood ordered the antenna be sent to the surface and a message explaining what had transpired be broadcast at full power.

The two aircraft swung around and headed directly towards the oil slick. At an altitude of less than one hundred feet, both dropped their last bombs, one of which slammed into the base of the conning tower blowing it completely off. The sub was immediately flooded and plummeted toward the bottom.

From the *Atlantis*, the German crew had been watching the attack. After the Japanese seaplane landed by the cruiser and were picked out of the water, Rogge spoke, "They must have gotten the boat they were after."

Seeing the Japanese ships push away, Rogge realized they were not about to look for survivors. "Head to the attack point," he ordered. "We'll look for survivors."

As the *Atlantis* slowly entered the immediate area where the American submarine had last been seen, Captain Lewis and the other British nurses were called on deck to assist the ship's doctor, in case any survivors were picked up.

Peering over the side at the floating debris, Lewis asked, "What happened here, Doctor?"

"The Japanese attacked a submarine here a few minutes ago, and from the looks of things, they sank it. The *Kapitän* is looking for any survivors. But I doubt if there will be any. Seldom does anyone escape from a boat when it is hit underwater."

Lewis felt sick. Had this submarine come in response to her message, and if so, did it have time to relay her warning to other ships in the area before it was sunk?"

"Where are the Japanese now?" she asked.

"Over there to our stern. They are headed back home now."

Lewis leaned over the rail and looked back. She could see the Japanese warships fast pulling away from them. As she glanced down, she let out a small gasp. Floating in the water was the body of a man. Looking closely she recognized the uniform of an American sailor. No survivors or other bodies were found, and in a few minutes Lewis could feel the rumbling of the engines picking up as the *Atlantis* turned and headed west.

LONDON

The fifteenth of December was a day of celebration throughout most of Great Britain. At 10:00 A.M., the Prime Minister announced over the BBC that the last of the British Army had been withdrawn from both France and Italy. The Royal Navy was being pulled back from the line off the coast of Normandy, but was still within striking distance should anything go wrong with the evacuation of the American Forces. With thousands of Americans on the British Isles, the Prime Minister and his cabinet thought it would be prudent to show they could still be counted on in case Hitler went back on his word. But, the last communiques coming in reported the German Army had not advanced any farther toward the coast from the position where they had stopped when fired upon by General Patton.

At 2:00 P.M., The Duke of Windsor was crowned King of the British Empire in West Minister Abbey. He had been the King once before. Thousands had camped out all night, in spite of the winter cold, around Westminster Abbey, which had been patched up as best as it could be for the big event. Eisenhower, who had been invited to the coronation, had politely declined, asking to be excused due to the pressing problems surrounding the eviction of his troops from Normandy. Since President Kennedy had not yet appointed a new ambassador to Great Britain, there was no high-ranking American at the coronation. The Prime Minister recognized this action as a snub.

All over the British Isles the day and evening were filled with celebrations. Food and drinks that had been horded away were brought out and a good time was had by most of the population.

WASHINGTON, D.C.

President Kennedy and his military and scientific advisors were meeting in the East Room of the White House. The President was being briefed on the status of events in Europe, the coming invasion of Japan, and the development of the nuclear device in New Mexico.

General Groves had just finished his briefing on the development of an atomic bomb in New Mexico, explaining that they thought they were on the right track, but still could not give a firm date of when a device would be ready for test. Just then a message was handed to the President.

"Gentlemen, I have some new information that has just come in. The Japanese have crossed the Amur River between Mongolia and Siberia, and have captured the Russian cities of Chabarovsk and Blagovescensk. They have also seized the railhead at Ussurijsk just north of Vladivostok. Unconfirmed reports state that they are also moving up into the Russian half of Sakhalin Island."

As the group broke into many discussions, President Kennedy raised his hand. "Gentlemen, please, there is more. This is evidently a planned and coordinated attack, for the Germans have also launched another massive attack along the Baltic Sea toward Leningrad and are massing troops in the southern sector."

Secretary of State, Cordell Hull stood up. "I'll attempt to contact Moscow and see if the Russians will provide any additional information. Ah, perhaps this may be the time to inform the Russians we are in the final stages of planning an assault on the Japanese mainland in the near future. It will remind them that we are still in this struggle with them and provide them some encouragement."

"Good idea, Cordell. But, of course, don't give any indication of a date," said the President.

"Right. Of course, I will use our code."

"Now," continued Kennedy, "any opinions on how this new Japanese attack on the Russians affects our plans for the invasion of their Home Islands?"

General Marshall walked over and pulled down a large wall map of Eastern portion of the Soviet Union.

"Evidently, the invasion force must have been elements of the Japanese Fifth Army, which has been guarding the border for some time. We have had no reports of the Japanese moving any outside forces into the region. That being the case, we are still facing the same number of troops on the home islands themselves. However, this new front will undoubtedly require a significant amount of materials to be used and will probably draw down the reserves on the Home Islands."

Kennedy looked around the room and noticed that the military men were nodding their heads in agreement.

Marshall continued, "We are still holding to our original invasion date and, barring any unforeseen events, should be able to meet it. Do you agree General MacArthur?"

"Yes, the forces we had for the Philippine campaign are being brought together. We will be ready."

"What about the transfer of the German Atomic device to the Japanese? Any news on this issue?"

Admiral King stood up and walked over to another map.

"We know the device was transferred from a U-boat to the raider *Atlantis*. We also have an unconfirmed report from one of our submarines operating in the area, that the device has since been transferred from the German Raider, *Atlantis*, in the East Indian Ocean to a Japanese ship. We have all of our ships in the area on alert with orders to stop and inspect the cargo on all ships of unknown origin. But it is a large area, and we have few ships there. However, they are probably headed for the Strait of Malacca, which would be the shortest route to Japan. They could, of course, deliver the weapon to their forces in Burma, or anywhere along the West coast of French Indo China here. But, to transfer the device overland for any distance would present serious problems. I am betting they will stick with a sea shipment all of the way to the home Islands."

"Unless," suggested Admiral King, "they are planning on taking it directly to where they plan to use it."

A general murmur ran through the room.

"That being the case," continued the President, "it is more imperative than ever that we intercept the ship carrying the device."

"We have notified the British and Australian naval forces in the area," announced Admiral Nimitz, "and they have agreed to assist us in the search."

"I guess that is about all we can do there," concluded the President. "Just wait and pray we intercept her before it is too late. Now what is going on in Western Europe?"

General Marshall took the Admiral's place at the map wall and pulled down the map of Europe.

"With our withdrawal from France and per the British request, we are transferring General Patton's Third Army to Italy to replace the British Eighth Army which is being withdrawn. The balance of our land forces and the Eighth Air Force, which were stationed in England, are being transferred as quickly as possible to the Far East to support the invasion of the Japanese home islands. They, of course, will not arrive in time for the initial assault, but will be available as replacements."

As Secretary Hull walked back into the room, everyone turned to him.

"Mr. President, I was able to contact Molotov, the Soviet Foreign Minister. He confirms the attacks by the Japanese, but claims information coming in is very sketchy. He does indicate the situation is very grave both on that front, and on the northern sector of their western front, where the Germans are steadily advancing in spite of stiff opposition from the Red Army. Furthermore, he wants to know what we can do to help."

Before anyone could answer, Hull continued, "I believe the Soviet situation must be very, very grave. All of the usual belligerent talk was gone. Molotov was almost pleading for assistance. I think we must do something as quickly as possible or the Russians could pull out of the fight like they did during the First World War."

"That would be a disaster," commented General Marshall.

Even the President, who still secretly wanted the United States out of the European War, could see the results if the Russians quit.

"What can we do to help?" he inquired.

"We could increase the pressure in Italy," speculated Marshall. "But as we have previously discussed, it would probably be of little value. If we concentrated sufficient forces for a major drive north, we would present an inviting target for another atomic attack. Or, the Germans could just fall back knowing full well we could never push through the Alps, even if we had elephants," he added to bring a little humor to the otherwise somber discussion.

Everyone again nodded in agreement.

Marshall continued, "Any invasion of Greece or Yugoslavia by sea would be very difficult under the circumstances."

"What if we could get Turkey to agree to let us launch an attack through their country on the Germans in Bulgaria and Greece?" asked Nimitz.

"That would certainly help the Russians, especially if we could cut some of the German supply lines supporting their southern offensive," offered Marshall.

All eyes turned to Kennedy.

"Set up a meeting for me with the Turkish Ambassador as soon as possible. I'll see what he says."

Cordell Hull spoke up, asking, "What if Turkey refuses? Remember they were Allies of the Germans in the previous war and have not been very cooperative so far in this one. Are we prepared to push them?"

The President thought for a moment and then decided. "No, I won't push them. That's what this war has been all about. One country pushing around another smaller one."

Although that would be the idealistic thing to do, many in the room were secretly of the opinion that drastic situations like they were now facing sometimes required drastic actions.

"Oh," added Secretary Hull. "Molotov had another piece of

information for us. It seems they had a freighter in the East Indian Ocean which picked up a distress signal from our submarine, *Swordfish*. The *Swordfish* reported that it was under heavy attack from the Japanese after witnessing the transfer of what they assumed was the atomic device, from the German Raider, *Atlantis,* to a Japanese cruiser. This confirms the previous report we had."

"I'll notify our naval forces, as well as the British and Australians that a Japanese cruiser is now our primary target rather than the German Raider," responded Admiral King. Of course, any Japanese warship would be a primary target, but it will be important to know if we find this particular one. Do we have the name of the cruiser?"

"Not that I know of," answered Hull.

"Well," continued King, "I doubt if there are many Japanese Cruisers in that general area."

Everyone nodded in agreement.

MOSCOW

Stalin had convened an emergency meeting of the Politburo along with his military advisors. As Stalin paced the floor, Field Marshall Zukov explained the current situation on the European Front. It was all bad. The Germans were advancing almost unopposed as the Red Army continued to retreat along the entire front, despite what Molotov had told the Americans. In the northern sector, Field Marshall Model's forces had pushed the Red Army out of the Baltic states of Latvia and Estonia, and were again on Russian soil with the thrust running along the south from Pskov to Novgorod and then swinging north to the Baltic Sea. They were once again just sixty kilometers west of Leningrad. With their reinforcements from the west. The Germans were deep in the Ukraine in the southern sector, threatening to once again cut off Crimea. As Zhukov continued with the bad news, an aide slipped in a side door and motioned to Molotov, who got up and walked over to the door.

"*Da*, what is it?" he inquired.

"We just received a radio message from the Germans, Comrade. It was very brief but they said they would call back in half an hour and want to talk to you or the Generalissimo."

"I had better take it. Would you bring me something to eat while I wait for the call? I assume it will be in the communication room?'

"*Da*, it will, and I will get some food for you."

"Whatever they have on hand in the kitchen will be fine."

Molotov was eating some soup when the radio came to life.

A heavy German accent asked in Russian, "Who is there please?"

"Tell them," instructed Molotov to the radioman.

"Our Foreign Minister is standing by."

"*Gut*. Do you have an interpreter there?"

"*Da*."

"Please stand by for *Feldmarschall* Rommel."

"Rommel?" questioned Molotov.

A voice came over the radio speaking slowly and pausing so that his words could easily be interpreted.

"*Herr* Minister, this is *Feldmarschall* Erwin Rommel speaking," began the interpreter. "For obvious reasons this message must be short and to the point. Please believe me, this is no trick. You must evacuate Leningrad as soon as possible. The *Führer* is going to destroy it with another atomic device within the next few days. Though we may be enemies, I cannot sit by and see several million civilians killed like this. Please believe what I am telling you. I must now sign off."

"He has signed off, Comrade Minister."

"Did you get down his exact words?"

"Yes. If you can wait a couple of minutes, I'll type them up for you. My scribbling is difficult to read."

"I'll wait."

As Molotov reentered the Ministry chamber the briefing on the Eastern Front was being summed up.

"In short, Generalissimo, the Japanese have cut the trans-Siberian railroad and also have Vladivostok surrounded. Unless we can rush a number of divisions to the end of the rail line and push through to Vladivostok, we will lose our only seaport to the Pacific within thirty days."

Seeing Molotov come in, Stalin turned to him and asked,

"Was that word from the Americans?"

"No, but this came in, Comrade," replied Molotov, as he handed Stalin the message from Rommel.

Stalin quickly read the message and tore it up. "Just another Fascist trick to get us to pull back our forces in the area."

Even Molotov was shocked that Stalin would not give the message any consideration, potentially risking the lives of the brave inhabitants of the entire city, which had held the Nazis at bay for so long. It was then that Molotov finally admitted to himself, that like their arch foe, Hitler, Stalin had little, if any, feelings for the people of his own country and would fight this war to the last Russian, if need be.

NORWEGIAN COAST

The American Destroyer, *Prince*, was at dead stop as the squad of Rangers slipped over the side and into three rubber rafts. In less than two minutes, each raft was loaded with six forty-pound packs of high explosives and manned by four Rangers. The rafts then quietly pulled away from the *Prince* and disappeared into the dark, moonless, and overcast night. Less than a mile ahead was the Norwegian coast. The lights from the small village of Norsk could be seen blinking off and on as banks of fog rolled between the Rangers and the village. North of the village, there were several lights from homes a short distance from the village itself, but the lights on the south side of the village ended abruptly marking the small port itself and the entrance to the fjord. The fjord was the Rangers' destination. One and a half miles up the narrow twisting fjord was a well hidden facility, which by all information available to the Americans, was the one and perhaps only plant producing the so called "heavy water" required in the production of the German atomic devices.

Before the British had dropped out of the war, they had attempted to destroy the plant several times. On October 18, 1942, under the code name Operation Freshman, two teams of paratroopers in gliders crash landed in the fog and were captured and later executed by the Nazis. Four months later, on February 16, 1943 the British employed specially trained Norwegians, organized as a commando team to destroy the plant, under the code name of Operation Gunnerside. The Norwegians succeeded in disabling the plant, and destroying all of the heavy water on hand. However, most of the Norwegians were killed in the attack, and the Germans had the plant back in operation by April.

The plant itself was built along a ledge protected by another overhanging ledge. The plant was strung out and only one room wide so it could not be hit by high-flying bombers. Low level attacks required flying up the fjord, which in the mile and half to the plant had four severe bends. The plant was on the inside of the last bend. Moreover, the Germans had a number of anti-aircraft batteries perched along both sides of the edge of the fjord from the sea to the plant.

But, now thanks to a Norwegian electrician, who worked at the nearby hydroelectric plant, and had helped wire the heavy water plant, a layout of the building had been smuggled out of Norway and into Sweden. Although the Swedes were technically neutral, the drawings ended up in the hands of the American Ambassador. The drawings showed where the power lines had been run over the edge of the fjord upstream of the plant and then run along the face of the cliff to the plant itself. Although cutting the power lines would be relatively simple, it would be just a minor inconvenience to the Germans, who could repair them in short order. More importantly, the Germans had been forced to build a narrow ledge where the lines ran along the face of the cliff. By going past the plant, scaling the cliff up to this small ledge, and then working their way along the ledge to the plant, the Rangers might just be able to gain access into the otherwise heavily fortified and guarded facility.

The attack was timed just as the tide was coming in, so once the rafts had safely passed the fishing village and were into the mouth of the fjord, the surge of water helped move the rafts up the fjord. Within less than forty-five minutes after going over the side of the destroyer, the Rangers had slipped past the facility by hugging the far side of the fjord, which was less than two hundred yards wide at this point. After going another one hundred and fifty yards, the Rangers crossed the fjord and edged up to the almost vertical cliff. Each man strapped a forty pound pack containing high explosives to his back. One Ranger from each raft started climbing the cliff to the ledge, which thanks to the high tide, was now only fifty feet above them. Once the three men had reached the ledge they lowered a rope back down to the others to climb. As the next three Rangers reached the ledge the men in the rafts began attaching the explosives to the ropes which were then hauled up. In the meantime, the three rafts were secured together. Leaving one man to move the rafts to a more secure hiding place, the remaining Rangers climbed up the ropes.

With Lieutenant James Reed leading, each of the Rangers carefully made their way along the ledge towards the electrical transformer station, their first destination. As expected, no German guards were at the station. Placing three of the explosive packages in and around the main transformers, the Rangers set the timers for thirty minutes and then moved on, knowing that in case they were detected, and captured or killed, the transformers would at least be knocked out.

As they approached the main building, Reed carefully crept along the building to the window near the door. Looking in he could see two German guards sitting at a table against the far wall playing cards. Realizing it would be next to impossible to dispose of the guards before they could send out an alarm, Reed motioned for his Platoon Sergeant to come up. After explaining his plan the sergeant made his way back to his men and two of them started to climb the steep incline above the ledge. The remaining men approached the building and flattened out against the wall. When everyone was in place, Reed flashed his flashlight quickly on and off. Whereupon the two men up the incline began digging under a large rock. Although five precious minutes were lost the large rock was finally dislodged and began rolling down the incline, starting a small land slide. As the rocks hit the ledge and rolled over the cliff the noise attracted the attention of the guards, who got up and opened the door.

"*Mein Gott*," exclaimed one, "the mountain is sliding down."

As the second guard pushed passed the first to see what was happening, two of the Rangers leaped forward and grabbing the guards from behind, quickly cut their throats. The two Germans slid to the ground without a sound, as Lieutenant Reed and his other men slipped into the room. Knowing the facility was laid out with a large hall running the full length of the building, with various rooms off the hall dug into the hillside, the Rangers passed out of the storage room they had entered and quietly moved down the hall. The first room was a small exercise and entertainment room which was vacant at this time of night. As they passed the second room which was the dining room from the kitchen they could hear the cooks preparing breakfast. The next room was the control room, one of their main objectives. Through the window in the door they could see four civilians sitting at desks, monitoring the main dials on the wall. Separating the control room from the main equipment room was a heavy glass panel, through which several other civilians could be seen working on the equipment that extracted the heavy water from the sea water.. At the end of the hall was a door which Reed knew led to the living quarters for the civilian staff and military attachment.

Reed motioned to two of his men, who quietly slipped down to the door at the end of the hall and placed two of their explosive parcels next to the door. Returning, one of the Rangers handed Reed the electronic detonator for the charges.

Dividing his men into three groups of four men. Reed positioned one group by the door to the control room and the other at the door leading into the equipment room. He and the other three Rangers positioned themselves to cover the door leading from the living quarters. At his signal the two groups burst into the two rooms. One of the Rangers in each group quickly cut down the surprised and unarmed workers, while the other three men quickly began planting the remaining charges around the rooms.

Within seconds of the sound of gun fire the door at the far end of the hall opened and armed German troops poured out. Reed hit the button on the detonator, and the end of the hall erupted into a ball of fire and debris.

"Let's get the hell out of here," yelled Reed. As the men ran down the hall, several cooks came running out of the dining room. When they saw what was happening they ran quickly back into the dining room.

"Let them go," yelled Reed. "Just keep moving."

Looking back down the hall, Reed could see several Germans running through the smoke. Reed fired a long burst from his Tommy gun into the group. Several fell, and the others turned and ran back into the smoke. Looking at his watch Reed realized that the explosives they had set at the electric transformers were set to go off in less than seven minutes.

"Hurry, to the boats," he urged his men. Placing the last charge at the entrance to the building Reed turned and ran after his men. At a safe distance from the building, Reed detonated the explosives left at the entrance of the building.

As the men repelled down the cliff and into the rafts, the transformer substation went up in a roar of flame as the oil in the transformers caught fire.

Once in the rafts the Rangers started paddling frantically away from the cliff and down the fjord. As they approached the center of the fjord, two searchlights on the ledge turned on and began sweeping the water.

"Damn!" exclaimed Reed. "They must have auxiliary emergency power."

One of the beams of light swept across one of the rafts. The light stopped, returned, and locked on the raft. Immediately, heavy machine gun fire opened up, cutting the raft in two. The Germans continued to pour fire into the men struggling in the water.

"Nothing we can do to help," said Reed, as he watched the last of the men go under. The other search light then caught Reed's raft. "Swim for it!" ordered Reed as he dived into the water. But the cold water soon numbed the men and one by one they were picked up in the beam of light and machine gunned. But it bought enough time that the remaining raft slipped away.

Aboard the *Prince*, once again at the mouth of the fjord, the explosions and following gunfire could be heard. Captain James Ford, turned to his First Officer. "They must have done it, Al."

"Yes, but it sounds like they are having trouble getting away."

"We must rescue at least one of the Rangers in order to get an assessment of the damage they were able to incur on the plant."

Realizing the risk he was taking, the Captain ordered the

Prince to be slowly backed up the fjord. Turning to his First Officer, he ordered, "Have a group on the stern keep an eye out for any survivors, and order the gun crews to be ready to respond to any fire we take from the German coast defenses if we are spotted."

"Aye, Aye, Sir."

Search lights on the beach near Norsk began turning on. But thinking any Allied ship must be off the coast, the searchlights first covered that area. In twenty minutes out of the darkness appeared one of the rafts. As the four men started to climb up the side of the *Prince*, Captain Ford ordered, "Flank speed. Let's get as far away as we can before they detect us."

The Germans heard the rumble of the *Prince* as it picked up speed but it was difficult to determine just where the noise was coming from over the water.

"The Germans must have heard us by now," observed Ford. "Fire on those searchlights before they pick up us. The second salvo from the destroyer's three inch guns knocked out two of the searchlights, but in less than a minute one of the remaining searchlights caught the *Prince* in its beam. In another fifteen seconds, Ford could see the flashes from the German guns.

"Order the gunnery office to concentrate the aft gun battery to continue to concentrate its fire on the searchlights and the forward battery to commence firing on the gun emplacements."

"Aye, aye, Sir."

The first round from the Germans passed well over the *Prince* and a little aft. The second round fell just short of the destroyer, causing her to rock. But before the third round could be fired the *Prince's* aft battery found its mark and knocked out the searchlights. Nevertheless the Germans had narrowed down the range and all batteries began firing for effect into the darkness. One of the shells hit the stern of the *Prince* knocking out its steering.

"Get the survivors into the radio room and have them report what they accomplished," ordered Ford. "Also notify fleet command of our situation. We can expect to come under air attack as soon as it is light, and without steering...." Captain Ford's voiced trailed off.

As Ford expected, with the first crack of dawn, six Junker-87

Stuka dive bombers swept over the *Prince* and then turned back for the kill. The first dive bomber missed and as he pulled up away one of the *Prince's* forty millimeter pom-poms found its target. The Stuka exploded in a ball of fire. The second and third Stukas where able to each hit the *Prince* with one of their one hundred kilogram bombs. As the *Prince* took on water and began to roll over, Captain Ford ordered the ship to be abandoned. As soon as the crew was in the life boats and rafts, the Stukas returned and began to strafe them. Those not killed in the strafing, soon succumbed to the cold Norwegian waters.

Two hours later, when the Martin PBY-1 flying boat arrived on the scene, no survivors were found.

BERLIN

Albert Speer, the Arms Production Minister, waited for Hitler and his aides to take their seats before he pulled down large photographs of the heavy water plant in Norway, before and after the American attack.

"How did this happen!" screamed a furious Adolf Hitler.

"Evidently," began Speer, "some American Rangers, which are an elite force, were dropped off at the entrance to the fjord and were able to make their way undetected up the fjord to the plant. Just how they got into the plant is not known, and since they were all killed as they tried to escape, we may never know."

"Someone will pay dearly for this!" Hitler screamed again. " Arrest whoever was in charge of the plant's security and have him executed! Now, how much damage was done and how long before it is repaired?"

"Explosives were set off at the power transformers, *Mein Führer*, and also at the extractors, but the most damage was to the control room. As to the time to repair the damage, it is too early to determine. But due to the remoteness of the facilities it will take several weeks before we can get the replacement parts there. So my best guess is that the plant will be down for at least six to eight weeks. "The good news is that all of the Rangers were killed and the destroyer that carried them was sunk, with no survivors. Also, sufficient heavy water was salvaged to complete another two or three devices."

"How many devices do we now actually have completed?" demanded Hitler.

"Well, we have, or rather did have the one we transferred to the Japanese. Then, there is the one headed for Leningrad. And we have a third one that will be finished within a few days."

"I want the Americans to pay for their attack in Norway," demanded Hitler. " How best can we use the new weapon on them when it is finished?"

Feldmarschall Keitel spoke up. "Short of an attack on America itself, we could use it in Italy. But in the long run, that would probably be a waste of a valuable weapon that might be put to a better use later on. Especially in light of the fact that we could rain havoc on the American lines in Italy with a combination attack using our V-1 and V-2 weapons, in conjunction with our jet powered aircraft."

Hitler thought for a moment, and then to everyone's surprise, agreed with the *Feldmarschall's* suggestion.

"Alright then. We'll pound the *hölle* out of the American lines and have Goebbels prepare a news release that the Americans broke the truce by their attack in Norway. How soon can we launch the attack?"

"It will probably take us a week to transfer the V-2s to Italy but if we only used the V-1s which we could airlift we could attack in forty-eight hours."

"How many V-1s would we have?" inquired Hitler as he settled down.

"Close to several thousand now."

"Also *Mein Führer*," interjected Goering. " I could have an additional seventy-five to one hundred jet bombers and fighters moved into position by then."

"*Gut, gut,*" responded Hitler. "A fast response is very important, so we will attack in Italy with just the V-1s and Jets. But what about transporting one of our atomic devices in a submarine and setting it off near New York?"

Hitler's suggestions, which usually meant he was going to do it, caught everyone unprepared.

After an uncomfortable long silence, Von Ribbentrop, the

Foreign Minister, finally spoke up. *"Mein Führer,* with all due respect to your suggestion, may I point out that such an action would so infuriate the Americans they would never come to terms with us. We would end up in a war of attrition until the Americans developed their own atomic weapons. And then what? They could deliver them here as well as we can there. I recommend we continue to try and work with the Kennedy administration and come to a settlement of the war."

Everyone looked at Hitler to see what his response would be. But to their surprise, Hitler said, "Your point is well taken *Herr* Minister. I agree with your recommendation."

Everyone present gave a silent sigh of relief.

"But," went on Hitler, "I still want the Americans hit hard and *kaputt* in Italy."

CENTRAL ITALY

General Patton woke up with a feeling that something was wrong. Looking out the window to the east, Patton could see the first hint of dawn breaking. Suddenly he realized what was wrong. It was the silence. Total silence. There was no gunfire going on. Ever since his Third Army had replaced the British Eighth Army, from Florence to the east, along the Arno River to Pisa on the west, there had been constant skirmishes along the line. No significant attacks, but just enough action to remind the other side that they were still being opposed. But now there was deathly silence from the German lines, just like there had been at Normandy proceeding the atomic detonation.

"Normandy!" shouted Patton. "My God, they are going to hit us again!"

Jumping out of bed, Patton began pulling on his trousers as his aide, hearing the commotion, rushed in.

"What is it, Sir? What's wrong?"

"Quick, call all the field commanders and tell them to withdraw from their positions as soon as possible. Leave all the heavy equipment that is not self-propelled. Tell them to pull back at least five miles, if they can, and dig in!"

"If they can? Sir?"

"Do it, damn it! We are about to be hit with another atomic device."

As the aide ran down the hall, Patton ran into the radio room next to his quarters.

"Get me General Clark," he barked to the surprised radioman.

In less than thirty seconds Mark Clark answered. "What is it George?"

"Mark, how far are you from the front?"

"About three miles George. Why?"

"Can you hear anything going on at your front?"

"No. It has been pretty quiet all night. What's going on George?"

"Mark, I am convinced the Nazi bastards are about to hit us with another atomic weapon. I have just ordered all of my troops to pull back five miles as quickly as possible. I strongly urge you to do the same!"

"Are you sure about this, George?"

"Damn it Mark, if I wasn't, do you think I would retreat for the hell of it?"

"No, George I know you wouldn't. I'll get the order out right now. Thanks George."

As Patton stepped out into the early morning mist, already some of the troops just forward of his headquarters were beginning to move out. As two infantrymen walked by, carrying a heavy thirty caliber machine gun, Patton yelled, "Drop that damn thing and run. Run for your lives."

The two surprised men dropped the gun, and each made a quick salute as they disappeared into the darkness.

As the trickle of men moving past his headquarters turned into a heavy stream of humanity, Patton walked over to his tank that was already manned by his crew and idling. As he climbed up to the turret, he yelled to some infantrymen passing by. "You there, as many as you can, climb aboard!"

Twenty-two minutes later, the first volley of two hundred V-1s were launched against Patton's eighty-five mile long front. Before the first ones reached their targets, three hundred others were in the air. Overhead ME-262 jets raked the retreating columns with cannon fire while several squadrons of the AR-

234 jet bombers raced towards the airfields of the Fifteenth Air Force at Foggia.

MOSCOW

Molotov woke up with a start as the small alarm clock went off, muffled by his pillow on his cot. Since the war began, many of the Soviet leaders, including Molotov, had sent their families east of the Urals for their safety. A select few had moved into vacated offices in the Kremlin itself. Molotov looked at the clock: 3:30. He quickly pulled on his pants and a heavy pair of socks, then pulled a heavy sweater over his head. After picking up a large flat leather pillow from his chair, he quietly walked over to the door. He listened at the door for a moment. Hearing nothing, he quietly opened it and looked up and down the hall. No one was in sight, as he knew was usual for this time of the night. Though the outside of the Kremlin was heavily fortified and guarded, the inside was not. The Communist leaders trusted only themselves and did not want anyone, including guards, to hear what was being said in these halls. Next to Molotov's office was a bathroom which he shared with Stalin. Molotov entered the bathroom and shut the door. Some light filtered in from the lights in Red Square through a small window high on the far wall. Although Molotov did not have a door from his room directly into the bathroom, Stalin did. Another sign of rank in the hierarchy. Stalin always locked his door to the hall but typical of most bathrooms, it locked from the inside only. Molotov took a deep breath and tried the door. It pulled open. Across the room, Molotov could see the simple single bed in the corner, where his old friend was lying on his back, snoring lightly. The two men had been close since the days of the revolution. So close in fact, that Molotov was one of the few that had escaped Stalin's ruthless purges. Molotov was even privy to the facts that Stalin had been responsible for his wife's death years before, and in 1943, had refused to exchange his son Jokov who was a prisoner of the Germans, for a captive German General. The Germans later reported Jokov had killed himself. But, this was no time for sentimental thoughts. What had to be done, had to be done, before all of the work of the revolution was destroyed by the Fascist hordes. Molotov slowly walked over to the side of the bed. Stalin's breathing came in short breaths. Years of heavy smoking had taken their toll on the sixty-five year old leader. Molotov, eleven years younger and thirty pounds heaver, quickly placed the leather pillow over Stalin's upturned face and then climbed onto Stalin's chest to hold the pillow tightly in place, while placing his legs over Stalin's arms. Stalin struggled, but the struggling only caused the need for more air. In less than a minute the struggling ceased. Molotov continued to keep the pillow in place while he slowly counted to one hundred. He then slowly reached down with one hand and felt for a pulse in Stalin's wrist. There was none. Slowly Molotov got off the body. There was still no sign of life. He then put Stalin's arms across his chest and straightened the blankets out over his body. Molotov then walked slowly backwards to the bathroom door which was still open. He entered the bathroom, shut the door and then opened the door into the hall. Safely back in his room, Molotov looked at the clock. It was now just 3:42. Only twelve minutes to end a lifetime friendship. As he slid back into his bed, tears ran down his cheek. It was the first time Molotov ever remembered crying.

THE WHITE HOUSE

President Kennedy sat in the Oval Office reading dispatches selected by his staff, in preparation for his weekly meeting with his Cabinet. The news from the Far East was mixed. The Japanese were steadily advancing up Sakhalin Island, and within the week would probably be in control of the entire island. On the mainland, their Fifth Army was advancing westward along the Trans-Siberian Railroad and were threatening Blagovescensk. Vladivostok was surrounded, and would soon be forced to surrender from lack of supplies.

The Australians reported the German Raider, *Atlantis*, which was thought to have been carrying an atomic device to the Japanese, had reportedly sunk another freighter, about two hundred and forty miles west of the position originally given by the captive nurse aboard the *Atlantis*. This seemed to confirm the

Russian report that the transfer of the atomic device to the Japanese had taken place and the *Atlantis* was moving back out of the area where it had been previously reported. The device was no doubt now in the hands of the Japanese.

In Eastern Europe the Germans were steadily advancing into Soviet territory. All was still quiet in Western Europe, and only a few thousand Americans remained on the British Isles. The stalemate in Italy continued. Meanwhile, the Turkish government had turned down the request to use their country for an invasion into the Southern Balkans. They invoked their neutrality and indicated their belief that they would be backing another losing side as they did in the first war, if they were to support the Americans.

The military had been pressing Kennedy to resume the bombing of the uranium processing plants in Czechoslovakia. Instead, he had agreed to the commando raid on the heavy water plant in Norway. Reports from the *Prince* stated that the attack had been a success, shutting the plant down. But, Kennedy knew the plant would be back in service in a few short months. Also, all of the Rangers had been killed, along with the crew of the *Prince*, when it was sunk.

From New Mexico came the best news. The processing of turning U-235 into Plutonium was working out. This meant that once the problem of setting them off was mastered, the bombs could be produced very rapidly. "American mass production again rising to the occasion," thought Kennedy.

Kennedy got up, gathered up his notes, and then walked down the hall where his cabinet was waiting.

MOSCOW

Molotov cautiously eyed each member of the Politburo as they each entered the hall for the emergency meeting he had convened. Word of Stalin's death had quickly spread after his body had been found by his secretary when he had brought in breakfast.

From his chair to the right of the vacant chair at the head of the table, Molotov reached over and picked up the gavel, and lightly tapped for order.

"Comrades," he began. "This is truly another tragedy that has been thrust upon us at an inopportune time."

Everyone politely nodded their heads in agreement. Molotov also noticed, to his satisfaction, that no one seemed to be taking Stalin's death too hard.

"No doubt," continued Molotov. "The strain brought on by the recent events on the Western Front and the Japanese trickery was too much for the Generalissimo's heart."

At this point, Molotov decided to take a chance.

"Of course, I don't really know if it was his heart or not. So what are your feelings Comrades? Should we order an autopsy or not?"

Nikita Khrushchev spoke up first. "Comrades, we all know the Generalissimo was getting up in years and was in poor health to start with. I, therefore, am opposed to mutilating his body for nothing."

"Thank you, Comrade, I am inclined to agree with you," ventured Molotov. "Is everyone in agreement with Comrade Kruschchev's proposal?"

Everyone raised their hands in support of foregoing an autopsy.

Molotov hoped his relief was not visible.

"Before we move on with the business of replacing the Generalissimo, I have some information I must share with you. Our opinions as to what to do about this information will be very valuable to whoever assumes the Chairman's seat, and I believe we will all speak more freely before we have a new Chairman."

Everyone leaned forward as Molotov picked a paper out of his briefcase.

"This recently came in, and so the Generalissimo did not have time to really consider it," he continued.

With that introduction, Molotov read the text of Rommel's call regarding the imminent destruction of Leningrad. Following the reading, a silent shock come over the gathering.

"Comrades, before I resign my office as Foreign Minister, so that the new Chairman can freely pick his own man, I wish to offer my last opinion as Foreign Minister. In light of what is happening on the Western and Eastern Fronts, together with this information from Field Marshall Rommel, which I believe is truthful, I propose it is time we seriously consider the possibility of coming to terms with the Fascists. Then we will be in a position to deal with the new Japanese threat. We may be able to reach a reasonable agreement with the Germans concerning our western territories. But there is no telling how far the Japanese thrust may extend. And, if they become firmly entrenched in the east we may never be able to dislodge them. Also we now have information which indicates the Germans actually transferred an atomic device to the Japanese."

A gasp escaped from several of those present.

"Where, or when, the Japanese will use the weapon is anybody's guess. But one thing we can be sure of is: they will use it."

"Even so, what if the Americans still are able to defeat the Japanese?" asked Beria.

"That is a possibility, Comrade; however, we have no idea as to what the final terms of such a victory may be. Remember, the Western Allies threw Austria and part of Czechoslovakia to the Fascists, in return for what they thought would protect their own interests."

"True, true," murmured several.

"Comrade Minister, your proposal to meet with the Fascists does have some merit," offered Andrei Vishinsky. "But, let's at least call in our Generals and get their opinions."

Everyone present knew the Generals were always reluctant to admit things were going badly and probably would get worse. But, perhaps with the Generalissimo gone, and no new leader yet, they may be more candid now.

"Fine," agreed Molotov. "Let us adjourn until 6:00 this evening, when our Generals can be here. Time is of the essence, but maybe by then, the Generals will have time to get their facts together."

The Soviet Politburo was reconvened along with the General Staff. Molotov called the meeting to order, and after reading Rommel's warning to the Generals, he asked. "What, if anything, Comrade Generals, can we do to prevent the Nazis from carrying out their plot against Leningrad?"

Always fearful of being the bearer of bad news, the Generals were reluctant to speak up. Realizing the problem, Molotov prodded them. "Comrades, the Generalissimo is truly dead. We here, are trying to fill the gap until a new leader is selected. But, we need your help, as will the new leader, who most likely, is someone in this room. If we are too weak to stop the Fascists, we may have to do something else."

Molotov quickly glanced around the room. If anyone caught the drift of his suggestion, they must be in agreement for he couldn't detect any surprised or shocked looks.

Field Marshall Zhukov broke the silence. "We did have a few minutes after we were contacted to discuss the situation among ourselves before we came over."

"And?" coaxed Molotov.

"We all agree, that there is probably nothing we can do to stop the destruction of Leningrad, short of a lucky successful attack on whatever is being used to transport the device. We are being driven back rapidly along the entire northern and southern sectors. Our troops are exhausted and our air force has been all but swept from the skies by the enemy's high speed jet-powered aircraft. Thousands of our troops that were exposed to the atomic blast are still dying every day, and hundreds more are still becoming ill. Moreover, with England out of the battle, recent American convoys bringing us supplies have lost half of their naval escorts and all of their air cover in the eastern portion of the Atlantic. We understand their losses have been very heavy and are fast becoming unsustainable."

"I was not aware of the problem with the convoys," said Molotov as he looked at the other political leaders. All shook their heads, confirming their ignorance also.

"We have been able to monitor some of the Americans' radio transmissions from their ships and also have had first hand reports from the Americans that made it through to Murmansk and Archangel. Both sources confirm the heavy losses."

"Ah, I am positive that these reports were forwarded to the Generalissimo," offered Zhukov.

"I am sure they were," reassured Molotov. "But, obviously not everything filtered down to the rest of us. Now, before we dismiss our Generals, does anyone else have any questions for them?"

"I have one," said Vishinsky. "In the southern sector, where do you plan to form a new line that can be held?"

Walking over to the wall map, Zhukov drew an imaginary line from Rostov-on-Don on the east coast of the Sea of Azov eastward to Astrachan on the coast of the Caspian Sea. "We must, of course, keep our lines open to our oil fields in the Caucasus. And, unless our forces are hit with another atomic device, we feel we have a good chance of holding this line, but at a heavy cost."

"Of course. Thank you."

As the door closed behind the Generals, Molotov turned to his associates. "Well Comrades?"

Beria was the first to speak. "What I would like to know, is what you had in mind, Comrade, when you said if we couldn't stop the Fascists from destroying Leningrad we may have to do something else?"

Before Molotov could speak up, Vishinsky did. "I am sure what Comrade Molotov has in his mind, is the same thing I, and probably nearly everyone else does. We may have to come to terms with the Fascists like the British did."

To Beria's surprise, everyone else nodded their heads in agreement.

Seeing the support he had, Molotov spoke up. "We all remember what happened in the last war, when the Czar pushed our troops too hard. They finally had enough of the slaughter, and deserted the lines by the hundreds of thousands. Fortunately, the Germans were as bad off as we were, and couldn't follow through. But, if that were to happen now, there is no telling when the Germans would stop."

Everyone except Beria agreed.

"You may capitulate to the Fascists," he shouted as he got out of his chair and started towards the door, "but I will have no part of it!"

As the door slammed behind Beria, Molotov turned to the others, and asked. "Well, should we contact the Germans and save Leningrad, or not? And if so, when?"

"I think we should do so in the morning after the morning newscasts and the newspapers are out," suggested Vishinsky.

"Why so?" asked someone from the rear.

"So that when the Germans are contacted, they will officially know Stalin is gone and it is new leadership they will be dealing with."

"Ah, how do you propose we select our new leader, Comrades?" asked Molotov.

"Certainly not the way Comrade Stalin took over after the death of Lenin," responded Vishinsky. "I must admit the Capitalists are way ahead of us in the selection of their leaders. So I propose we, those of us here, have a secret vote and whoever receives the most votes will become the new party chairman and head of state. Does anyone have a better idea?"

"Well we certainly could not leave it up to the masses. That would result in chaos," voiced one.

"That would also take weeks and there is not that much time to act," offered another.

"Then, if no one is opposed to it, we might as well do it right now," offered Molotov. "I am sure it has crossed all of our minds at one time or another, who we would be the most comfortable with in succeeding the Generalissimo, if anything happened to him."

Everyone acknowledged that the thought had crossed their minds.

"Wait. Let me see if I can find Beria, tell him what we are doing, and see if he will rejoin us before we vote," suggested Vishinsky.

"Yes, we want all members of the committee to vote on this," agreed Molotov.

Even before the last votes were counted, the tally revealed that Molotov was going to be Stalin's successor. The final count gave Molotov all but three of the votes cast by the Politburo. In turn, each member of the Politburo came forward to shake Molotov's hand and pledge his support. They were followed by the military staff, who had no vote, but were allowed to witness the voting.

By the end of the week, Von Ribbentrop, the German Foreign Minister, and his staff were on their way to Warsaw, as were

Molotov and his staff. Two days later, the group began the negotiations for an armistice in the German Embassy Building, which had been hurriedly repaired.

After five long and hard days of negotiations, an agreement was finally reached. The Baltic States of Estonia, Latvia and Lithuania, along with Belarus, the Ukraine, and the Caucasus Republics of Georgia, Azerbaijan and Armenia would become independent countries but protectorates of Germany. The loss of the Caucasus Republics with their vast oil fields was an especially hard loss for the Russians, but, following intense negotiations, the Germans agreed to sell the Russians up to thirty percent of the output from the fields, providing the payment was in gold. The Russians were also able to negotiate the retention of the southern portion of the Russian Republic itself from Stalingrad southward, with the understanding that the Germans would have an unrestricted railroad right-of-way from the Ukraine to the Caucasus States, through which their oil would be transported. The Russians also retained shipping rights to and from the Black Sea, as well as shipping on the Black Sea itself. The Germans also agreed that the Russians could continue to defend themselves from the Japanese unhindered.

ALAMOGORDO, NEW MEXICO

James West had just finished his early morning chores, throwing the last bale of hay out to his cattle. As he straightened up and stretched his back, he was startled to see his shadow suddenly form on the ground in front of him, as the sky lit up behind him in the northwest. Turning around, he couldn't believe his eyes. The whole northwestern sky was lit up as if the sun was just coming up over the horizon. And then, almost as quickly as it had appeared, the light started to dim. Within thirty seconds all was dark as before. As he ran to the house, his wife, Sara, was standing on the back porch looking to the sky.

"What was it Jim? I have never seen such a bright light in the night sky. It lit up the kitchen even though I had the lights on."

"I don't know Sara. It may have been a large meteor. Turn the radio on and see if there is any mention of it on the air."

General Leslie Groves grabbed Oppenheimer's hand and began shaking it vigorously. "We've done it Robert! We've done it! I've got to call Washington."

"Yes, but what wrath have we really brought forth here General?" replied Oppenheimer as he removed his protective goggles but continued to stare at the dimming light.

"Damn it, man, we may have just saved Western Civilization as we know it. That's what we have done here!"

"For all of our sakes, let's hope you are correct," replied Oppenheimer as he turned and walked into the bunker that was collecting data from the blast.

THE WHITE HOUSE

President Kennedy was reviewing the morning reports that were always waiting for him when he came into the Oval Office. He picked up the intercom on the first ring.

"Yes, Wilson?"

"Mr. President there is a call for you from General Groves on the secure line."

"Thank you, Wilson."

"Good morning, General," answered the President.

"It is a very good morning, Mr. President, I want to report that the goal of the Manhattan Project has been achieved. We have just successfully detonated our own nuclear device!"

"That is the best news I have heard since taking over this job, General. Please pass on my heartfelt thanks to your staff for a job well done. How soon do you think you can have another one ready in case we need to use it?"

"In two to three weeks, and, in addition Mr. President, it will be much smaller in size than this demonstration device. Doctor Oppenheimer informs me it will be able to be carried by a B-29. In addition he believes we should initially be able to produce one every two weeks, barring any unforeseen breakdown in our manufacturing equipment."

"General, what you and your staff have accomplished will no doubt completely change the present military situation back to our favor. Again, please give my sincere thanks to everyone involved."

"Thank you, Mr. President, I will. I'll also, of course, keep you informed on our production progress."

As he hung up the phone, Kennedy realized he now had the necessary tool to bring the war to a quick, if not victorious, conclusion.

THE ANDAMAN SEA

The Australian Cruiser, *Sydney,* was moving slowly to the northwest through the gentle swells about seventy-five miles northwest of the northern tip of the Japanese occupied island of Sumatra. In the east the sun was just coming up over the horizon. At her slow speed, the *Sydney,* and her two destroyer escorts, were producing as little smoke as possible from their diesel engines. They were avoiding detection in the Japanese controlled waters. On the bridge of the cruiser, Captain Bernard Waterman was scanning the western horizon with his field glasses. Suddenly, he stopped and refocused his field glasses. "There!" he shouted to the others on the bridge. "Smoke on the horizon." Walking over to the radar screen, he studied it closely. Nothing was showing. "Continuously sweep that area," he ordered.

"Whoever they are, they must still be too close to the horizon to be picked up, but the amount of smoke they are producing certainly indicates they are in one hell of a hurry," mused the First Officer.

"Sir, we are starting to get a signal now," reported the radarman. "No, wait–we are getting three signals. One strong, and two weaker signals."

"Think they are the Japanese ships the Americans have asked us to help locate, Captain?" asked the First Officer, as he studied the smoke on the horizon.

"They could very well be. They are obviously old coal burners and they are throwing caution to the winds, so they must be Japanese, thinking they are secure here in these waters. Bring her back to a heading of 360 and reduce speed to one eighth. Man all battle stations and prepare for a broadside. As soon as we are in range open fire with main batteries and order the destroyers to attack at flank speed. Concentrate all fire on the cruiser."

The *Sydney* rolled port side from the recoil of the six main eight inch guns.

Not equipped with radar, and looking into the sun, the *Togo* was unaware of the threat until the first shells passed over the ship and exploded harmlessly off her stern. However, as the shells whistled overhead, it was apparent that they were being fired upon from head on.

"Damn, the sun must be right behind them, I can't see a thing," cursed Admiral Yamashita. "Take evasive action and launch the aircraft. Notify our base at Banda Aceh we are under attack!"

"Slightly long on that round," said Captain Waterman to no one in particular, knowing the gunnery officer knew his job and would make the necessary range corrections.

Again, the *Sydney* rolled from the recoil of the main batteries. This time, the range was correct. However, due to the sharp turn to port the *Togo* was making, only one shell found its mark. Falling on the stern, it took out the *Togo's* rudder control. With the rudder being locked in the hard over position, the *Togo* commenced circling.

As the two Australian and Japanese destroyers raced at each other the Australian warships separated, each heading for either side of the circle the *Togo* was trapped in. Seeing the Australians' plan, each of the Japanese destroyers changed course to intercept one of the Australian destroyers. However, the Japanese destroyers were now in range of the *Sydney's* secondary batteries, which concentrated their fire on just one of the destroyers. The second salvo caught the destroyer at midship, breaking it in two. As the second Australian destroyer crossed the port side of the remaining Japanese destroyer, the Japanese destroyer fired its four torpedoes, one of which caught the bow of the Australian warship, stopping it dead in the water as it began to sink. The *Sydney* now brought its secondary batteries to bear on the second destroyer, while continuing to hammer away at the *Togo* with its main batteries. Now having the range, the *Sydney* locked onto one point on the circular wake being left by the *Togo* and had only to wait until the *Togo* swung around on its next pass around the same point. This time, two of the eight-inch shells found their mark and the *Togo* stopped its pitiful circling and began to list to port. Immediately, the Japanese Destroyer, *Koza,* broke off its engagement with the Australian destroyer and sped to the *Togo*.

As the Australian destroyer raced in for the kill, it was suddenly attacked by four Nakajima Type 97 bombers from the Japanese base at Banda Aceh. By the time the last bomber had made its run, the destroyer was in flames and the bombers headed for the *Sydney*.

Seeing what had happened, Captain Waterman ordered, "Break radio silence and report what has happened. Flank speed on course 270. Let's get out of here."

But it was too late. The *Sydney* was able to down two of its attackers before it too took two torpedoes and lay dead in the water and sank.

THE WHITE HOUSE

President Kennedy was shocked as he was briefed on the events of the last two days. The Germans and Russians had actually signed an armistice. The German attack in Italy had caused almost twenty thousand casualties. Only General Patton's quick evacuation efforts had kept the number from being much greater. The only other good news was an unconfirmed report that an Australian warship may have intercepted and sunk the Japanese cruiser carrying the German atomic device.

Turning to General Marshall, the President asked, "What is the latest from Italy, General?"

"Well, new information just received indicates the German attack, although very intense, lasted less than an hour and was limited to buzz bombs and artillery fire along the front and air attacks just behind the lines. By the time our fighters reached the front it was all over. Even the German jet- powered aircraft had left. However, a large number of aircraft of the Fifteenth Air Force were caught on the ground and destroyed. The attack came so quickly only a few of our P-38s were able to get into the air to provide some defense and they were overwhelmed by the German Jets. And, per your previous directions, there was no hot pursuit. General Patton and Clark are forming a new defense line south of their previous positions. But as you know, General Patton is giving up very little territory. No German ground troops were involved, so there was no attempt on the enemy's part to take back any territory. There is now essentially a no-man's-land between the two armies. According to a broadcast by Goebbels himself, the attack was in response to our attack on the German heavy water plant in Norway.

"Now," continued the President, "Admiral King, what about the report from the Australians?"

"Their Cruiser, *Sydney*, with two destroyer escorts intercepted a Japanese Cruiser with her escorts making a run for the Strait of Malacca and possibly Singapore. One of the Japanese destroyers was positively sunk and the cruiser badly damaged and possibly sinking, before the Aussies were attacked and sunk by torpedoes and shore-based aircraft."

"Why do you think the Japanese ship was the one carrying the atomic device?" asked the President.

"Well sir, we don't have any positive proof. But we do know the German Raider that had the device must have transferred it, as the Raider moved back to the western half of the Indian Ocean where it is still operating. Neither our ships, the British or other Australian ships or aircraft have spotted any other Japanese ships in the eastern Indian Ocean. So it is only by a process of elimination that we think this was the ship. We have sent out reconnaissance aircraft to the area of engagement. There is a lot of debris floating in the area but no sign of the Japanese Cruiser. Also our agents in the area have not reported seeing any large cruisers. So we feel it must have been sunk. Of course, there is a possibility the Japanese were able to transfer the device from the cruiser, before it sank, to the remaining destroyer."

The President stood up and said, "Gentleman in light of these recent events, I think it is time to meet with our Allies to lay out a plan of action. Secretary Hull, would you please arrange that as soon as possible?"

"Of course, Mr. President."

Everyone left as Kennedy turned and walked to his living quarters in the White House. His wife, Rose, was sitting in the living room as he walked in.

"Well, Rose, I think the needless slaughter in Europe is finally about over."

"Oh, how is that?" she asked.

"Well, with the Russians finally out of the fighting, the Germans will be able to withdraw so many of their troops from their Eastern Front they will be able to strengthen their positions facing us in Italy to the extent that even the most hard liners in the military and Congress will see that the cost of us winning a ground war in Western Europe would be too costly. And I mean not only in lives and materials, but also financially. I am convinced that such a prolonged struggle would bankrupt this country."

"But what about the threat of their, ah, what do you call it, atom device?"

"Well, my dear, I haven't told you before, but I am happy to tell you now, that our scientists have unlocked the secret of its manufacturing and we have successfully tested one out in the New Mexico desert."

"That is good news."

"Yes, and there is more. The Convair Corporation in Texas is working on the development of a very long-range bomber they are calling the B-36, that will be able to fly from bases here in America to Europe and back while carrying an atomic bomb. Northrop Aircraft in Southern California, is working on an even more exotic long-range jet-powered bomber. They call it the Flying Wing."

"What is the next thing you have to do, dear?" Rose asked.

"First, I must convince the hardliners in Congress that we must come to terms with the Germans. Then, possibly as early as next week, I am meeting with representatives of all of our Allies to tell them our plans, and to formulate a general policy for future dealings with the new German Empire."

"That may present some problems for the Western European nations now under German control."

"Yes, I suspect it will. But we can't do much else at the present time. Besides, no political situation lasts forever. Seventy-five years ago who would have suspected that Great Britain would have been brought to her knees with her empire in tatters?"

"Well, let's hope the present situation doesn't last for the thousand years Hitler boasts about, or even seventy-five years for that matter," responded Rose.

"It won't, I can assure you that."

ALGIERS, NORTH AFRICA

General Charles de Gaulle sat facing his previous co-president of the Free French, General Henri Giraud. Following the withdrawal of the British from the war, de Gaulle had left London and returned to the capital of the French colony.

"Thank you for coming on such short notice, *Mon* General."

Giraud merely gave a slight nod. It was no secret that Giraud despised the man sitting across from him. The previous year, the two Generals had founded the French Committee of National Liberation in Algiers. Later, after maneuvering Giraud out of the organization, de Gaulle became the sole president of the committee and moved its headquarters from Algiers to London where he diligently worked to have the Free French as a primary partner among the Allies. With England out of the war, he found himself no longer welcome in London and so he returned to Algiers.

"As you probably have heard," continued de Gaulle, "the Russians have also now come to terms with the Germans."

"So I hear."

"Yesterday, I received this communique from the Americans stating they want to hold a meeting next week to discuss the situation in Europe."

"So?"

"So, we both know that the new American President, Kennedy, never was in favor of America entering the war with Germany."

"And you think this meeting is to force the remaining Allies into accepting some kind of truce with the Germans?"

"I am positive of it!" declared de Gaulle as he brought his fist down on the table. "The Americans are going to sell us out. And if they do, you know where that will leave us? No foothold on the continent, and British troops in control of our colonies of Syria, Madagascar and even Morocco."

"Yes, I see the potential problem, *Mon* General," said Giraud as he started to warm up and forget their past differences. "I assume you are going to this meeting?"

"Of course. And that is where you come in, *Mon* General. I want you to put together a group of men we can trust and have some of them travel to each of our colonies and size up the situation and report back to me what they have found so that I may know, while at the meeting, where our strengths and our weaknesses are. Will you help?"

As much as he detested the man, Giraud's love of France overcame his reluctance to help his adversary.

"Yes, General I will help. Viva La France!"

SOUTH WESTERN INDIAN OCEAN

The *Atlantis* had finally received word that hostilities with England were over and it was being recalled home. That evening, Kaptain Rogge had requested the ships regular cooks to prepare a special dinner for his officers and the English nurses. As they all took their places, Rogge picked up his wine glass and asked everyone to please join him in a special toast. The English nurses were somewhat reluctant.

"Please," asked Rogge.

As Captain Lewis slowly raised her glass, her fellow officers followed suit.

"I have some very special news for all of you. Three hours ago, I received a special communique stating that the British and German governments have signed an armistice and are no longer at war. Here is to peace between our countries."

"To peace," all repeated.

As they sat down, Rogge continued, "I don't know any of the details of the armistice, but I do know we have been ordered to return home. Our mission is accomplished, at least for the time being."

Everyone again raised their glasses.

"To home."

"Since we are no longer at war, I can tell you we are headed for the Red Sea. Presumably the English will permit us the use of the Suez Canal, reducing our return trip home by three weeks."

Then turning to the English Officers, he went on, "It is my plan to put you *Frauleins* ashore at the port of Suez. From there, I am sure your government will provide you transportation to Cairo for your flight home."

Several of the nurses started to dab their eyes.

"Thank you, Captain that is very kind of you," responded Captain Lewis, who had a difficult time maintaining her composure herself.

As the group excitedly began to discuss the happy turn of events, Captain Rogge felt the *Atlantis* begin to swing to starboard on the new course he had set for the Suez Canal and home.

THE WHITE HOUSE

Although it was inconvenient for the leaders of the free world to come to Washington on such short notice, President Kennedy insisted upon it. He felt that being on his own turf would give him more advantage in the negotiations with the other leaders. He realized it would be a difficult task to get the other Allied Leaders, whose countries were occupied, to agree to an armistice with the Germans. But, he was determined to end what he considered to be a needless slaughter. The majority of Republicans in Congress were against the armistice, as were a number of Senior Military Officers, who didn't want to go down in history as commanding the only American Army that was defeated in a war. This made the President's task even more difficult. As the Commander-in-Chief of the armed forces, Kennedy knew the military men would hold their peace; he also knew the more radical Republicans would be up in arms.

As the leaders of the Allied nations entered the East Room of the White House, Kennedy greeted each one and their aides, who by request were limited to three each. Each country at war, or occupied by Germany, was present, with the exception of several of the Balkan nations, which had no organized government in exile. Although no longer at war with Germany, Great Britain was represented by the Foreign Secretary. The Soviet Union, although invited did not send a representative. At the head of the table

Kennedy was flanked by two of his Cabinet Members, Cordell Hull, the Secretary of State, and Secretary of War, Henry L. Stimson. Also present was General George Marshall.

After allowing the leaders to socialize among themselves for a few minutes, Kennedy sat down at his place. The other leaders followed suit, and took their places.

"Gentlemen," began the President, "as you all are aware, we are facing a grave situation unparalleled in the annals of recorded history. The Germans, with their new jet powered aircraft, have the ability to sweep our aircraft from the sky over the battlefields while their atomic weapon of mass destruction can destroy entire armies at one stroke. Worse yet, we have reports that the Germans are testing rockets with the potential of traveling several thousand miles. If, and I suspect a better word would be when, they are able to combine their long-range rocket and atomic weapon, very few places in the world will be beyond their ability to annihilate. Even without resorting to further use of their atomic weapon, now that the Russians are out of the struggle, the Germans will be able to concentrate their forces against us in Italy or wherever else they choose."

"Monsieur Le President," asked de Gaulle, "what is the status of your atomic development? We understand that there have been reports of strange flashing bright lights in the southwest of your country. The Lights have reportedly lit up the sky for hundreds of miles."

Kennedy had not planned to bring up the status of the American atomic device. He had hoped that it was still more or less a secret. But he suspected de Gaulle knew more than he had revealed.

"Yes, General, we have had a successful test of our own atomic device. It is much smaller in size than the German's. In fact, our scientists inform me that the next model will be small enough to be carried by one of our heavy bombers."

Everyone in the room began talking to one another.

de Gaulle pressed on, "Surely Monsieur Le President, does not the industrial might of the United States, which has not been damaged at all, have the capacity of out-producing the Germans in the creation of these atomic devices?"

"Especially if we keep sabotaging the German facilities in our country," interjected the Norwegian representative.

"What you both say is true," admitted Kennedy. "The ability to produce one hundred airplanes or tanks to your enemy's ten is only one part of what we must consider. When we are dealing with atomic weapons it doesn't matter if you produce one hundred to the other side's ten. The destruction the enemy can cause you with those ten is still unacceptable. Think what ten such explosions as what occurred over Normandy would do if they were spread over France, or Italy, or even a country as large as the United States."

"What you say is true, Monsieur Le President," admitted de Gaulle.

Drilling in, Kennedy turned to the Italian representative, "Mr. de Gasperi, would you be willing to let us use an atomic device to blast our way through the German lines in your country?" Before de Gasperi could answer, Kennedy went on, "And what if we had to do it three or four times before we finally pushed the Germans back out of your country?"

"I see your point, Mr. President," responded de Gasperi. "The destruction that would be incurred on our country would, indeed, be too high a price for us to pay."

"Exactly my friend. That is the point I am trying to make. In time, we would be able to overcome the Germans and push them out of your respective countries. But are any of you willing to pay the enormous price required by your country? I have even asked myself if the Germans were to destroy New York City with an atomic device, how long would it be before my own fellow citizens would be demanding a settlement with the Germans? And if I may add, the agreement would contain worse terms than at the present."

He had finally gotten to what was the heart of the meeting: coming to terms with the Germans.

The room was unusually silent as each man was lost in his own thoughts. Finally de Gaulle spoke up, "Exactly what do you have in mind, Monsieur Le President?"

Addressing the assembled group, Kennedy answered de Gaulle's question. "I believe it is time to end this hopeless struggle, and end the needless killing, by following the example of England and Russia. We should all sign an armistice with Germany."

"But!" protested de Gaulle, "where would that leave those of us whose countries are now occupied by the Germans? Are we to agree to let the Germans control our lands forever?"

"Nothing is forever," responded Kennedy. "Every empire of the past, Greek, Roman, or whatever, has finally collapsed. And if I may, even today the Empires of France and Great Britain are teetering."

de Gaulle winced, while his aides and the British representatives all twisted nervously in their seats.

"An empire as evil as Hitler's Third Reich cannot possibly exist for long. Once the grandeur of battlefield victories is over and the day-to-day realities of running such an empire sets in, the German people themselves will grow weary of it. Millions of their sons and husbands will be tied up for years in occupational armies. The cost of being more or less on a continuous wartime alert will grow burdensome."

"Since you brought up the subject of the French Empire, Monsieur Le President...Does your proposal include turning France's colonies, along with those of the English and Dutch, in Indo China over to the Japanese as well?"

"No," responded Kennedy, "We will continue to not only drive the Japanese out of the occupied territories, but take the battle to the Japanese Home Islands until they unconditionally surrender."

"What about the reports that the Germans have given the Japanese an atomic device?" someone asked.

Before Kennedy could answer, the Australian Prime Minister spoke up. "We have reason to believe that one of our vessels intercepted that Japanese cruiser carrying the weapon and sank her, along with the weapon."

"But, you are not positive that happened and so what if the weapon did get delivered?"

"It is a chance I am willing to take," responded Kennedy. "The Germans now have the ability to deliver an atomic weapon by submarine to any of our coastal cities. Soon they will have the ability, with their rockets, to deliver such a weapon even further inland. On the other hand, it is a much more difficult problem for the Japanese to bring such a weapon to our Western Coast by crossing the Pacific Ocean, which is fast coming under our complete control. In fact, the chance of the Japanese being able to transport such a weapon to our shores, diminishes every day."

de Gaulle and the other representatives invited to the meeting all realized they were at the mercy of Kennedy. Without the active participation of the United States, it was doubtful that even if all the rest worked together, they could defeat the Nazis. None-the-less, de Gaulle could not abandon France to occupation for an unknown length of time.

"Monsieur Le President," he asked, "we Europeans, with the exception of England and her naval forces, would be of little use to you in your struggle with the Japanese. Would you, therefore, be willing to let us continue to resist the Germans while you concentrate on the Japanese?"

"How would you propose to do that General?" asked Kennedy.

Looking around for possible support from the other European leaders, de Gaulle went on. "What if the rest of us pooled our forces and replaced your army in Italy?"

"Well, I suppose that is your prerogative. But what about the supplies your forces would require?"

"We still have a small fleet at Dakar as well as several vessels that survived Normandy," replied de Gaulle.

"And we still have several warships," added de Gasperi. "Plus, we do have some of our industries still functioning in Southern Italy."

Even Jan Smuts, the South African Prime Minister, offered his willingness to support the effort with troops, supplies, and financing from the large gold mines in his country.

Kennedy thought the Europeans and others were reaching for straws to keep afloat, yet he could not help but admire their determination. The fact that most of the other European representatives were nodding in agreement did not escape his notice either.

"Well, get together and see what you can work out among yourselves. We certainly won't stand in your way. But don't count on us to supply you with armaments of any kind."

"But, Monsieur Le President," interjected de Gaulle, "would you at least be willing to leave what weapons you now have in Italy for our use until we get on our feet?"

Kennedy thought for a few minutes, and decided it would be to his advantage to have the others leave the conference on an upbeat note. "Well, yes, I think we could do that, couldn't we, General Marshall?"

"I believe we could, without seriously affecting our efforts in the Pacific, Mr. President. Nearly all of our materials for the invasion of Japan are being shipped out of our west coast ports anyway."

"Very well, General, we will leave you what we have on hand for your use. Let me know by next week how soon you can replace our forces in Italy, since this will obviously be a factor in my negotiations with the Germans. And good luck to all of you."

As they all filed out of the room, General Marshall pulled his superior, Secretary of War, Henry Stimson, aside. "Mr. Secretary, what should I do about the convoy now in the western Mediterranean headed for Italy? There are over fifty Liberty Ships, all loaded with everything from tanks to small arms and ammunitions?"

"Let them deliver their cargo," responded Stimson, "de Gaulle and the others are going to need everything they can get."

"I was hoping you would say that, Mr. Secretary."

"Oh, General, also tell General LeMay that we will be leaving what is left of his Fifteenth Air Force there as well."

"Knowing General LeMay and his feelings about what is happening, it will likely take a direct order from the President himself to even get him to pull out his airmen."

"Along with General Patton," laughed Stimson.

"You realize Mr. Secretary, we could actually face the problem of large numbers of American troops becoming mercenaries and continuing to fight alongside the resistance. This talk of an armistice is not going down very well with a number of our military leaders. Especially those who served in the First War and remember that the armistice was nothing more than a twenty-year truce."

"Yes, I have thought of that too. We may be repeating history again, but at much higher stakes."

PEACE

On the fifteenth of March, 1945 President Kennedy, Secretary of State Cordell Hull, and a number of aides flew to Reykjavik, Iceland, where they were to meet with Adolf Hitler, his Foreign Minister, Joachim von Ribbentrop, and their aides. Hitler had initially demanded that the President of the United States travel to Berlin for the meeting, but President Kennedy held firm to his position that the meeting must be held on more neutral territory. Both parties would travel approximately the same distance. As the proposed meeting was about to collapse before it even started, Ribbentrop and others were finally able to convince Hitler that this was too important a meeting to jeopardize over the location of the meeting place. Hitler reluctantly agreed to the location, and the meeting convened on the sixteenth.

Hitler, outraged, after finding that the United States had not forced the other Allies to cease hostilities against Germany in Italy, informed the President that this left him with no other choice but to continue his active support of his Japanese ally. Kennedy, upon assurance from his own military advisors that it was highly unlikely that any significant amount of advanced German armaments could get through the blockade that was about to be set up around the Japanese Home Islands, decided not to fight this issue. However, during the last session, Kennedy, knowing that Hitler was aware of the fact that the United States had detonated an atomic device in the New Mexico desert, informed the German leader that if he detonated another atomic device anywhere, including in Italy, the United States would respond in kind.

Thus, on the nineteenth of September, Kennedy and Hitler signed a peace treaty ending the war between the two countries. The terms of the treaty left occupied Western Europe under German control, but with some degree of autonomy. Kennedy explained that the Americans would withdraw from Italy, but troops from other nations, notably the French and Italians, would replace them. In return for the United States agreeing to not supply the Allied troops in Italy, Germany agreed to terminate the development of longer-range rockets. But Hitler insisted that the situation in Eastern Europe was not open to discussion. President

Kennedy did not bring up the "Jewish" question, much to the dismay of the world-wide Jewish community, including the Jewish population in the United States. Demonstrations were held in New York City and in Washington D.C. to protest his decision.

Kennedy returned to Washington and a nation that was sorely divided over the treaty. The millions of Americans of German descent were, of course, relieved that the war with the homeland was over and their friends and family members in Germany would be spared further bloodshed. The other Americans of European descent felt betrayed, and plans were immediately started to organize a volunteer liberation army once the war with Japan was over. Nevertheless, on the twenty-seventh of September, the treaty was ratified by the United States Senate by the narrow vote of fifty to forty-six.

Two days later, amid widespread celebrations across Germany, Hitler addressed an estimated one hundred and twenty-five thousand Germans massed in the giant Grunewald Stadium in Berlin. An equal number surrounded the stadium, and listened to him by loudspeakers. His two hour speech was broadcast over every radio station in every country under German occupation.

On the same day that the United States Senate was voting on the treaty, the Japanese Destroyer, *Koza,* steamed into the port of Nagasaki on the southern Home Island of Kyushu. As it docked, it was surrounded by security forces, while the majority of the remaining Home Island air defense aircraft patrolled overhead, lest the harbor come under an American bombing attack. In less than an hour, the cargo the *Koza* had been carrying was transferred to a large truck, and under heavy guard, was on its way north.

TOKYO

By the end of March the Japanese advance in Eastern Siberia had ground to a halt, as a very heavy Siberian storm moved in. However, the majority of the Japanese goals had been attained. The three southern Kuril Islands, as well as Sakhalin Island, were in their hands. On the mainland, the Russians had been driven from everything east of the Amur River from Chabarovsk to Nikolaevsk on the coast. The Trans-Siberian railroad from

Chabarovsk to Blagovescensk was also under Japanese control. However, there were confirmed reports that the newly-formed, Russian Twenty First Army was rapidly being transferred eastward on the railroad.

In Tokyo, the Japanese warlords were now faced with two threats. From the south and west, the relentless American offensive was fast closing in what the Japanese realized was soon to result in a massive invasion of the Home Islands. In the west, they were faced with a possible Russian winter offensive which would commence along the Trans-Siberian railroad.

As his Admirals and Generals completed their briefings of the situation, General Hideki Tojo, head of the Japanese military cabinet, polled each of his advisors for their opinion of the oncoming disaster. All agreed there was little that could be done to prevent the American invasion, and once it occurred, it would gradually roll across the islands with an enormous loss of life and property.

"What if we used the atomic device the Germans gave us?" asked General Tojo.

"If we were positive where the invasion was to take place," offered Admiral Amau, "we could get it in position somewhere off the coast. However, the question remains where would we position it? And what if there are several simultaneous landings?"

"We must also seriously consider the reaction of the Americans to such an attack," warned Admiral Kichisaburo Nomura. "Prior to the war, as you know, I lived for some time in the United States. Its industrial capacity is unsurpassed. The reports, although not confirmed, of the Americans developing their own atomic device must not be dismissed either. We all are aware that a number of the great scientists of Europe moved to the United States where they are assisting the Americans in the construction of an atomic device. Such a formidable array of scientists combined with their American counterparts, are sure to soon duplicate the achievement of the Germans, if they have not already done so. And once they have fully mastered the problem, these devices will roll off their production lines in terrifying numbers. If we use our one device against them, they will eventually utterly destroy us with their almost unlimited quantity."

The assembled body sat in silence for a few moments,

considering Nomura's remarks. Finally, Prince Konoye, who had headed the government before it was replaced by General Tojo and his military cabinet, spoke up. "Our nation is already in shambles. Every day enemy bombers are overhead, flying unchallenged at times. Many of our large cities have water and electrical power for only a few hours a day. Our supply of petroleum has been reduced to a trickle, and food rations are being reduced every month. I would like to propose that we not surrender the Home Islands, but we declare them to be open and now neutral in the war. If we were to withdraw all our combat troops from the Home Islands, as well as from other parts of the Empire, and concentrate them in Korea, Manchukuo, and the Russian occupied territory, we would have an army of several million men in an area of rich natural resources and with some industrial capacity that has been spared from destruction. The homeland would be spared further destruction, and it is doubtful the new American President, Kennedy, would want to become engaged in a land war on the Asian Continent itself."

"An interesting possibility, but what about the Russian army that is moving toward the area?" asked Nomura.

"Perhaps this is where our present from Germany could best be put to use," suggested Tojo. "We know where the Russians must concentrate their forces along the Trans-Siberian Railroad for an offensive. We could place and use the device in a critical location along the route."

"But we have only one device," objected Nomura. "When it is gone, it is gone, and our chance of ever receiving another one from Germany through the American blockade is very remote, as is our own chance of duplicating it."

"That may be true, Nomura," conjectured Tojo. "But perhaps we may not have to use it, only threaten to use it, if the Russians step over the line. After experiencing its force once on the battlefield, Molotov may be reluctant to suffer the same disaster a second time. Stalin, yes. Molotov, probably not."

"How would the Russians know we actually have the device?" someone asked.

"That is a good question," responded Tojo.

"Perhaps I could offer a suggestion," said Konoye. "While in college I took several courses in physics where we studied some atomic theory. Radioactive materials such as are found in the atomic device, naturally emit small particles. As I recall, there is a device...a scintillation counter, I believe it was called, that can detect these small particles. Some Russian scientists must have these counters. All we would have to do is let several of them with scintillators, get in the area of our device and they would pick up the emissions. They would verify we have the device."

"And also return with aircraft to bomb it," added Tojo.

"Surely, that is a minor security problem that could easily be solved," responded Konoye.

"Yes," added Nomura. "Possibly as simple as not letting the Russians know where they were taken to run their test. It could be done."

"I'll have to think about all of this," concluded Tojo.

Two weeks later, before Tojo had made a decision, it was too late. Although he had agreed to the transfer of the atomic device from the Home Islands to Vladivostok for possible transportation by rail to the Siberian front, no orders were given to consolidate the Japanese Army on the Asian mainland. On the morning of October 10th, a single American B-29, named the Enola Gay, flew unopposed over the city of Hiroshima. Being a flight of one, the Japanese Air Defense Force decided it must be on a surveillance mission and was therefore no threat. With gasoline reserves very low all across the country, it was decided to save what fuel was left to oppose more serious threats. It ended up being the largest threat of all to the Japanese war effort. In a flash, Hiroshima, for all practical purposes, ceased to exist.

Three days later the city of Nagasaki met the same fate. The following day, Emperor Hirohito ordered the civilian members of the government to contact the United States about ending hostilities.

BERLIN

Hitler and his military staff were reviewing their options in Italy. For the past several weeks the American troops, in accordance with the peace agreement, had been pulling out as fast as they could be replaced with Italian and Free French troops as well as some French Colonial Troops from Africa.

"How many troops do you think de Gaulle has, and how many can the Italians, and the others, round up?" asked Hitler.

"It is difficult to say, *Mein Führer*," responded *Feldmarschall* Keitel. "Certainly not as many as the Americans they are replacing, and except for a few units, not of the same quality. I am sure that once the Americans leave and we hit this rabble with a major offensive, they will melt away like butter, and we will be, for all practical purposes, unopposed in our advance down the boot."

"I expect no less," replied Hitler. "I want to end this once and for all, and as quickly as possible."

As the discussion turned to the establishment of puppet governments in the occupied western countries, *Reichmarshall* Goering strode into the room. "*Mein Führer*, General Hiroshi Oshima, the Japanese Ambassador, has just given me some disturbing news. Two days ago the Americans destroyed a major Japanese city with an atomic weapon and just this morning another city was similarly obliterated."

"*Mein Gott!*" exclaimed Hitler. "The Americans destroyed two cities with atomic devices in such a short time?"

"Evidently, and furthermore the Americans have informed the Japanese that if surrender is not forthcoming, another city will meet the same fate in the next few days, to be followed by another and another."

"The Americans are...what is the word? Bluffing, that's it. Bluffing. They can't possibly have that many atomic devices."

"Not just devices, I am afraid, *Mein Führer*, bombs. Both weapons were evidently dropped from one of their large B-29 bombers. The Japanese are, of course, stunned by these disasters, and General Oshima says the Emperor, who is taking the American threat seriously, is suing for peace."

"The Emperor?" questioned Hitler. "I thought General Tojo was running their government."

"He is...or evidently was. The Emperor has gone around him and seems to have the support he needs. Oshima says General Tojo and his military cabinet have fled Japan for Manchukuo, where they plan to continue to fight."

"What about the atomic device we shipped to them?"

"We have had no further information on its status since *Kapitän* Rogge informed us it was transferred from the *Atlantis* to a Japanese cruiser in the Indian Ocean."

"Since we no longer have a monopoly on atomic weapons, it is all the more imperative that we reoccupy Italy as soon as possible. Instruct *Feldmarschall* Kesselring to start the offensive as soon as the last American leaves! What forces did you say he has?"

"The First and Nineteenth Armies which are now at full strength, *Mein Führer*," replied Jodl. "They should be sufficient for the task, with proper air support from the Luftwaffe."

Goering glared at Jodl. "In two days the Luftwaffe will sweep the skies over Italy clear of all opposition, giving us air superiority over the front."

"Let us hope so," replied Jodl, remembering the disaster at Stalingrad, when the Luftwaffe failed to support *Feldmarschall* Paulus, and the entire Sixth Army was lost.

WASHINGTON D.C.

Never before in the memory of its inhabitants had the mood in the Capital been so festive. In less than six weeks the war with Germany had ended, and the last American troops had been withdrawn from the continent. The United States had broken Germany's monopoly on atomic weapons, and the Japanese were now at the negotiation table. Although there were reports that the Germans had launched an offensive in Italy against the Italians, Free French, and their Allies, the United States was no longer involved. Riding high on a wave of popularity, President Kennedy held a rare press conference. After reviewing the world situation in general, Kennedy took several questions from the press.

"Mr. President," asked one reporter, "it has been reported that over eighty thousand Japanese civilians were killed in the bombing attacks on Hiroshima and Nagasaki. Did you have any idea the casualties would be so high when you authorized the attack?"

"My military and scientific advisors had estimated the number of deaths would exceed fifty thousand and perhaps approach one hundred thousand. However, had we proceeded with the actual invasion of the Japanese mainland, it was estimated that before the islands were secured, we could suffer close to one hundred thousand American lives and over another five hundred thousand wounded. The Japanese casualties, both military and civilian, would probably have been, two to three times that many. Also, since the Japanese warlords would have fought for every inch of the homeland, the islands would have been devastated from one end to the other. With their food production reduced to practically nothing, millions would have gone hungry, possibly even starved to death, before we could have shipped in sufficient food to alleviate the situation.

"Also, we had to demonstrate to the Nazis that we not only had atomic weapons, but also our will to use them, if necessary."

"Mr. President, speaking of the Nazis, how can you be sure they are living up to their agreement and are not continuing to secretly develop long-range missiles or even bombers, capable of hitting the United States?" asked another reporter.

"That is a good question. The missile would be much the greater threat. However, to develop such a missile would require extensive testing. Fortunately this type of testing would be extremely difficult to conceal. We are confident that our sources in and around the German test facilities at *Peenemünde*, along the Baltic Sea, would be aware of such tests and let us know. Detecting the development of a long-range bomber would be more difficult, but not impossible. But, remember the Germans are still using a large number of forced laborers from Eastern Europe in their industries, and many of these workers would be aware of what is happening and pass the information to us. Also, the new jet-powered interceptors we are now beginning to produce should greatly reduce the risk of bombing attacks."

"What could we do about any of this, if they did resume development, Mr. President," the same man continued.

"Well, we do have some options. For obvious security reasons I am not free to discuss them here."

"Mr. President, what about the rumors that the Japanese

warlords are going to continue to carry on the war on the Asian mainland, in spite of the Emperor surrendering the Home Islands?" questioned a representative of one of the major radio networks.

"The Emperor appealed to the Japanese military everywhere, to lay down their arms. From what we can tell, they are doing so in the Philippines and throughout Southeast Asia in general. The only places it may be a problem is in Northern China, Korea, Siberia, and their puppet state of Manchukuo. But the Russians are preparing to launch an offensive against the Japanese in Siberia right now. How the Japanese Army there reacts, and what the outcome will be, should be known in a couple of weeks."

The next question came from another member of the press, "Are you going to assist the Russians in their offensive, Mr. President, and if so, how?"

"No. We will provide no direct assistance. The Russians pulled out of the war with Germany without giving us any advance warning, just like they did in the first war. As far as I am concerned, what happens in Siberia between them and the Japanese is their own affair."

Someone from the back of the group called out, "Mr. President, you warned the Germans, that if they used another atomic device, the United States would respond in kind. What if the Japanese did manage to take possession of the atomic device the Germans were sending them and did use it against the Russians? Would you still hold the Germans responsible?"

"Since we have no proof the Japanese acquired the weapon, it would be premature at this time to comment on what our response would be. I would rather defer that question until, if and when, it actually becomes an issue."

"Thank you, ladies and gentlemen, it has been a pleasure to meet with you," concluded the President, who then turned and walked out of the East Room of the White House.

SIBERIA

General Tojo stood in the heavy snowstorm just west of the Russian village of Belogorsk. Gathering his coat more closely around himself, he watched intently as his troops carefully unloaded the German atomic device from a railroad car parked on a siding, and moved it into a damaged stone home. The Russian inhabitants of the home and nearby village had fled a number of weeks before with the approach of the Japanese Army which was being reinforced daily by more troops fleeing the Home Islands in advance of the American Occupation Army as it moved across the islands.

Seventy-five miles to the west, the Japanese Army was holding a line along the east bank of the Selemdza River from Svobodnyi on the main line of the Siberian Railroad, to Blagovescensk where the Selemdza River joins the Amur. Although the river was frozen over to the extent it could be walked across, the ice would not yet support heavy trucks and tanks. With the bridges across the Selemdza all down, the Japanese had been able to halt the Russian advance. However, each morning the Russians tested the ice, as day after day it slowly thickened. Once it was thick enough to support their tanks, the Russians would be able to resume their offensive. With the atomic device in place Tojo would be ready for the Russians. During the night of April sixteenth, the Japanese Army quietly withdrew from Svobodny to form a new line east of Belogorsk where the Trans-Siberian rail line cut through some rolling hills.

Upon realizing the Japanese had retreated, the newly appointed Russian Field Commander, Marshall Semen Timoshenko, ordered temporary bridges thrown across the Selemdza, in an attempt to engage the retreating Japanese before they had time to establish a new line. By the evening of the eighteenth, advance elements of the Russian Army could see the lights of Belogorsk in the distance.

Assuming that the Japanese had fortified the city, Timoshenko ordered a halt to the advance, until his front line forces were up to full strength. The morning of the twenty-first dawned with a clear sky and a gentle wind blowing out of the north. Timoshenko split his forces with one mechanized and two infantry divisions driving south towards Blagovescensk. Another mechanized division and three infantry divisions drove east along the main rail line towards Belogorsk.

Tojo intently watched the Russian advance through his field

telescope from his position almost four miles east of Belogorsk. As the first Russian tanks approached the old stone farm house containing the atomic device, Tojo yelled, "Now!" But, incredibly nothing happened. Turning to his aides he repeated, "Fire the device now, before they destroy the building and the device!" Again nothing happened. "What is happening, you fools?" roared Tojo. "The Russians are almost to the building!"

"We don't know what is wrong General. It appears that the firing mechanism has malfunctioned. The firing signal appears to be going out, but nothing is happening on the other end."

"Keep working on it!" replied Tojo as he ran back to his telescope. "Hurry, I can see a Russian tank approaching the building now!"

Horrified, Tojo watched as several Russian infantryman who were escorting the tank, cautiously walked up to the stone house. Kicking open one of the doors, they slowly entered. In a few minutes, one of the men exited the building and ran over to the tank where he carried on an animated conversation with the tank commander. As the tank commander climbed out of his tank and started walking over to the house, Tojo could tell by his uniform that he was an officer.

Turning to his staff, Tojo barked, "Order an immediate attack, we must drive the Russians back and reclaim the atomic device before it is too late!"

Within ten minutes, Japanese tanks and troops were advancing towards Belogorsk. After ensuring the attack was under way, Tojo returned his attention to the stone house where the atomic device still sat, in spite of the attempts of his engineers and technicians to detonate it. There were now a number of Russians swarming in and out of the building, and a more senior officer had also arrived on the scene. Suddenly, several of the Russian tanks turned and began firing over the small city at the Japanese advancing out of the low hills to the east. From the gestures the Russian officers were making, Tojo realized that the Russians were aware that the Japanese attack must have something to do with the device in the building before them. In minutes, several other Russian tanks had been brought up and positioned side-by-side all around the old home. Men were busy filling sandbags with soil and stacking them against the building in an effort to prevent possible damage to the building and its contents, in the event of a Japanese attack on the building itself.

As the Japanese troops entered the east side of Belogorsk, the Russians entered the west side. For the next four hours, the battle for the city raged. As the long shadows of the early evening at that northern latitude crept across the city, a cold wind began to blow across the battleground. In less than a half hour, the cold front had dropped the temperature to fifteen degrees below zero, forcing the troops of both armies to seek whatever shelter they could find among the ruins of the city.

After reviewing the weather forecast for the next few days, Tojo realized that his chances of driving back the Russians before they had time to remove the device were fast diminishing. Reluctantly, he picked up his field phone and ordered an air attack on the building the next morning. Although visibility was very low the following morning, and the temperature was down to minus twenty degrees, the Japanese ground crews managed to get the engines running on three Mitsubishi Type 96 twin engine bombers. Taking off from their base in Bei'an Manchukuo the bombers reached Belogorsk in a little over an hour. Being directed to their target by ground radio, the bombers came in low under the heavy overcast sky. Failing to recognize the target on the first pass, they turned and made a second pass and located their target. However, the stone house stood vacant and alone. No tanks or other vehicles were near the site and the winds and drifting snow had obliterated all evidence of any vehicles in the area. Nevertheless, the three bombers each made a bombing run over the building, which was left in absolute ruins. Realizing the only possible way the Russians could move the heavy weapon any distance was by rail, the bombers picked up the rail line that ran west out of town and followed it. Less than an hour later a plume of smoke was visible rising from a narrow but long canyon where the railroad followed the Amur River through a low, but long mountain pass. It soon became evident that their quarry had been found. A small coal fired 2-4-0 locomotive was pulling only two flat cars up the long grade and was nearing the summit. On the first flat car was a flat bed ten wheeled truck with a tarp covering a large object that took up almost the entire bed of the truck. The second flat car was manned with several anti-aircraft cannons and heavy machine guns. Captain Mori glanced at his fuel gauge and out of habit taped it to ensure it wasn't stuck at the one-quarter level. It wasn't. He didn't have sufficient fuel to make the attack and return to his base. Realizing the importance of destroying his target, Mori lined up his bomber with the train from the rear. As soon as he was in range of the Russian guns which opened fired he pushed the throttles of the bomber to the full-forward position, and pitched the bomber down into a steep angle with the nose of the plane centered on the first rail car. All the while his nose gunner returned the Russian fire. Without being ordered to do so, his two escorts plunged into the same kamikaze attack spaced at thirty-second intervals. Mori felt his aircraft shudder as the machine gun fire swept across his left wing, and he had to fight the controls to stay lined up with the moving railroad car. Fortunately the train was moving slowly up the grade, and he was not forced to make any major corrections in his deadly plunge to death. The bomber hit the covered target and the remaining bombs and fuel detonated on impact. The explosion was sufficient to rupture the case of the atomic device and set off the internal explosives that would normally be used to drive the two fifteen kilogram halves of the Uranium U-235 together and initiate the chain reaction. However, since the explosion was not controlled, the Uranium was blown to pieces instead of detonating. The second bomber plunged into the fire ball and pulverized the Uranium even more.

Seeing that the target had been destroyed, the third bomber pulled up and dropped its remaining bombs into the conflagration before turning back to Belogorsk. The pilot realized he had no hope of reaching his base at Bei'an, but perhaps by reaching Belogorsk he could at least be close enough to report that the target had been destroyed. Twenty minutes later the pilot of the bomber pancake landed in the deep snow behind the Japanese lines.

When he heard from the pilot that his atomic weapon had been destroyed, Tojo decided he had no option but to order the withdrawal of his army back down the Amur River.

As the fire at the site of the attack on the train burned itself out, hot particles of the Uranium, up to the size of marbles, melted down through the snow to the ground. Others that had been thrown into the river rolled along the bottom of the river until they became caught in rocks. From one side of the narrow canyon to the other a thin blanket of U-235 granules and dust settled onto the snow, and were blown down the canyon.

GULF OF SUEZ

The *Atlantis* slowly approached the British controlled port of Suez, at the head of the Gulf of Suez and the southern entrance to the Suez Canal. Their journey through the Gulf of Aden, up the Red Sea and Gulf of Suez, had been uneventful. Still, Captain Rogge was apprehensive as he approached the port where several British warships lay at anchor. As a safety precaution, Rogge had invited the British nurses to be on the front deck with their gear. Their presence, Rogge hoped, would ensure that no hostilities would break out, even though he had radioed his desire to use the canal and had been granted permission several days ago. It was his intent to put the nurses ashore at Suez, where after hearing their report of their voyage, the British would not interfere with his passage through the canal. He would cross the Mediterranean Sea to his destination of Toulon, the great French Mediterranean naval base.

Rogge requested, and was granted, permission to dock. He desired to put his prisoners ashore, and also be resupplied with sufficient fresh water, foodstuffs, and sufficient fuel to reach the German-held port of Toulon, France. He was, however, previously informed that all provisions would have to be paid for in hard western currency, as an official exchange rate between the English Pound Sterling and the German *Reichmark* had not yet been established.

As soon as the *Atlantis* docked, the German's captives lined up to go ashore. Rogge and his First and Second Officers stood at the head of the gangplank and shook the hands of each of their former captives as they left the ship. Debbie and Fritz stood talking and exchanging addresses until the last possible moment, when Captain Lewis motioned for her to disembark. As Captain Lewis approached Captain Rogge, she gave him a smart salute which Rogge returned. She then offered her hand and thanked him for the courtesies he had extended them.

"*Auf Wiedersehen, Käptain*," replied Rogge.

Rogge stood on the deck until the buses carrying his former prisoners pulled away. Then he went to the ship's safe were he counted out the various currencies he had to pay for his supplies. Going ashore, he was met by the British Supply Officer. After exchanging salutes, Rogge offered his hand and introduced himself.

"After searching for you for so long Captain, it's good to meet you face to face. I am Major Bradshaw."

"It is good to feel solid ground under my feet once again," responded Rogge.

"I am sure it is, Captain. Especially in light of the fact that most of your associates will not have that opportunity."

"What do you mean, Major? I am afraid I have been out of contact with much of what has happened for some time now."

"Oh, I'm sorry, I just assumed you knew about the *Pinquin, Kormoran* and *Stier*. They were all sunk. You may be the only Raider to have survived."

"The *Pinquin* was sunk? What happened to *Kapitän* Kruder? Ernst-Felix Kruder is one of my closest friends."

"I believe he was rescued. Most of the Raiders were sunk in fairly close combat and many of the men that survived the actual battle were rescued."

"I hope so," responded Rogge. "As you saw from the number of prisoners we just put ashore, the *Atlantis*, and I am sure the other Raiders, made it a point to rescue the survivors of ships we sank."

"Yes, I noticed, and I understand that Captain Lewis gave a favorable report on the treatment she and the other nurses received. Otherwise, you and your men would be held and tried for misconduct."

Rogge did not respond, but merely changed the subject. "Well Major, now that you have reviewed my list of needed supplies, can you tally up what I owe you?"

"Of course, please come into my office. I am sure my staff will have the bills tallied in short order. You were informed that you must pay in hard currency, were you not?"

"*Ja*, and I am sure I have sufficient funds to cover the supplies. Unless you have orders to confiscate my ill-gotten gains," Rogge responded with grin.

"I don't believe the armistice agreement between our two counties got down to that level of details, Captain," a smiling Major Bradshaw replied.

The Major watched with interest as Rogge paid for the fuel, water and food he was to receive with a mix of American and Australian Dollars, British Pounds, French Francs, and Dutch Guilders. The currency had been taken from the various ships he had captured. It will take us a few minutes, Captain, to figure out the exchange rate for these various currencies."

"That will be fine, I am sure they will be through before the supplies are all aboard."

"If I may be so bold Captain," inquired another nearby British Officer, "how many ships did you sink on your tours?"

"Well, I assume that is no longer a military secret," responded Rogge. "The total number was twenty-two, which represents a total of more than 145,000 metric tons."

"That's a large number," reflected the officer.

"*Ja*, but it is not in the same league as some of the U-boats. *Kapitän* Kretschmer sank forty-four ships for a total tonnage of over 265,000 metric tons. Of course, there were many more targets in the north Atlantic than in the Indian Ocean where I was assigned. However, I didn't have to contend with dozens of escort warships or aircraft either. My targets were almost entirely single ships."

"But how did you get close enough to them to attack?"

"Many times I didn't, and they escaped, but you must remember, most ships followed regular shipping lanes that are the shortest routes between the various ports. I would wait near one such shipping lane until a ship came by and then would attack it. I would then switch to another lane to avoid being tracked down. I know that at one time there were three or four warships looking for me. In fact, on one occasion, I was in an actual battle with one of your light cruisers, but we got a lucky hit on it early in the exchange and were able to get safely away."

"How many miles did you sail to sink so many ships?"

"I estimate it was a little over 80,000 kilometers," responded Rogge.

At this time Major Bradshaw spoke up. "Captain if you have some hard currency left, and since it will be several hours before the loading is completed, you are welcome to go into town and do some shopping. We have had a couple of supply ships come in during the last couple of days, and some of the stores have some things you and your men may be interested in obtaining. I understand many things are still not available in your homeland. Also, there are a couple of pretty good restaurants and pubs in town. Your men may enjoy the Egyptian belly dancers."

"Danke, Major. I think we will take advantage of your generous offer, if you don't believe our presence will present any problems," responded Rogge thoughtfully.

"I don't think there will be any problems. Especially if you keep your officers and men pretty much together."

Leaving several officers and half of the crew to assist in the resupplying of the *Atlantis*, Rogge and the rest of the officers and men prepared for a time on the town. Rogge reviewed what American and English money he had left after paying for the supplies. Dividing it up, he gave each enlisted man the equivalent of approximately fifty American dollars, and each officer about sixty. He then went with the first group into the small town, after informing those left behind that they would be relieved later and have some time in the town themselves before they left port.

As the Germans walked into one of the larger pubs, everyone turned and looked at them. Even the small band that was playing for the belly dancer stopped their music. The manager quickly waved to the musicians and dancer to continue. Walking over to the Germans the manger said, "Welcome to my humble establishment, *Mein Herren*. If you will please wait here a moment, I'll have my help arrange some tables for you."

"*Danke*," responded Rogge.

Looking around the room Rogge noticed a few Egyptian men sitting at the bar, while at several tables were English sailors. One table had five army officers. Sitting at the bar, and waiting on the tables, were the usual complement of barmaids.

While the tables were being rearranged for the Germans, the

English officers all arose and walked over to Rogge and his officers.

"Good day, Captain," said the senior English officer, who was a Major. He extended his hand. "I am Major Samworth."

"I am *Kapitän* Rogge of the *Atlantis*," responded Rogge as he took the Major's hand.

As the other German and English officers all introduced themselves, Major Samworth said, "We would be happy to have you join us at our table, if you would care to. We heard you were arriving and watched you pull into port."

"*Danke.* We would enjoy that very much. Perhaps you would be so kind as to bring us up to date on what is happening around the world. We have been somewhat out of contact with things."

"I am sure you have," concurred the Major.

Seeing the officers intermingling, several of the English sailors walked over to the German seamen and introduced themselves. They were quickly followed by the barmaids. In a few minutes the German and English Sailors were all sitting and talking. However, Rogge noticed that several of the English sailors got up and walked out the door. Rogge also noticed that in a few minutes a member of his crew got up and walked up the stairs with an Egyptian barmaid on his arm.

As the officers and men enjoyed the company of one another, as well as the entertainment, food, and drink, one of the officers that had been left on the *Atlantis*, walked into the pub carrying a large pouch. Rogge excused himself from the group and walked over to his second officer. "*Ja*, what is it?" he asked.

"*Herr Kapitän*, shortly after you left, the English delivered the mail they have been collecting for us. Evidently, it was known back home that we probably would be coming through here. In the letters, most of our families mentioned several things they are short of at home and asked that if we had the chance purchase some of these things and bring them home with us. I thought your *Gruppe* might like to read their mail and pick up a few needed things before you come back to the ship."

"Good thinking. If things are in such short supply in the Fatherland, perhaps we should divide up the rest of our money among the officers and men and all go on a spending spree. No telling what the officials will do with any money we brought home anyway, right?"

"*Jawohl.* Shall I go back and divide up the rest of the money, and bring you and your *Gruppe* their share?" asked the officer.

"*Ja,* and divide it up equally among the men and officers."

"*Jawohl.*"

"By the way, how is the loading going?"

"It is about half way completed."

"If it is completed before we finish our shopping, leave a few guards on board and let the rest of men and officers come into town. Several of us will hurry back to the ship as quickly as we can to relieve them. We have been treated so nicely here, and the men are so enjoying themselves, I have decided we may as well spend the night in port and leave the first thing in the morning."

"*Genau, Herr Kapitän.* I'll inform the men, and have the money back here in fifteen minutes."

Rogge walked over to his crew and began passing out the mail. He also informed them with a wink, of their "back pay" that would soon be coming. They were given the freedom to spend the rest of the evening in town. The crew stood up as one, saluted Rogge, and then gave a cheer.

As Rogge walked back to the table and passed the letters to his officers, he said to the English Officers, "*Danke,* for your hospitality. Some of us must be leaving now, but I wish to buy another round for everyone."

As the barmaids distributed the beer, Rogge asked, "Some of our families back home have asked us to pick up a few things for them. Are there any stores in the area?"

"Yes," responded Samworth, "but they are not too plentiful. Let me see what I can do, if you will excuse me for a minute." The Major walked over to a telephone and began talking. After a couple of minutes he returned. "I just called our commissary and explained the situation to the officer in charge. He said you and your men are welcome to shop there. It is about a quarter of a mile north of where your ship is docked."

"*Danke, Herr* Major. That was very kind of you. Is your commissary open to both officers and enlisted men?"

"That is so. It's one of the few things in our military that is not segregated," answered Samworth.

"That is more than I can say for our military establishment," responded Rogge.

With that, one of the German Officers got up and walked over to where the crew was sitting and explained what was happening. As he was doing so, the Second Officer walked into the bar with the extra money. As the crew got up and walked over to him, Rogge explained. "I decided to give all of you your back pay while we are here."

Rogge hoped his story of back pay was believable, and that the Englishmen did not realize it was mostly plunder from captive ships. If any of the Englishman were suspicious, they didn't indicate it.

As Rogge got up to leave, he turned to the English Officers. "If any of you would like to have a tour of the *Atlantis*, you are most welcome. I should be back aboard by 1800 at the latest."

"Thank you Captain," responded Samworth. "I am interested and am sure several others would be."

All of the other officers nodded their heads in agreement.

As Rogge and his fellow officers left the pub a number of the crew followed them.

"Is someone remaining to inform those who are occupied upstairs what is happening?" he asked.

"*Jawohl, Herr Kapitän*," responded one of the officers. "I think I'll do it myself," he smiled.

As they entered the commissary, the Germans received a few looks of curiosity and of disdain, but they were welcomed by the manager, who evidently had been informed of their pending arrival. Once inside, everyone gradually drifted apart. Rogge stood by a counter and for the first time read the letters from his wife and children. As he made note of the several things his family had informed him they were in need of, he was startled to hear someone call his name. Turning toward the feminine voice, he was surprised to see Captain Lewis walking toward him.

"Captain what a pleasant surprise to see you in here," said Lewis.

"And you also, *Kapitän*. I guess from being at sea so long, our money is burning a hole in both of our pockets," he laughed.

"So it would seem. I'm happy the authorities have allowed you and your men to shop here. I have been here for some time and already have taken an armful of things back to my quarters. Is there anything I can help you find? You know us women, we like to shop, even if it is someone else who is actually doing the buying. Besides, I might see some more things I want."

"You must have received some of your back pay too," observed Rogge.

"Yes, we did," laughed Lewis, "and it is the most money that any of us have had in years. By the way can I help you find what you are looking for?"

As she grabbed a shopping cart, Rogge said, "We found mail from home waiting for us when we got here, and my *Frau* and *Tochers* asked me to bring home a few things."

"Like what?" Lewis asked.

"Some foodstuffs and clothing."

"Well, let's save the best for last. The groceries are over this way. What is first on your list?"

"Canned meat."

"Here we have a selection of some canned fish and up there is 'Escallop of Spam'."

"Escallop of Spam?"

"That is the joke name we gave it because we had it so often. Actually, it is an American product made of chopped ham and other pork parts. I see they sell it by the case, forty eight cans."

Rogge bought a case, along with one case each of tuna, salmon, and sardines.

"What are these?" he asked, picking up a small round can.

"Oh, those are another American product, Vienna Sausages."

"I have been to Vienna several times and have never seen a product like this there."

"The Americans have a way of giving romantic or foreign names to their products."

"Well, I might as well give them a try," said Rogge as he lifted a case into his cart. "The only other things on the list were coffee and sugar. We have hundreds of pounds aboard the *Atlantis*, but when we get home I suspect they will be taken from us, so I better get some other brands and a receipt so I can prove it is my personal supply. What brands do you recommend, *Kapitän*?"

"To me, sugar is sugar, and you probably don't have any Egyptian sugar on board so you might as well get some of it. As far as the coffee is concerned, the Turkish brands are all very good. You probably don't have those aboard either."

"No, I'm sure we don't. Maybe I'll get a hundred pounds of sugar and a case of this coffee, whatever it is. Well, that finishes the food list. Now for the clothing."

"This being a military establishment, the selection of civilian women's clothing is very limited Perhaps you could do better in some of the local private shops. But does your wife sew? They have some nice Egyptian cotton and wool here."

"Yes, she is a good seamstress; let's take a look at what they have."

"I'll let you pick out what you think is nice," said Rogge. " I don't have much experience in this sort of thing."

Lewis picked out several partial bolts of different patterns of cotton and wool cloth.

"Your wife will probably need thread and needles, too, but I imagine she has been saving her old buttons."

After purchasing a few more things, Rogge said, "Well, I think that should do it for here." As they walked back to the counter and checked out, he said, "I would appreciate it if you would accompany me to the small shops you mentioned. My *Frau* and *tochers* all said they need underclothes and I am a little embarrassed to purchase such things."

"Do you know what sizes they wear?"

Without saying anything, Rogge handed Lewis the letters he had received which detailed the sizes.

As they entered a shop, Lewis said, "Why don't you go look for some nice dresses for your wife and daughters while I purchase the other things?"

"That is a good idea," responded Rogge.

In a few minutes, Lewis returned with several packages. "What have you found?" she asked.

"I like these," said Rogge holding up several dresses. I selected two for my *Frau* and each *tocher*."

"They are very nice. I especially like this one. And it is my size. Do you mind if I try it on? I may purchase one for myself."

"Please do," responded Rogge.

In a few minutes Lewis returned, looking stunning in the pretty dress. As she swirled around for effect, Rogge said, "Yes I think you need one just like that. And for being so helpful it is my treat. And no argument, for I insist on buying it for you."

"Then I will at least help you get all of your purchases back to the ship. They will let me take a couple of the shopping carts and I can return them on my way back to my quarters."

"It is, as you say, a deal," responded Rogge.

As they were leaving the store, Lewis nudged Rogge and nodded her head to one side. Following her gaze, he noticed Ensign Stuben and Lieutenant Debbie Johnson, the English nurse. They were at the jewelry counter.

"Maybe you are not only going to be asked permission from one of your crew to marry, but asked to perform the marriage, Captain," teased Captain Lewis.

"I hope I am not put in that position," responded Rogge. "I have never done that before."

As they got back to the ship, Rogge noticed a few of his men had already returned, but most were still ashore. Rogge then let all of the men who had been on watch go ashore but reminded them to be back by two bells.

Just as Captain Lewis was about to leave, Rogge noticed Major Samworth and several of his fellow officers walking toward the *Atlantis*.

"You might as well stay for the tour Captain, or have you seen enough of the *Atlantis* for a lifetime?"

"Maybe I will stay," responded Lewis. "I noticed that Major Samworth is not wearing a wedding band and I find him quite attractive."

"Too bad you are not wearing your new dress. That would really catch his eye," joked Rogge.

Lewis blushed slightly, and said, "I shouldn't think out loud like that should I?"

"No harm done," responded Rogge. "He might be a good catch at that."

As the English Officers came aboard, Rogge welcomed them, and introduced them to Captain Lewis.

"Ah, Captain Lewis it is good to meet you. I hear they are going to ask you to tell about your war experiences in the officer's club this weekend. Is that correct?" asked Samworth.

"I haven't heard anything about that," replied Lewis.

"Oh, it seems I have let the cat out of the bag, haven't I? Oh, well, consider this advance warning."

"That will also give us time to get out of town, in case she tells on us," laughed Rogge.

"From what little we have heard, I don't think you have any worry there Captain," responded Samworth.

For the next hour Rogge and a few of his officers showed the English officers around the ship. They explained how they managed to disguise the ship in so many ways. Captain Lewis insisted on showing her fellow officers the quarters where she and the other nurses had lived while aboard. She also told of the transfer of the atomic device to the Japanese.

"Speaking of that transfer," inquired Rogge, "what did the Japanese do with it?"

"Oh, I guess you didn't hear," responded Samworth. "The Japanese transported it to Siberia, where they were going to use it against the Russians. But the Russians somehow got control of it and in the fighting it was destroyed."

"It exploded?" asked Rogge.

"No, it didn't explode. It was destroyed in a bombing attack, but left a lot of what they call radiation in the area."

"What else is happening in the Pacific war?" asked Rogge.

"Didn't you hear that the Americans have developed their own atomic bombs, and have destroyed two Japanese cities with them?"

"*Mein Gott!*" exclaimed Rogge.

"The Americans have also given the Japanese an ultimatum, that if they don't unconditionally surrender immediately, one city after another will likewise be bombed until the country is utterly destroyed."

"I wonder if now that the Americans have an atomic weapon of their own the war in Europe will resume," mused Rogge.

"Let's hope not," responded Bradshaw.

"I agree," added Captain Lewis. "I have seen enough suffering for a life time."

After about an hour aboard the *Atlantis,* the English officers, including Captain Lewis returned to shore.

The following morning, an English port pilot came aboard to direct the *Atlantis* through the canal. As the *Atlantis* was pulling away from port a large crowd, including the nurses, were on the dock to watch the *Atlantis* enter the Suez Canal.

"*Herr Kapitän*, I must confess, I am going to miss our lovely prisoners," offered the First Officer.

"*Ja*," responded Rogge.

As the *Atlantis* entered the "The Great Bitter Lake," the English pilot informed Rogge that they would be held up for a day as a large fleet of American ships was headed south and needed to pass. As the convoy made up of warships as well as freighters passed, Rogge assumed they were headed for the Pacific to reoccupy the islands that had previously been under Japanese control. Rogge was also slightly nervous about his own situation. But the Americans, to his relief, ignored him. Two days later the *Atlantis* docked at Port Said at the north end of the Suez Canal, where the pilot disembarked. As he left, Rogge asked him which was the safest route for him to take to Toulon to avoid more American war ships.

"I would suggest," said the pilot, " that you hug the northern coast of Africa until you are west of Sardinia and then make a dash for Toulon at night. Some people are still nervous and have their finger still on the trigger, so to speak."

"*Danke*," replied Rogge, "I appreciate your advice."

"Good luck to you Captain," said the pilot, as he shook Rogge's hand and climbed down into the small boat that had been sent out to pick him up.

Eight days later the *Atlantis* pulled safely into the French Port of Toulon after being at sea one hundred eighty-seven days. Due to their success in sinking twenty-four ships, second only to the *Pinquin's* thirty-two, and the important part they played in the transportation of the atomic weapon to the Japanese, the entire crew was called to Berlin for a welcome home celebration and all were awarded Iron Crosses. Rogge was offered the command of a new warship being secretly built. He declined, and offered his resignation to be able to spend time with his family. Hitler accepted his resignation and gave him a full lifetime pension. Ensign Fritz Stuben took a three week leave, and after visiting his widowed mother, traveled to England to look up a certain British nurse.

ITALY

As the Japanese withdrawal began, a quarter of the way around the world, the German Army Group G, comprised of the First and Nineteenth Armies, under *Feldmarschall* Albert Kesselring, began to relentlessly drive the Italians, Free French, and their Allied forces down the Italian peninsula. The Italian and French fighter pilots, together with some from South Africa and Poland, made a heroic stand against the much larger German fighter command which also included a number of the new high performance ME-262 and AR-234 jets. But after just five days, the Germans were in complete control of the Italian skies. Having very few experienced bomber crews, most of the B-17s left behind by the American Fifteenth Air Force were captured by the advancing German troops as they overran the airfields in and around Foggia. With no air support, and being outnumbered two to one, the Allied retreat became a rout, and by the first of December, the remains of the Allied troops were pressed into Reggio di Calabria at the toe of the Italian boot. Under relentless air attacks, there was little hope of evacuating the troops across the Strait of di Messina to Sicily. On the fifteenth of May, after their ammunition and food were depleted, the exhausted Allied army was forced to surrender. The war in Europe was brought to an end the war after sixty-eight months of continuous fighting.

EASTERN SIBERIA

Marshall Timoshenko shipped in hundreds of slave laborers to remove the debris from the destroyed train and to repair the one hundred meters of track destroyed by the Japanese attack. He had given orders that despite the blowing snow and cold temperatures the work was to continue twenty four hours a day until the job was finished. His engineers estimated that in spite of the bad weather, the jobs should be accomplished within seventy-two hours after the receipt of the necessary railroad ties. In the meantime, the debris would have to be removed by hand as well as the regrading. During the first day both the workers and the guards drank from the river, and also breathed in the powdered snow that was mixed with U-235 dust. By early evening nearly all of the men were experiencing severe nausea. Before the end of the second shift, half of the men of the first shift were extremely ill. Timoshenko, who was familiar with the effects the nuclear explosion had on the Soviet troops on their western front, realized that the sickness had something to do with the destruction of the nuclear device.

A call back to Moscow confirmed his suspicions. After being provided the details of the destruction of the weapon, Dr. Sakharov explained, "Comrade Marshall, the cause of the sickness, which by the way will soon result in the death of a high percentage of the victims, is due to their ingestion of the residue of the uranium from the bomb remaining in the area. It may be from either breathing the dust, or as you mentioned, drinking water from the river which has been contaminated. The blowing snow is spreading the dust over a larger area which is bad, but it is also diluting the concentration, so I don't know if the over-all situation is getting better or worse. As far as the river is concerned, there may be some small pebble-sized particles on the river bottom. As long as these particles are there, the water will continue to be contaminated, perhaps for years, or even dozens of years. It is difficult to say."

"Years?" responded Timoshenko. "How can we rebuild this section of railroad, if the problem is going to remain for years?"

"I realize the dilemma you are facing Comrade Marshall. But you do have several options that you could use. One is to equip all of your workers with gas masks that will filter out some of the dust. Another is to make sure that no one uses the river water for bathing or drinking. Also I would limit the number of hours the men are working in the contaminated area to just a two hours each shift. Another option, which I am for humanitarian reasons not in favor of, is to pull your troops out of the area and throw in as many of your laborers as you can to get the job done as quickly as possible. You must realize that most of them will suffer greatly and possibly be killed."

"Thank you for your assistance Comrade Sakharov. I will take your suggestions under advisement," said Timoshenko, as he concluded the conversation.

Realizing the pressure he would soon be under to complete the repair and resume his offensive against the Japanese, Timoshenko knew what he had to do. Most of his laborers were expendable, being either captured German soldiers, that in spite of the treaty had not been returned, Japanese prisoners of war, or political enemies of the state from the labor camps.

Unbeknown to Timoshenko, the Japanese had tapped into his telephone lines and had monitored his entire conversation with Sakharov. Within the hour, Tojo had a copy of the entire conversation. Whichever method the Soviets used to repair the railway, Tojo realized that his best option was to continually attack the work area and delay the completion of the repair as long as possible. He would keep the workers exposed to the contamination for as long as possible. Since the Amur flowed toward his position he immediately sent out orders that all of his men were to avoid the river at all costs. Since the repair area was beyond the reach of his artillery, Tojo would have to rely on bombers to continually attack the work area. Consequently, a number of bombers were sent up the valley every few hours throughout the nights, laying out strings of one-hundred kilogram bombs along the work area. On a number of occasions, suicide missions were sent out with mortars to shell the area. These constant attacks not only continually damaged the work that had been accomplished during the day, but also kept the radioactive debris continually stirred up. As a result, the repair of the railroad stretched from days to weeks and then to months, while the toll in sickness and death among the workers continued to climb.

By early May, it became apparent to both the Japanese and Russians that they were at a stalemate. Neither army was in a position to push through the canyon where the tracks were still damaged. The radiation continued to take a heavy toll on the slave laborers being used by the Russians. In fact, to avoid the radiation sickness many of the workers were escaping to a certain but merciful quick death in the coldness of the surrounding hills. Many were shot in the attempt to escape.

The Japanese, on the other hand, under constant pressure from the Chinese, had been slowly forced, over the preceding months to withdraw most of their troops from China. They consolidated their forces in Manchuria and Korea to make a final stand.

On the fifteenth of May 1945, Tojo sent feelers out to Moscow concerning a cessation of hostilities.

MOSCOW

On the twentieth of May, Molotov convened his Cabinet and military leaders to review the Japanese proposal. Unlike Stalin, who would continue a battle until his last troops were killed, Molotov could assess a situation and make a compromise when necessary. Carefully and methodically, Molotov reviewed the situation in the far east with his advisors. The remnants of the Imperial Japanese Army did occupy areas blocking the Soviet Union's access to the Pacific Ocean. The American-Japanese peace treaty did not directly address the status of the Japanese occupied Russian Islands, but Tojo was in a poor position to defend any of the islands should the Americans decide to invade them. Of course, at the time the Americans had not foreseen Tojo continuing to pursue the war on the Asian mainland. The Americans were continuing to supply the Kuomintang government under the leadership of Chiang Kai-shek, while the Soviet Union was now having a difficult time supplying the Chinese Communists under Mao Tse-tung. As long as the two opposing factions concentrated on fighting the Japanese, Molotov reasoned, the Japanese under Tojo would eventually be defeated and the Soviet Union could then regain its lost far eastern territories.

Several questions remained as to what would happen to Russian territory if the Kuomintang army, or even Mao Tse-tung's army for that matter, crossed into Russia to defeat the Japanese. The Sino-Soviet border had been in dispute in several places for many years between the two countries. The Chinese might well decide now was the time to settle the border dispute once and for all in their favor. Also, there was the question of the American occupation army taking control of the Russian off-shore islands. Would the Americans give them up? There were many pieces to the puzzle. Molotov, being a dedicated Communist, was certain time was on his side. Consequently, Molotov was able to convince the leaders of the Soviet Union that a peace treaty with the Japanese warlords was in their best interest.

Molotov, and several of his political and military advisors, flew to Irkutsk on Lake Bajkal, where they met with Tojo and his advisors. After over three months of negotiations, on Wednesday, September 5, 1945, the Soviet Union and the remains of the once great Japanese Empire signed a peace treaty. It was forty years to the day after the signing of the Portsmouth Treaty that ended the Russo-Japanese war of 1904-05.

OCCUPIED EUROPE

For the remainder of 1945 and 1946, Germany was able to control the destiny of most of Western and Eastern Europe through their collaborators in the conquered nations. The leaders were Ante Pavelich in Yugoslavia, Clausen in Denmark, Pierre Laval in France, Anton Mussert in Holland, Szalassy in Hungary, Vidkun Quisling in Norway, and Sim in Romania.

By the spring of 1947, some semblance of normality was returning to the devastated continent. Farmers were able to prepare more of their fields for spring planting, as the land was gradually cleared of unexploded mines, bombs and shells. Although the acreage under cultivation was increasing year by year, some certain types of seeds were still scarce. Most draft animals which had been killed, either during the battles, or for food, were becoming more plentiful. Surplus military vehicles, the four-wheel drive American Jeep being the most favored, were being used to pull plows and other equipment. Gasoline and oil from the Romanian fields and refineries were becoming more plentiful and some petroleum products from the captured Russian oil fields around the Caspian Sea were beginning to arrive in Central and Western Europe. In addition, the I. G. Farbenindustrie,

Germany's great chemical combine, had resumed the production of the synthetic rubber, Butyl, and synthetic petroleum from Germany's and Poland's vast coal reserves. Although neither synthetic product was not yet competitive in price, with the natural rubber and petroleum, the Butyl furnished Germany with all of its rubber needs. Since the large rubber plantations of southeast Asia were still not back in full production, natural rubber was scarce. Other foreign chemical companies had been trying to get permission from their respective governments to purchase production rights of the Butyl from I. G. Farbenindustrie.

However, all was not well within the Third Reich. While the people of the conquered countries tackled the repair of their homes, small industries, and businesses with enthusiasm, reconstruction of the basic large industries languished. The main problem was money. President Kennedy insisted on an American ban on large investments in Europe, including England. But many Americans of European descent continued to send dollars or relief packages to friends and relatives in their home countries. Thus, small private businesses were slowly being rebuilt. On the other hand, the large industries of Krupps and the other industrialists suffered from lack of capital. The rebuilding of the great industries in the Ruhr was almost at a standstill. After his conquest of most of Europe, Hitler had insisted that back in January 1945, all of the currencies of the occupied countries had to be converted to *Reichmarks*. The conversion ratio was not only based on a fictitious value of the *Reichmark*, but it had no real backing to speak of. In order to finance the war, Hitler had stripped the national treasuries of the conquered lands while confiscating the property and wealth of the Jewish population of Europe. Even the gold fillings of the victims of the massacres were removed from the bodies and melted down. But, by the end of 1945, the foreign treasuries had been spent, as had the funds raised from the sale of Jewish property. In fact, less than 100,000 Jews were still alive in Europe. With nothing to back the artificial value of the *Reichmark*, the few countries that had been trading with the Nazi Empire demanded to be paid in gold or hard currencies. Between the summer of 1945 and the beginning of

1948, the inflation rate in conquered Europe jumped over one hundred percent and continued to rise every week. Fear of repeating the runaway German inflation of the 1920s became widespread.

Although the occupied countries were relatively peaceful with the general populace primarily concerned in rebuilding their countries, the German military remained at a level of just over three million troops. Since Hitler still did not trust the Soviet Union, two million troops were spread along the Soviet border, and within the occupied countries of Eastern Europe. Another million were used to garrison the occupied Western countries. Nearly three million members of the *Wehrmacht* and one half million German civilians had been killed in the war. Now with the still large army of occupation, the country faced an acute shortage of workers. This shortage was being compounded, as under the terms of the peace treaty the forced laborers from the western occupied countries, and prisoners of war were being returned to their home lands. As a result, the rebuilding process of Germany itself, was proceeding at a slower rate than in the occupied countries. Moreover, in spite of his agreement with the United States on terminating the development of atomic weapons and long-range missiles, Hitler continued to pour scarce funds into their clandestine development. By the early summer of 1946, the heavy water processing plant at Norsk, Norway had been returned to full production, as were the pitchblende mines and uranium processing plants in Czechoslovakia. Near Nordhausen in the Harz Mountains of central Germany, production of the V-2 rockets continued.

As Commander-in-Chief of occupied Western Europe, *Feldmarschall* Erwin Rommel, spent much time since the end of the war touring the territories under his jurisdiction. Rommel was especially interested in the success that the American General Douglas MacArthur was having in the occupation of Japan and its reconstruction. His counterpart in Eastern Europe, *Feldmarschall* Erich von Manstein, was having a very difficult time, as the peoples of the occupied territories chaffed under their still harsh occupation. In addition, von Manstein had to fortify his front with the Russians, who under the leadership of Marshall Georgi Zhukov had fortified the Russian lines.

In September of 1948, Erwin Rommel again made a tour of Denmark, Holland, Belgium, and France to see first hand how the fall harvest was going. Tractors were now being used in some areas now. The harvest was going very slowly, as the farmers were still fearful of mines and live bombs and shells laying in their fields. During the past two seasons hundreds of farmers had been killed or seriously injured by exploding mines and bombs. Recognizing the problem, Rommel ordered his mine sweepers to clear as many of the fields as possible before the fields were worked. For this act, the locals were thankful. And it gave his troops something useful to do rather than be conspicuous as merely an occupational force. As a result, the tension between the occupied citizens and the German troops, was greatly reduced.

As Rommel, along with several of his aides, checked into their hotel in Paris in the early afternoon of the fifteenth of September, Rommel was surprised to see that he had a message to call Dr. Wather Funk, the Minister of Economics for the Reich, who was staying in the same hotel. Normally, they would have stayed in the German Embassy. However, the reconstruction of the embassy was going very slowly, due to the poor state of the Reich's economy.

Since Funk was a high-ranking member of the government, Rommel called Funk's room himself rather then going through his aide. "*Herr* Minister, this is *Feldmarschall* Rommel. I just got into the hotel and was informed at the desk that you had left a message for me to call."

"*Jawohl, Herr Feldmarschall,*" answered Funk, "it is good to hear from you. It is imperative that we meet as soon as possible. Would you be available for dinner tonight here in the hotel?" he asked.

"I could make that, *Herr* Minister. I have no special plans for the evening."

"Excellent. Shall we meet at 6:00 in the Parisian Room? We have reserved the room. Oh, one other thing, please give your staff the evening off and come alone. I'm sure your staff will only be too happy to have an evening on their own in Paris."

"I am sure they will find something to entertain themselves," laughed Rommel. "I understand that there are a lot of friendly French girls around these days."

"*Gut*, your men can enjoy themselves while we talk over some business. We will be expecting you at 6:00 then."

As Rommel hung up he was curious as to what business Funk had that would involve him.

After his staff had brought in his personal things and put them away, Rommel said, "It has been a strenuous few days for us. How would you all like the rest of the day and evening off? I understand Paris is getting back to normal now."

All of the staff were obviously enthusiastic about the offer.

"The offer extends to you as well, Oberst," Rommel said to his Chief-of-Staff, *Oberst* Kohler.

"Thank you *Herr Feldmarschall*, but as you know, I am more than willing to stay and help you, if need be."

Laughter from the other men embarrassed Kohler. The other officers took Rommel's offer to mean that he, too, might have his own ideas about a night on the town. Rommel went on with the little joke.

"*Danke* for your concern *Oberst*, but even at my age there are a few things I can still do by myself."

With that, everyone, including Rommel, had a good laugh.

After everyone had left, Rommel stretched out on his bed and mentally reviewed what he had seen on this tour and what he could do to expedite the rebuilding of Western Europe. He received information that the Americans were pouring millions of dollars into the reconstruction of their former enemy, Japan. The United States came through the war with their industries not only intact, but greatly expanded. After a short nap he got up, showered, and put on his best dress uniform. There was no telling who might be in the meeting, so he wanted to look his best. After some thought he pinned on his medals and battle ribbons.

At 5:50, Rommel entered the Parisian banquet hall. He was surprised to see he was the last to arrive. Nazi protocol stipulated that the higher one's position, the later he would arrive. In addition to Dr. Walter Funk, the Reich Minister of Economics, Wilhelm Keppler, one of Hitler's senior economic advisors, and several others Rommel did not know were present.

Funk and Keppler, both of whom Rommel knew, came over to greet him. Instead of giving the customary Nazi salute, they shook his hand.

"*Feldmarschall*, may I introduce you to these other gentlemen?" offered Funk.

"Please do, *Herr* Minister," replied Rommel.

"This is Baron Kurt Von Schroeder, President of the Bank of *Köln*," continued Funk.

Offering his hand the banker said, "It is a pleasure to meet you *Feldmarschall*. I followed your exploits during the war very closely."

"It was too bad I didn't do as well in North Africa as we did in Normandy," smiled Rommel.

Funk then proceeded to introduce Rommel to Albert Voegler of the United Steel Works and Fritz Thyssen, the head of the German Steel Trust. Also present were Karl Goerdeler, the one-time Mayor of Leipzig, who in the mid-thirties had been the Reich's Price Controller until he resigned over the anti-Semitic Nazis policies.

Just as the introductions were completed, in walked General Ludwig Beck, who had been the Chief of the General Staff, until he, like Goerdeler, had resigned his position in the thirties. He was later recalled as the head of the German First Army. Accompanying Beck was Lieutenant General Hans Speidel who was Rommel's Chief of Staff during the war.

"We are sorry for being late," Beck apologized, "but I had a call from Berlin at the last minute, just as we were leaving."

Seeing the concern on the faces of several of those present, Beck quickly added, "It was nothing of real importance."

Beck and Speidel saluted Rommel in the usual military fashion, rather than with the Nazi salute. Rommel returned their salutes, and the friends shook hands.

"It is good to see both of you again, " offered Rommel.

"*Ja*, it has been a long time since we have seen each other," replied Speidel.

Funk then spoke up, "*Herren*, if you would follow me, we have dinner waiting for us in the next room."

Following the dinner, where the men enjoyed themselves visiting with one another, the men returned to the sitting room. Funk suggested, "Please sit anywhere you would like. The time has come for us to get down to serious business."

"Several of you know why we are here. The others have their suspicions. Erwin, you are probably the least aware of why you have been asked to join us."

Rommel nodded his head in agreement.

"The simple fact is," continued Funk, "we won the war. But it is obvious we have lost the peace. And, even as we speak, we are headed toward another disaster."

Rommel noticed that everyone, including Generals Beck and Speidel, nodded in agreement. Although he didn't disagree with what had been said, Rommel realized that the topic was just short of treason.

Sensing Rommel's hesitance to agree, Funk tried to reassure him.

"We can speak freely here, Erwin. The room is not wired and we have friends outside and around the building, as well as within to make sure we are not disturbed." He then continued, "As we all know, in our travels throughout Western Europe, including Italy, the reconstruction of the occupied countries is proceeding at a much faster pace than in the Fatherland itself. Much of this is due to funds being sent from individuals in America to relatives still living in the occupied countries."

"What about Americans of German ancestry?" asked Voegler of the United Steel Works. "I understand that more Americans are of German descent than any other nationality except perhaps British?"

"That is true," responded Keppler, "but unfortunately the vast majority of them do not want anything to do with the Fatherland now. And those who would like to financially help their close relatives are forbidden by the American government to do so. That is not to say some funds aren't being smuggled in, but nothing of any significance."

"Moreover," Funk added, "we have reason to believe that the American Government itself is providing funds to the puppet governments of the western nations. Probably in an attempt to strengthen these countries at the expense of the Fatherland. All the while, the Fatherland is facing an economic repeat of what happened after the first war. The *Mark*, is for all practical purposes, worthless on the world market."

"And may I add," interjected Karl Bosch of the chemical cartel, "it is nearly impossible to get any of our suppliers to accept the *Mefo Bills*."

"*Mefo Bills?*" questioned Rommel.

"The *Mefo Bills*," explained Funk, "were how we were able to financially disguise our rearmament during the thirties. The Mefo Bills were essentially a currency of their own. To avoid the necessity of flooding the country with *Reichsmarks* and driving down their value, it was agreed among the various major industries that they would accept from the government partial payment for their goods in what become known as Mefo Bills. They would, in turn, use the *Mefo Bills* among themselves wherever possible. The *Mefo Bills* really were not much more than IOU's, but as long as everyone accepted them they served their purpose. Of course, the government paid the various companies for some of the goods in *Marks* so that the German workers and stock holders could be paid in negotiable money. However, since the majority of the workers in many industries were forced laborers, they were paid next to nothing and what little they did receive, they were paid with *Mefo Bills*. The *Mefo Bills* could only be used in the government stores located in the camps where they were being held captive."

"I had often wondered," replied Rommel, "how in the early day of the Reich the government had enough funds to pay for the enormous amount of armaments being produced...especially since the whole world was in a serious depression."

"Now you know," said Funk. "There are the equivalent of some twelve billion *Marks of Mefo Bills* still in circulation. Of course, one by one as the various countries fell under our control we confiscated their gold and silver reserves to be used in the rearmament."

"To say nothing of the tens of millions in currency and property the government also confiscated from the Jews," added Goerdeler.

Several of those present knew Goerdeler had resigned his former government position over the Jewish question, as it was originally called. Among those present, some were sympathetic toward the Jews and some were not. Not wanting the group to be splintered over the Jewish issue, Funk merely stated, "That is also correct. We built ourselves a financial house of cards, thinking that when we won the final victory we would have the entire resources of our conquests to build the thousand-year Reich. However, with the terms of our settlement of the war, we fell short of what we thought we would have at our disposal."

"So what you are saying," stated Rommel, "is that the Reich is essentially bankrupt?"

"That is correct, Erwin. And we are going down the drain more every day. The *Führer*, in spite of agreements, is still building new armaments. Werner Heisenberger, the head of our atomic research projects, informs us they are still developing new improved atomic weapons. General Dornberger, who is in charge of the rocket programs, informs us that they are developing a rocket which could reach the eastern coast of the United States, while carrying one of the new improved atomic weapons. The forced laborers from Eastern Europe have not been returned to their homes and are still being used in this effort."

Turning towards Rommel, General Speidel asked, "Erwin, what do you think the Americans' response will be once they become aware of this continued arms development?"

"I suspect they will have no choice but to consider it to be a threat to themselves," responded Rommel. "However, as long as Kennedy is their president, they probably will not do anything drastic. But, once he is replaced, the American response is anyone's guess."

"Exactly," replied Speidel, "and that is why we are all here. We must take action quickly and decisively to avoid another catastrophe, especially since the Americans now have atomic weapons as well."

Everyone nodded in agreement, except for Rommel.

"Erwin, I must confess," continued Funk, "all of us, except for you, have been discussing this for some time now. We are unanimous in our decision that the *Führer* must be eliminated. In fact there have been several attempts on Hitler's life already. But for one reason or another, nothing ever came of them. This time we have thought out everything and are almost ready to act."

"Are you not taking a chance telling me of your conspiracy?" inquired Rommel.

"We don't think so," answered General Speidel. "Knowing you as well as I do, I told the others that I believed you were behind the warning to the Russians that Hitler was planning on destroying Leningrad with an atomic device. That, in itself, put your life at risk."

Rommel didn't respond to the remark, but asked, "What then do you need from me?"

"We need you Erwin, to agree to become the new head of state once we have disposed of Hitler and his cronies."

"Me!" exclaimed a surprised Rommel. "Why me? I know nothing about politics. I have been a military man all of my life."

"We are aware of that," responded General Speidel. "In fact we did give serious consideration to asking Louis Ferdinand."

"He is the grandson of Kaiser Wilhelm II, is he not?" asked Rommel.

"That is correct. In fact, he is just one of many involved in this operation. But let's face the facts, Erwin. You are known by everyone in the Fatherland, and by all of the leaders of the other major world powers. You were one of the few *Feldmarschalls* that did not join the Nazi Party. You are a hero in the eyes of the German people, and highly respected even by our enemies. Even Churchill once made reference to your abilities during the Africa Campaign. If you were to take over the leadership of the country the entire army would back you including many in the S.S. The population in general would support you also."

"Erwin," added Funk in all seriousness, "we are not asking you to be a new dictator for years. Once we have consolidated our position, we will call for a general election. Of course, I would be very much surprised if you were not elected, if you chose to run. In the interim, you would be free to pick a cabinet to assist you. There are many good and able men who are willing to assist you in any way. Even *Herr* Ferdinand thinks you are the man of the hour."

"If I agreed to do this," asked Rommel, "what would be our long term political goals, other than getting rid of Hitler?"

"As you know," replied Funk, "we have much more in common with the western democracies than with the Bolsheviks, who are our only real threat. The democracies, deep down, do not trust the Bolsheviks either. Therefore, one long-term goal, will be to convince the democracies that we stand as a front line guard against any Bolshevik western aggression. Now that the fight against the Japanese in China is all but over, it is only a matter of time until the Chinese Bolsheviks and Nationalists resume fighting among themselves, and, with the help of Russia, the Bolsheviks will take over China. That alone, will convince the democracies that the Bolshevik threat against Western Europe must be taken seriously."

"And, if I may?" added Keppler, the economic advisor to Hitler, "we have already discussed that the country is technically bankrupt, but Hitler insists on printing more and more money. That is one of the major causes of the inflation we are now experiencing. The fact is, we are overextended in trying to control such a large area and so many people."

"Are you suggesting that we withdraw from the occupied countries?" questioned Rommel.

"Not completely. And not all of them of course. We propose to grant France, Belgium, Denmark, The Netherlands, Norway, and Italy some degree of self-rule. We would retain complete control of Eastern Europe as presently defined by our treaty with Russia. This will provide us with the industrial capacities of Poland and Czechoslovakia, the oil of Romania and southern Russia, and the food producing capacities of the Ukraine and other areas. With such an industrial and agriculture base, we would still be the dominant power of Europe and, within a decade, we would be the natural leader of Europe."

"In addition," General Speidel added, "without having to tie up so many troops occupying the western countries, we would have a larger work force to rebuild our Fatherland. Perhaps the Americans might even drop their embargo on German-Americans sending funds to us. Erwin, you simply must join us in this endeavor. With the development of the longer-range rockets and an atomic device that can be carried in it, sooner or later Hitler is going to insist on testing one or both of them. Such a test cannot be hidden."

"We must not overlook the American political situation either," added Funk. "President Kennedy has been very lenient toward us. But, next year, the American Presidential election will be held again. From what we can determine, the Republican challenger, Thomas E. Dewey, is going to defeat Kennedy even though he lost in 1944. Dewey has been a hard liner all of his political life and has been critical of Kennedy's past dealings with us. If Dewey is elected, I'm afraid there will be a drastic change in American policy towards us."

"I can see that what you are proposing is probably a good idea," conceded Rommel. "I read up on this Dewey fellow during the 1944 election, just in case he was elected then. But how do you propose to remove Hitler?"

General Beck spoke up. "On January 12th, less than three months away, it will be Goering's birthday. As usual, his staff is throwing a big party for him. From 2:00 to 6:00 P.M., there will be an open house at Karinhall, his country villa. Then at 7:00, there will be a large banquet for a few special guests. We know the guest list includes the *Führer*, Himmiler, Goebbels, von Ribbentrop, Hess, the General Staff, Martin Bormann, and other civilians including one or two of us. Of course, you will probably be invited as well."

"How could I become the new head of state if I am on a suicide mission before hand?" inquired Rommel.

"Have you had your appendix removed?" asked Beck.

"*Ja*, during the war. Just when I was needed most at the front, I may add."

"In that case, you will have to conveniently come down with gallstones a couple of days before the party and will be admitted to the army hospital in Berlin. We have several doctors who will confirm your illness."

"Please continue with your plans."

"With all the coming and going of people at the open house, it will be easy for one of us who will be invited to plant a bomb under each end of the long table. As usual, Hitler will sit at one end and Goering at the other. Either bomb will be capable of destroying the entire room. In addition we will have a bomb full of poison gas. During the main course, when everyone is at the table, whichever one of us is there, will pretend to start choking and excuse himself. Just down the hall is the men's room. Hidden in one of the stalls will be the electronic detonator that will set off the bombs. Even those who escape the blast with their lives will most certainly be injured to the extent that the poison gas will overcome them before they can drag themselves to a door. The men's room is far enough away from the dining hall that whoever assists with the bomb can escape the blast, and be out of the building before the gas has time to spread down the hall."

"Also, I will have the villa surrounded by troops loyal to our cause," added General Beck,. "just in case anyone of the leaders may still escape the blast and gas. They will all be shot on sight, except for any of the *Frauen* who should survive."

"How many *Frauen* will be at the banquet?" inquired Rommel.

"Since this will be a night of revelry, the men's *Fraus* will not be there, but their mistresses will. Eva Braun with Hitler, Manja Behrens with Bormann, Maria Masenbucher with Eichmann, Lida Baarova with Goebbels, and Hedwig Potthast with Himmler. *Prostituierens* from the Kitty Bordell in Berlin will probably be provided to any of the others that come alone and desire some company," said Beck.

"Kitty's?" inquired someone. "Is that place still open? I mean with all of the bombing in the area?"

"Not only still open, but thriving. The only damage it suffered during the entire war was a couple of broken windows. In fact, it was considered to be one of the safest places to be during an air raid."

"So all the men in the area flocked to it during a raid, hence the thriving business?" laughed Rommel.

"There is evidently some truth to that," confirmed Beck, with a smile.

"Getting back to the banquet," said Rommel, "I assume that most everyone else will have left the open house by the time of the banquet."

"Everyone except the servants," noted Beck.

"At the time the villa is destroyed," picked up Funk, "we will have you outside a radio station in Berlin. You will simply announce that Hitler and several of the leading party members have been killed in an accident, and until a senior political official reaches Berlin, you will be temporarily acting as the head of state. Of course, all of the high Nazi leaders, as well as all senior military officers from *Kornel* on up, and not involved with us, will be taken captive immediately after the explosion. All Gestapo headquarters will be surrounded by loyal troops just prior to the explosion so will all Waffen S.S. units, with the exception of those along the Russian border. They may be needed in case the Russians attack after hearing of Hitler's death, and try to take advantage of the situation.

"By the following morning, the government will be completely in our hands and you will make an announcement over Radio Berlin, explaining what has taken place and that you are now the new Chancellor. After that, we expect to be hearing from the western democracies. We will then enter into a new set of negotiations with them."

Everyone now turned and look at Rommel, obviously waiting for his decision.

"I take it you will like an answer right now."

"*Ja*," replied Funk. "Every day is critical now, not only from a security point of view, but once you agree we can proceed to get everything else ready. Of course, you are the last major link in the chain. All of the other senior officers that we felt we could trust have been contacted, and all have agreed to join us. Of course most are very fearful of their safety, which is another reason we must get this over as soon as possible."

"I can appreciate their concern," smiled Rommel.

The room was silent for a few moments while Rommel gave thought to the proposition. Finally he stood up and said, "Gentlemen, I see what you are proposing must be so. I accept your offer, on one condition."

"What is that?" asked Funk.

"That we hold a general election as soon as possible. If I am to be the new leader of the nation, I prefer to be an elected one with the support of the people."

"Agreed," said Funk, offering Rommel his hand.

Everyone crowded around Rommel, thanking him and shaking his hand.

"Now what do you want me to do?" he asked.

"Only one thing," replied Funk. "Go back to your regular duties and work on your talk for the radio broadcasts. Two days before Goering's birthday, someone will pick you up to take you to the military hospital in Berlin for your 'operation.' The doctors that will admit you are with us and will provide the necessary answers to inquires about you. The afternoon of the party you will be taken to a radio station outside Berlin where you will wait for word that Hitler is dead."

"Now I think it is time we break up this little meeting, and get down to some serious work," recommended Funk. "We still have a lot of work to do before the big party."

"One last question, if I may?" inquired Rommel. " Goering has stolen many works of art from various museums around Europe. How many of these masterpieces are going to be destroyed?"

"A good question Erwin, and one we have considered. The Mayor of Berlin, who is with us, has asked Goering if he would loan a number of the masterpieces for the New Year celebration in Berlin. Naturally, the most valuable works have been requested and Goering has agreed. They were to be returned the day before his birthday celebration. But for obvious reasons they will be several days late in arriving."

"It looks as if you have thought of everything," responded Rommel.

"Let's hope so."

With that, the group all shook hands and went their various ways.

The next morning, Rommel's staff kidded him about how he enjoyed his night out in Paris.

"It was an evening, I will never forget," laughed Rommel. "Someday I will have to tell you about it."

As expeted, in November 1948 Thomas E. Dewey was elected President of the United States with General Douglas MacArthur as his running mate.

As planned, on the morning of the ninth of January, Rommel was admitted to the military hospital. Once he settled into his room, the head doctor came to inform Rommel that an "operation" to remove his gall bladder would take place that afternoon. Since the hospital staff was greatly overworked due to the large number of injured war veterans in the hospital, no one paid particular attention to the fact that Rommel's operation was being performed by the head doctor himself, assisted by just one other doctor and a nurse. Rommel was nervous as he was rolled into the operating room, wondering if they were really going to remove his gall bladder. After the door closed behind him, the two doctors and the nurse removed their masks.

"I am *Doktor* Joregson, *Herr Feldmarschall*, and this is *Doktor* Barth and Nurse Solf."

Rommel shook hands with each of them.

"What you are doing is the greatest thing that has happened to the Fatherland for many years, *Herr Feldmarschall*. We are happy to have a small part in it," said Joregson.

"How many others here know about the plan?" asked Rommel.

"Only the three of us here, and the head of hospital security. After our little 'operation' is over, you will be returned to a private room and two guards will be posted outside your door. You will be attended by one of the three of us plus the hospital staff who will bring you your meals. I am afraid the meals will be the most unpleasant part of your stay. To avoid any suspicion, you will be on the same soft, bland foods as you would be if you had really been operated on. The guards, who do not know about our little charade, will be given orders that due to your condition you are to have no visitors unless they are escorted by the head of security. Your admittance to the hospital has already been passed on to your superiors, who no doubt will pass the information onto the press."

After visiting with their famous patient for fifty minutes, Dr. Joregson announced, "Well, I suppose it is time to call our little operation a success. To complete the deception, I am going to have to give you a sedative. You will be out for approximately one hour. That way, any early visitors will find nothing amiss. Now have a pleasant sleep."

When Rommel regained consciousness, he found his wife Lucie and son Manfred at his side, along with Nurse Solf. For the next two days, Rommel had a string of visitors, many of which he found to be collaborators. Mostly his visitors were family members and other senior military officers. For the sake of appearance, Lucie Rommel stayed at the bedside of her husband. She slept in another bed that had been set up in his room for her.

On the morning of the twelfth of January, the day Operation *Valkyrie* was to be implemented, Rommel and his Lucie were just finishing their breakfast when the door suddenly opened. To their surprise and horror, in strode the *Führer* himself. Rommel and his wife were almost in shock. Hitler walked over to Lucie, and taking her hand, asked if she was taking good care of his famous *Feldmarschall*. Before she could recover her composure and answer, Hitler turned and walked over to Rommel.

"This is a fine state of affairs, *Herr Feldmarschall*. You go through the entire war safely, only to be hospitalized after it is all over."

"Well, it is," stammered Rommel. "However, it is much better than the alternative, *Mein Führer*."

"*Jawohl*, it is at that," responded Hitler. "But we are going to miss you at our little party tonight. I asked the head doctor if you couldn't be moved to Karinhall by ambulance and at least be with us on a couch."

"What did he say?" asked Rommel, trying to sound hopeful of the proposal.

"He said that even though you are doing fine, the incision he had to make was much larger than usual and there was a lot of infection in the area. So you need to stay here for another few days. Maybe when you are able to get up and around, you and your family could come up to Berchtesgaden and spend a few days with me."

"We would enjoy that," spoke up Lucie, after regaining her composure.

"Then it is as good as done. You can relax there. And I could go over a few issues with you and get your opinion on them. You know I always have highly valued your opinion. Now I must be going, I have several other stops to make before we drive out to

Goering's. It is a lovely day for early January and should be a nice drive. Mercedes has given me their first automobile produced this year. Can you believe it even has air conditioning? Of course, I won't be needing that for a few months."

"That is quite an innovation," marveled Rommel. "I could have certainly used that in my tank in North Africa."

Hitler laughed, "I bet you could have at that."

Hitler shook hands with both of them, then turned and walked out of the room.

Immediately, General Beck walked in from an adjacent room.

"I thought we were *kaputt* there for a few minutes, Erwin. When I got word he was on his way here I rounded up as many loyal troops as I could, and stationed them down the road. If Hitler had taken you, I was prepared to start a civil war right here and now."

"*Danke Gott*, it did not come to that," responded Rommel. "He was evidently truly concerned about my condition."

"*Ja*, even the most terrible men do have some good qualities remaining within them. But now, it is time for you to get dressed. We will sneak you out through a side door in disguise and proceed to a location near the radio station we have under our control. *Frau* Rommel, I suggest you return to your home. Your son is there and you will find we have some loyal troops in and around your house, just in case."

"I appreciate that," replied Lucie.

KARINHALL

After passing through the reception line at Goering's villa, and offering his congratulations to Goering, General Beck made his way into the dining hall. The table was set, ready for the food which would be served within the hour. Already, many of the visitors who had not been invited to the dinner, were leaving. As he walked around the end of the table, Beck "accidentally" dropped a folder from which a number of papers spilled out onto the floor. One of the serving *Fraüleins* quickly walked over.

"Let me help you pick up your papers, *Herr* General," she said.

"I'm sorry *Fraülein*, but these are classified state papers I'll have to pick up myself. That's what I get for being so careless."

As the young lady walked away, Beck couldn't help but hope she would be far away in the kitchen when the bombs went off. As he picked up the papers Beck was able to get a quick look under the table. Both explosive bombs were in place near each end of the table. In the center of the table was a canister containing a newly-developed nerve gas. If the heavy table shielded some from the blast so they would not be killed outright, they would still suffer serious wounds to their feet and legs. Before they could drag themselves out of the room, the nerve gas would do its job. *Oberst* von Stauffenberg had done his job as planned. Beck got up and noticed no one was paying any attention to him. Placing the papers back in his folder he turned and walked out of the dining room and into the reception hall. The last of the visitors, Wilhelm Keppler, was passing through the line. As a close advisor to Hitler, Keppler was the conspirator who would be at the dinner and who would set off the bombs.

Beck walked out the front door. It was 6:15 P.M. It was now dark and a heavy snow was falling. "Perfect," Beck thought to himself. "The snow will muffle the explosion and keep any of Goering's roving guards under cover. The snow will make it that much easier to track down any who should escape the blast and try to flee into the woods." Beck got into his staff car and instructed the driver to wait until the last of the visitors left before the dinner started. By 6:30, Beck was sure the last of the visitors had left. Through the window he could see shadows moving out of the reception room and down the hall leading to the dining room. He instructed his driver to drive slowly away and proceed down the long driveway to the highway. At the guard gate to the villa, the two sentries snapped to attention as Beck's automobile passed through the gate. Beck returned their Nazi salute. "That should be the last time I have to do that," he thought to himself.

Down the road less than two kilometers, Beck came upon *Oberst* von Stauffenberg. He was in command of the troops and armored vehicles that would move into the villa as soon as the explosion occurred.

"Everything all right, *Oberst?*"

"Everything is proceeding as scheduled, *Herr* General.

Feldmarschall Rommel is in place near the radio transmitter, and our loyal troops are all in position around the key facilities." Looking at his watch, he added, "It ought to be all over in a less than an hour."

"I hope so," replied Beck. "But one always wonders if we have overlooked something."

After the soup and salad had been served, Keppler noticed that the servers had all left the dining room to bring in the main course. Keppler took a spoonful of soup and immediately started to cough as if he was choking. Instinctively, von Ribbentrop, the foreign minister, who was sitting next to him slapped Keppler on the back.

"Are you alright, Wilhelm?" he quietly asked.

Keppler nodded his head yes, but excused himself and got up and walked out of the room. Much to his dismay, von Ribbentrop got up and followed him.

"I just want to make sure you are all right," he explained, "I once had a cousin choke to death while eating at a family dinner."

Again Keppler nodded his head and added a couple of feigned coughs for good measure.

When they entered the men's room, Keppler walked into the stall in which the detonator was hidden and shut the door. Sticking his finger down his throat he feigned that he was about to vomit. Quickly he took a deep breath and grabbed the detonator. Quickly he pushed the plunger all the way in. The resulting blast shook the room so violently that plaster fell from the roof.

"*Mien Gott!*" exclaimed von Ribbentrop. "Wilhelm! Are you all right?"

Keppler grabbed the Luger pistol that was also hidden in the stall. As he exited the stall, he saw von Ribbentrop standing in the door looking down the hall toward the dining room. As von Ribbentrop turned towards Keppler, his eyes widened as he saw the Luger in Keppler's hand.

"You!" he exclaimed, before he was cut off with a bullet in his forehead.

Keppler ran down the hall and out the front door, keeping ahead of the poison gas. Turning, he ran down the side of the house and positioned himself near the outside door to the dining room, where he would be able to see if anyone had made it out. None of the intended victims were outside. He could see several of the cooks and servers running out of the door from the kitchen. All of the windows in the dining room were blown out, but it was impossible to see anything in the room itself because of the smoke and dust. At the same time, he heard a number of shots coming from all sides of the villa as Beck's troops fought their way through the villa's guards. In less than a minute a number of Beck's troops came through the trees and approached Keppler. Keppler motioned for several to watch the door he was near. Several others followed him to the kitchen door.

"Most of these people here are harmless members of the house staff," he yelled over all of the screaming. "I'll point out anyone else."

As soon as he heard the explosion, Beck ordered the driver of his staff car to proceed to the entrance of the villa. He was followed by several armored vehicles and a fire truck to put out any fire. They wanted to save the works of art Goering had in his possession. As Beck approached the gates, the Luftwaffe guards hesitated for a moment as they saw the four stars on his license plate. The machine gun on the armored vehicle following Beck chattered, cutting the guards down. As the vehicles drove around the circular driveway, armed troops wearing gas masks and led by *Oberst* von Stauffenberg, jumped from the trucks and made their way into the building. Beck was pleased to see that smoke was coming out of only the blown-out dining room windows. The fire appeared to be restricted to the dining room and possibly the kitchen. Following the armed troops, another twenty-five unarmed troops wearing gas masks entered the home and then emerged with the art treasures Goering had accumulated over his years in the Nazi reign.

In a few minutes, von Stauffenberg exited the building and came over to General Beck, who was standing by his staff car with his Luger in his hand.

"It appears, *Herr* General, that the bombs did their job. We could find no one alive in the dining room and Wilhelm, who escaped with his life, reports no one exited the rear of the building except for the cooks and most of the servers. I believe it would be safe to contact the other elements of our coup and tell them to proceed with their assignments."

"*Danke Oberst*," responded Beck. "I'll send out the code word right now."

By 8:00 P.M. all of the road stations and airports under Nazi control were in the hands of the rebels. Also, all of the S.S. units throughout Europe were surrounded by superior forces of the *Wehrmacht* loyal to the coup. Resistance by some of the S.S. units lasted until the late afternoon of the next day, when they were finally overrun by powerful *Panzer* units.

By 8:30 P.M., most of the people of Europe were aware that something was happening in Germany. All of the German radio stations had gone off the air. In Washington, D.C., in the Office of Strategic Service which monitored Radio Berlin twenty-four hours a day, the agents on duty decided after fifteen minutes of silence, to notify their chief, William Donovan, the chief of the Office of Strategic Services. Donovan, in turn, notified President Dewey at 3:20 P.M., Washington time. Dewey left the Oval Office and walked downstairs to the White House Communications Center, where the security agents were already busily scanning the various German radio frequencies.

"Hearing anything yet?" inquired the President.

"Not a thing, sir. It appears that every radio station in Germany is off the air," replied the agent in charge.

"Could it be some type of natural interference? I once heard that sunspots or solar flares can interfere with radio transmissions."

"That is a very remote possibility," Mr. President, "especially since we are still picking up London, Paris, and even Moscow. I believe it is a deliberate nationwide shutdown."

"I think I had better notify the Secretary of Defense just in case the Nazis are up to something. Will you please contact Secretary Forrestal for me?" requested Dewey.

"Yes, Sir."

At that moment Radio Berlin started to hum.

"I think they are coming back on the air!" exclaimed one of the agents, as he began to fine-tune the frequency.

"*Achtung* everyone who is tuned-in. There will be an important announcement in five minutes by Feldmarschall Erwin

Rommel." With that brief statement, Wagner's *"Ride of the Valkyries"* began playing.

Donovan handed Dewey some earphones. "Put these on Mr. President and a translator will translate Rommel's speech into English even as he is speaking."

"Thank you," responded the President as he adjusted the earphones. "I wonder why Rommel would be speaking?"

"If I had to guess," replied Donovan, "I'd bet there has been a coup in Germany, and the Nazis have been overthrown."

"I certainly hope you are correct," replied Dewey.

In the next couple of minutes, the phones in the office all lit up as calls from Canada, England, France and various other nations poured in. They wanted to ensure that the United States was aware of what was happening.

"I wonder if our Allies really think we are that much asleep at the switch," joked the President.

The music slowly died out, and a voice came over the airways. "This is *Feldmarschall* Erwin Rommel speaking. Within the last two hours, Operation *Valkyrie* has been successfully completed. This operation, which has been in the planning stage for several months has resulted in the overthrow and replacement of the Nazi regime throughout Europe. All of the hierarchy of the Nazi Party, including the *Führer* himself, have been either killed or taken captive while at a party at Hermann Goering's estate at Karinhall. In addition, almost all Officers of Field Rank in the S.S. have been taken captive. All S.S. units have been surrounded by units of the army loyal to our operation and are being urged to throw down their weapons or be destroyed. Officers of Field Rank in the *Wehrmacht*, who were not directly or indirectly involved with *Valkyrie*, have also been taken into custody until their loyalty can be established. *Valkyrie* has been planned by noted civilian leaders, as well as members of the military. It has broad support among both groups. I have been asked to assume temporary leadership of the country until a representative government can be formed.

"Again, I urge all S.S. units to surrender, and all other units of the *Wehrmacht* that are not involved in the operation, to remain in their camps. Those units in the occupied countries are to carry on their duties to ensure that peace and tranquility are maintained.

Within a short while, other leaders of the new government and I will meet with the national leaders of the occupied countries to work out our new relationship.

"We want to stress to our former enemies in the recent war, that this change of government poses no threat to the existing peace, and will in fact, eventually result in an improved relationship between our nations. However, we must stress the importance of the western democracies to not attempt to take advantage of the situation in the Fatherland. We are still organized and have the means to defend ourselves, if necessary.

"As things stabilize, we would encourage those countries that have not resumed diplomatic relations with us since the war, to do so now.

"Thank you, and good night," Rommel concluded.

"Well, you were correct in your assessment of the situation. This is a change of events, Bill," remarked Dewey. "It will be interesting to see how the cabinet and military advisors interpret this."

At a special cabinet meeting the next day, that included the Joint Chief of Staff, it was decided that the United States would do nothing and wait to see what transpired next in Germany. After discussions with the British government, it was decided that Great Britain would exchange ambassadors with the new German Government in an attempt to determine what was really transpiring within Germany. The United States would withhold recognition until it was determined what the new German Government was really going to do.

POST NAZI GERMANY

The next thirty days were hectic for Erwin Rommel. As his fellow senior officers were rounded up, he was at a loss as to what to do with them. Most of the senior officers of the *Wehrmacht* were Rommel's friends. Most of them took oaths of loyalty to the new government, but some had refused. Of the approximately two thousand generals at the start of the war, Rommel found, as he reviewed the statistics, over two hundred had been killed in action, while another thirty-eight had died of wounds. Twenty-three had been executed by Hitler and sixty-four had committed suicide. Three hundred six had died of other causes. In reviewing the records of each living *Feldmarschall* and general, Rommel felt at least another hundred should be brought to trial for what was becoming known as "war crimes." Therefore, he knew a tribunal would have to be set up and trials held to determine their guilt and punishment, if any.

Rommel spent the month of February organizing a new government. Rommel chose to be called Chancellor. The formation of the new government had, out of necessity, been organized as quickly as possible. Therefore, Rommel was granted the right by his fellow conspirators to appoint a temporary cabinet until a general election could be held.

After more than a decade of Nazi military control there were very few experienced civilian government officials that had not been mere stooges of the Nazi Party. Rommel selected an obscure, but upcoming politician, by the name of Konrad Adenauer, as his Foreign Minister, while Walter Funk retained his position as the Minister of Economics. Since the German economy was in shambles, Funk requested that Kurt von Schroeder, formerly the president of the bank of Cologne, and Wilhelm Keppler a former member of the Ministry of Economics, be appointed to assist in the rebuilding of the economy. Rommel agreed, although all three had been involved in the Nazi economic debacle. Still, they were capable men, and without having to follow the dictates of Hitler, Rommel felt they would be able to produce an economic turnaround.

For Home Minister, Rommel selected Carl Goerdeler, the one-time Mayor of Leipzig. One of Goerdeler's pressing tasks was to relocate those the Nazi's had declared as *"undesirables."* As soon as an agreement had been reached with the Italians on the use of Sardinia, they would be located there.

As Commander-in-Chief of all German military forces, Rommel appointed *Feldmarschall* Erwin Witzleben. He, in turn, selected General Ludwig Beck as his Chief of Staff, and Rommel's own former Chief of Staff, General Hans Speidel, was appointed commander of the German forces still guarding the Russian front. Admiral Karl Doenitz was retained as Commander in Chief of the Kreigsmarine.

In an effort to reduce Russian suspicions, Rommel contacted Former *Feldmarschall* Friedreich von Paulus who was living in Moscow. Rommel asked him if he would consider being the new German Ambassador to the Soviet Union. After von Paulus had surrendered the Sixth Army at Stalingrad, he had collaborated with the Russians. While living in the Soviet Union, he had learned Russian. He also knew most of the Russian leaders personally. Although von Paulus had been considered a traitor at the time, Rommel could see he was the best man for the difficult task of negotiating with the Russians. As an incentive to obtain von Paulus' agreement, Rommel informed him that his family was still alive and would be sent to Moscow to once again be with him. Hitler had placed his entire family under house arrest following word of his collaboration with the Russians, and had cut off all communication between von Paulus and his family. A very moved von Paulus agreed to his new position.

Rommel called upon several supporters of the coup, General Fabian von Schlabrendorff, *Oberst* Claus von Stauffenberg and *Oberst* Alexis von Roenne to set up a tribunal for the trial of all military and civilian personnel accused of war crimes. During their first meeting, the tribunal decided to allow victims of the accused to attend and testify. In an effort to show their sincerity in administering justice, all nations that had been at war with Germany were invited to send representative to attend the trials.

Great Britain was the only major western power that offered to exchange ambassadors with the new German Government. Rommel selected a talented young man by the name of Willie Brandt to serve as ambassador.

ATROCITIES

On the first of March, Rommel decided to take a tour of the country. He was accompanied by his Home Minister, Carl Goerdeler, and his Foreign Minister, Konrad Adenauer along with several aides. Although he had heard of the extermination camps, he was not prepared for what we saw when he entered the Buchenwald concentration camp, near Weimar.

"*Mein Gott!*" exclaimed Rommel as he walked through the

gate and saw the hundreds of emaciated inmates standing or lying about. They were surrounded by dozens of dead bodies. "What kind of a place is this?" he asked his aide, *Oberst* Alexis von Roenne. "I have been to several Stalags to visit captured senior Allied officers, but as bad as those camps were, they were nothing compared to this."

Before von Roenne could reply, Karl Koch the camp commandant, stammered, "Ah, this is one of the camps that has been exterminating the *'undesirables'* and other enemies of the Reich, *Herr* Chancellor."

"One of them?" questioned Rommel. "How many other camps are there?"

"I am not sure, *Mein Herr*. The main ones are Dachau, Auschwitz, Belsen, and Treblinka. But there are at least nine others that I know of."

"How many people have been killed in these camps?"

"Again I don't know, *Mein Herr*. I hear rumors of three to five million."

"Three to five million!" exclaimed Rommel. "*Mein Gott,* what is the world going to think of us when this is discovered?"

"If I may *Mein Herr*?" asked Koch, "the leaders of most of the major countries must know already. We have had many escapees who have made their way west and have told about these camps. Yet the Americans and British have never once attempted to destroy these camps or even the railroads and highways leading to the camps."

"That is strange," replied Rommel. "Who are these people?"

"Jews, Gypsies, those who were insane or mentally retarded, and Jehovah's Witnesses. We also have a large number of the Russian POWs who have refused to be repatriated under the terms of our treaty with the Russians. They claim they will be shot as soon as they are in the hands of the communists."

"I have heard reports of that happening," responded Rommel. Then turning to von Roenne, he ordered that food and clothing be immediately brought into the camp and distributed. "Don't wait to go through normal channels. Take some of these trucks here and go through the nearby towns to get what is needed. Charge the goods to the government. If need be, I will sign for them myself."

"I don't think that will be necessary, *Herr* Chancellor."

As they left the camp, Rommel turned to *Feldmarschall* Hans von Kluge, who was with him. "Hans, I want you to arrest Koch and all of the other officers in that camp immediately, and appoint a new camp commander. Keep the inmates locked up until we decide what to do with them, but see they are given medical attention and treated humanely. I want the same done at all of the other camps we have. Do we know how many there really are and where they are located?"

"We have captured Fritz Sauckel, who was in charge of the slave labor programs. He will certainly know," responded Kluge.

"*Gut*, get the information from him and implement my instructions as soon as possible."

"*Jawohl*, I agree with you wholeheartedly. We must eliminate these camps. *Herr* Chancellor may I suggest that when we arrest Koch, we arrest his wife, Ilse, as well. It is rumored that she is known as the 'Bitch of Buchenwald' due to her own cruel and perverted treatment of some of the prisoners in the camp."

"She is involved in this too? Well, I will take your word for it. It looks like we may have some civilian trials as well as more military ones to conduct in the near future."

"We are going to have to do something, if we ever expect to get accepted by the rest of the world again."

Rommel could not face inspecting the horrors of the other camps. He knew feelings against the inmates of the camps still ran high throughout the country and he had to come up with a solution, and soon. In a meeting several days later the problem was discussed among several of the new leaders of the country.

Rommel, who himself was not anti-semitic, stated, "I realize that with feelings as they are among our people we cannot simply turn the prisoners in these camps out on their own. But the killings I hope have now stopped."

"*Ja*, they have *Herr* Chancellor," reassured Adenauer, "and in case you don't know, during the late thirties, when the Jewish question first came up, someone, and I don't remember who, presented the proposal that Mussolini be talked into relocating part of the populace on the Island of Sardinia, and exiling all of the '*undesirables*' there at German expense. Since Mussolini was opposed to the liquidation of the Jews in Italy, it was thought this plan would appeal to him. Unfortunately, Mussolini was fearful that it would cause the populace of Sardinia to rebel if they had to move. But now that we control Italy as well as Sardinia, we could hold this carrot out to Italy in exchange for returning some of its sovereignty. This time Mussolini might accept the offer so he could regain control of the country by claiming he negotiated the treaty with us."

"I like that plan," responded Rommel. "By the way where is Mussolini?"

"Oh, ever since Hitler lost all confidence in him, he has been living in his villa at Lake Como with his mistress, Clara Petacci. His son-in-law Ciano, Count Galeazzo, the Foreign Minister, is running the government. He is under the watchful eye of *Feldmarschall* Kesselring."

"That is understandable. I had to work with Mussolini's so-called army in Africa for several years, as you may recall," said Rommel.

"That I do, *Herr* Chancellor. By the way, did you ever hear what Churchill said before the war about the Italian Army?"

"I don't think so," replied Rommel.

"Well, when our troops moved into the Sudetenland, it looked like that could cause England to take action. During the negotiations between us and the English, von Ribbentrop threatened the English by saying, 'If there is a war, this time it will end differently because this time the Italians are with us.' At that time, you may remember, Italy had the largest army in the world, even larger than ours."

"*Ja*, I was aware of that fact."

"Well, when Chamberlain returned home and reported what von Ribbentrop had said, Churchill piped up and said, "I hope you told him that was only fair, since we had them the last time."

All of the group roared with laughter.

"By the way," resumed Rommel, when the laughter had died down, "where is the Italian King, Victor Emmanuel III?"

"He is still living in Rome."

"How does he get along with *Feldmarschall* Kesselring?"

"Very well, from what we hear."

"Has Kesselring fully joined our cause?"

"Yes."

"Good," replied Rommel. "Ask him to meet with us as soon as possible. Maybe we can solve two problems at once. We'll have you and *Feldmarschall* Kisselring meet with the King and Count Galeazzo to offer the king his real kingship back along with the promise that he can form a new Italian Government. We'll let the Count continue in his position, if he cooperates. We will get rid of Mussolini for them and remove our troops. In return, they are to remove all Italians from their island of Sardinia. We will relocate all of the so called '*undesirables*' on the island like you said had been proposed years ago."

"What about Mussolini? You said we would get rid of him. Just what did you mean? We can't very well execute him and expect his son-in-law to cooperate with us."

"Well, to my thinking," offered Rommel, "he is one of the most '*undesirables*' of all; but, executing him could cause more problems for us. So, let's exile him and his mistress to Sardinia along with the others."

"Or, after thinking about it, we could offer him the old castle on Elba where the English exiled Napoleon. Maybe he would think that would be an honor," laughed Beck. "But, in any event, I think you have a good and workable plan here."

"*Ja*, Elba may be even better. Now," said Rommel, "what about these rumors that Hitler was violating the peace agreement and was still developing and producing vengeance weapons?"

"They are not rumors, *Herr* Chancellor, I have found that near Nordhausen in the Harz Mountains, there are underground caverns where the V-2 rockets are still being produced. I also understand that a new longer-range version of the V-2 is being developed," replied Beck.

"I want to see these facilities for myself, as soon as possible."

"We could drive over there in the morning if you like."

"That would be good. I would like to arrive without prior warning, so we can see exactly what is really going on before anything could be hidden."

VENGEANCE WEAPON PRODUCTION

The road to the V-2 facility was blocked and guarded by several military troops. As Rommel was recognized, the small group was waved through. After pulling into the parking lot, the group was surprised to see Doctor Werner von Braun walking from one building to the entrance of an underground facility. When von Braun saw the staff cars drive up, he stopped and started walking toward them. Stepping out of the Mercedes, Rommel met von Braun and extended his hand.

"It is good to see you again, *Herr* Doctor. But what are you doing here? I thought you were assigned to *Peenemünde.*"

"I usually am, Herr Chancellor. But we are having some problems down here and General Dornberger ordered me to come down and see what I could do to help out."

"Help out with what?" inquired Rommel.

"Well, we are finding that we cannot simply build a larger V-2 to increase its range and payload," von Braun replied in all innocence. "It appears that we are going to have to start from scratch and build what we call a multistage rocket. That is, we will have to place two or three rockets one on top of another. We will also have to change the type of fuel that we are using, to a more powerful type."

"I thought that our treaty with the Americans required that we were to cease all production and development of rockets?" Rommel inquired.

"I....I am afraid I know nothing about that," responded an obviously confused von Braun, "with my work taking up so much of my time, I have little time to follow what is going on outside of my little world here and at *Peenemünde.* It was only through your broadcast that I even learned about the overthrow of the Nazis. And the General has never even discussed that with me. I know we have quit producing V-1 and V-2 weapons. General Dornberger told us to concentrate on developing this new rocket, which will be able to put an artificial satellite in orbit around the earth."

"Artificial satellite?"

"Yes, a small man-made moon, if you will. It would rotate around the earth about every ninety minutes, and be about three hundred kilometers above the surface of the Earth."

"For what purpose?" inquired Rommel, but before a reply was given, he went on, "Never mind for now. I want to see inside this facility."

Inside the caves, which had been enlarged to immense caverns, Rommel was conducted through rooms where dozens of engineers and draftsman were busily working on drawings. In one large cavern, he was shown the prototype of the first new large rocket.

"As you can see, *Herr* Chancellor," explained von Braun, "this new missile is three meters in diameter and will be twenty-five meters long when fully assembled."

"Who are these people that are doing the work on it?" asked Rommel.

"For the most part, they are former Russian prisoners of war, who refused to be sent back to Russia after the peace treaty was signed. They were certain that the Communists would kill them for being allowed to be taken prisoner. Since we are short of help, the General decided to put them to work here."

"I have heard elsewhere that captured Russians have refused to be repatriated," noted Rommel. "Who are the rest of the men and women?"

"Mostly common criminals. However, murderers and those serving life sentences for other crimes are working in some of the machine shops."

"Why in the more skilled jobs?" inquired Rommel.

"We are working here with some very toxic materials. The dust and fumes resulting from machining these materials are very hazardous to the lungs. Most of these workers are incapacitated within six or seven months and are dead within a year."

Rommel made no response, but asked, "When do you think you will have this new rocket ready to test?"

"*Ach*, we are about nine months away, I would say," responded von Braun.

"Since we are not supposed to be developing such rockets, how are you planning on testing it without others finding out? You obviously can't fly this from *Peenemünde* without being detected."

"According to General Dornberger, the plan is to conceal it aboard a ship and take it to Argentina. Near the town of Rio

Grande in the state of Del Fuego, which is the southernmost portion of Argentina, Juan Peron, the country's leader, is helping us build a launch complex. From Del Fuego we can fly this rocket undetected down along the coast of Antarctica."

"An interesting plan," observed Rommel.

After leaving the facility, Rommel commented to the group in his automobile, "This artificial satellite business is interesting, but I think Hitler had other plans for the rocket. The Americans developed an atomic bomb that can be carried in a bomber. It appears to me, if that rocket back there can put up a man-made moon, it could carry an atomic bomb a long way."

"I am sure you are correct," agreed Beck.

"Where is our atomic research going on? I know we were getting the ore from Czechoslovakia and the heavy water from Norway, but where are the devices actually put together?"

"From what we have been able to determine," offered General von Thoma, who had succeeded Rommel as commander of the Africa Korps years before, "there are at least three locations where research and possibly production is going on: Hechingen, Bisingen, and Haigerloch. Haigerloch is where our first chain reaction took place. To help keep away the curious, they called the place 'The Virus House'."

"I can see where a name like that might deter curiosity seekers, but not knowledgeable spies," observed Rommel. "But I wasn't aware that you knew so much about these things."

"I didn't until after the first device was set off at Normandy. Then I started doing more research on atomic energy. Physics was my major in college, anyway."

"Well, what else do you know about these places?"

"Only that at Haigerloch they did not provide for protection from the radiation, and as a result, many were exposed to lethal doses of radiation poisoning. Even a number of our leading scientists were killed."

"Who was, or is, the head of this atomic program?" continued Rommel.

"*Doktor* Werner Heisenberg. I think he still is."

"Where would we find this *Doktor* Heisenberg?"

"Probably at Haigerloch."

"I think that we had better have a talk with *Herr* Heisenberg in the near future."

"I'll arrange it," offered von Thoma.

"No. I would prefer to just drop in and see what is going on and find out what he has to say."

"Very good. If your schedule is such, we could be there the day after tomorrow."

"Well, I can't think of anything more important right now. Perhaps later in the week we should visit the other two places as well."

HAIGERLOCH

Haigerloch was a small unassuming town. It was still in good condition since it had not been a target of Allied bombers. Just off the main road south of the town, they turned off to the research center. A sign to the side of the road displayed the universal skull and cross bones indicative of a dangerous place, and another a second sign simply stated, "Virus House." Another half a kilometer down the road was a heavily guarded gate.

As they drove up to the gate, Rommel asked, "Are these guards our people?"

"I don't know," replied Beck. "There are so many guarded facilities that we haven't gotten around to all of them. But the guards certainly know who you are. I don't expect we'll have any problem."

Beck was correct. The cortege was waved through, after a very brief examination of everyone's papers.

At the main office, the secretary escorted the group to a conference room. She invited everyone to make themselves comfortable, while apologizing that she had not been made aware that they were coming and so was not properly prepared. She said that she would call *Doktor* Heisenberg, who was in one of the labs.

Rommel and his staff looked around at the displays in the room, which were set up much like a museum. In less than ten minutes, in walked Heisenberg and several of his chief scientists and engineers, still in their white work smocks.

"*Herr* Chancellor, may I welcome you to our laboratory?" he said. "I was not aware you were coming to visit us, so please excuse our appearance."

"That is quite alright, *Herr Doktor*," reassured Rommel. "We have been spending the last week getting acquainted with the various research facilities. We have not been able to establish a firm schedule."

"I see. Well what do you want to see, or hear, about our little facility here? I don't know how much you already know about us. Perhaps it would save some of your valuable time if we were to show you a short movie of our project first. In early 1942, when we started this project, *Herr* Goebbels sent crews to all of our facilities and filmed everything. We have taken all of these films and edited them into one film that runs for about forty-five minutes."

"We would be very much interested in seeing this film," offered Rommel.

The film opened with an explanation of the potential power of atomic energy by *Doktor* Heisenberg, followed by a tour through the mines in Czechoslovakia where the pitchblende ore containing the Uranium was mined. This was followed by a tour through the Norsk Plant in Norway, where the deuterium oxide or "heavy water" was extracted from the sea water.

"Is this the plant the American Rangers attacked?" asked Rommel.

"*Ja, Herr* Chancellor, but it was up and running about six months later. I understand the security was increased dramatically afterwards," replied Heisenberg.

The plants at Hechingen and Bisingen, where the Uranium 235 was produced were shown as well as the "Virus House" at Haigerloch where the atomic devices were actually produced.

"The Americans evidently learned what we were mining and processing here and did bomb the mines before the treaty. But we were able to get them up and running in short order," informed Heisenberg.

"That was very interesting *Herr Doktor*," said Rommel, thoughtfully, "and it prompts me to ask if we know where the Americans produced their atomic device and who is in charge of their program?"

"Well, our sources tell us that they have plants at Oak Ridge, in the state of Tennessee, and at Hanford, Oregon. The Americans also have abundant deposits of high-grade pitchblende, the ore which contains the uranium, in several of their western states. Utah is one of the larger producers. Their bomb was evidently assembled at Los Alamos, near Santa Fe, New Mexico. They also were able to test their first device at a place called White Sands near Alamogordo, New Mexico. The over all development is obviously under the direction of the American Military but a physicist by the name of Robert Openheimer is directing the scientific research."

"I have noticed that many of the scientists the Americans have working on their atomic program are Europeans. How is that?" inquired Rommel

"Ah, well you see," interjected General Beck, "Many of them are Jews. When Einstein left for America he started a flood of his fellow Jew scientists that follow him."

"We just let them go?" asked Rommel.

"Well if they hadn't left on their own they would have been arrested and sent to one of the extermination camps you visited a while back," answered General Beck.

"I can't believe the short sightliness of our previous leadership," exclaimed Rommel.

"Everyone who knew, was afraid of going against the *Führer*, *Herr* Chancellor."

"You are probably correct. I have been subjected to several of his tirades myself," continued Rommel. "By the way, did the first device the Americans tried work?"

"We really don't know. But we do know that the first one the Americans dropped that destroyed Hiroshima, obviously worked. It, like our own weapons, utilized Uranium-235. More disturbing is, according to reports from the Japanese, the second one used on Nagasaki used Plutonium. That means the Americans can produce Plutonium bombs much faster than we can produce our Uranium bombs."

"How is that?" asked Rommel.

"There are essentially two types of Uranium," answered Heisenberg. "The most common has an atomic weight of 238. Unfortunately, it is not fissionable, and so, cannot be used in a weapon. However, mixed in with the 238 is a rare isotope of Uranium with a atomic weight of 235. The U-235 is fissionable and so we use it. But to extract the U-235 from the U-238 is a very complex and time-consuming process.

"Another, even more rare element, Plutonium, is found with the U-238 and it is also fissionable. One of the American scientists, perhaps it was Enrico Fermi, concluded that if you would take some U-238 and bombard it with neutrons in a reactor, you could convert some of the U-238 to Plutonium. It is a much faster process."

"I must confess I don't fully understand all you told me, *Doktor*. It sounds like alchemy to me."

The *doktor* laughed and said, "I guess in a way it is."

"Just how many bombs do we presently have?" inquired Rommel.

"I haven't been keeping track, but close to fifty now."

"And where are they stored?"

"Right here, *Herr* Chancellor. Would you like to see one?"

"Of course."

Heisenberg led the group down a long hall to a room that was heavily guarded. Once inside the storage room, they could see several large devices sitting side by side. "These are some of the first few devices we produced. They are identical to those used at Normandy and on the Russian front." explained Heisenberg. Directing their attention to the far side of the room, he continued, "These other rows are our new bomb-sized weapons. As you can see, they don't look much different from our large one thousand kilogram conventional bombs."

"*Nein*, they don't," responded Rommel. "I wouldn't have detected any difference. But tell me, isn't it dangerous for us to be this close to these things? I understand they give off a radiation that can be deadly."

"That is true *Herr* Chancellor, but the Uranium is encased in a heavy lead shield that absorbs nearly all of the radiation. Of course, we limit the time anyone is in the area to just a few minutes."

As the group walked back to the front office, Rommel noted many engineers and scientists working in several offices. Curious he asked, "Now that you know how to make these weapons, what are all of these people working on now?"

"*Ach*, we have several programs going on, *Herr* Chancellor. We believe it may be possible to reduce the dimensions of the bombs down to the size of a large artillery shell. Of course, most of our effort is devoted to the development of what we call a thermonuclear device. From what we hear, the Hungarian physicist, Edward Teller, who is now working in America, believes that by using a regular U-235 or Plutonium fission bomb as a trigger, it would be possible to set off a fusion of hydrogen surrounding the trigger bomb. Fusion of hydrogen into helium is what powers the sun you know?"

Rommel didn't know, but asked, "And what would be the advantage of that?"

"Theoretically you could build a bomb of almost any size simply by putting more hydrogen around it. Where a fission bomb can produce the equivalent of thousands of tons of dynamite, a fusion bomb could produce the equivalent of millions of tons."

"Millions of tons?" asked an astounded Rommel. "I was a witness of the Normandy explosion. It is difficult to even imagine something a thousand times more powerful."

"Well it might work and it might not," responded Heisenberg. "And we might never know, since we have no place to test a weapon of that size, unless we took it far out into the ocean."

BERLIN

On Monday, the third of April, 1949, Rommel met with his new cabinet and military leaders for the first time. They reviewed the progress the new government had made in solving the numerous problems facing the nation. After discussing his findings at the concentration camps, vengeance weapons factory, and nuclear development facilities, Rommel asked the Home Minister, Carl Goerdeler to report on his and *Feldmarschall* Kettering's meeting with the Italians concerning the relocation of the *"undesirables"* to Sardinia.

"I am pleased to report, *Herr* Chancellor," began Goerdeler, "that *Feldmarschall* Kesselring and I have most everything worked out. We do not need the entire Island of Sardinia. The Italians agreed to exile Mussolini to Elba, and Mussolini is happy with the arrangement. He evidently feels it is an honor to live in the same villa where Napoleon did. As far as the Jewish problem goes, they, with the help of the American Jews, have set up a plan to establish a new home land for themselves in Palestine."

"But isn't that area presently occupied by Arabs?" inquired Rommel.

"*Ja*, it is. It is still an English Protectorate, so the English have the final say. We hear the English are not too happy with the situation. They feel it will cause troubles with the Arabs and make Palestine even more difficult to govern."

"Then why are they doing it?" asked Rommel.

"Evidently the Americans pressured to English into doing it in return for aid in rebuilding their country."

"Money talks," commented Rommel. "How soon will they be ready to start transporting the Jews to Palestine? How many people are we talking about?"

"If all of them want to go, and I suspect under the circumstances most of them will, it could be several hundred thousand."

"Who would pay for such a migration?" asked Funk the Economic Minister. "We do not have the means to pay for such an expense."

"The Jews have been doing their homework," responded Goerdeler. "They have been working with rich Jews in America. Bernard Baruch, one of the most important Jews in America, has assured us that he would personally see that sufficient funds are raised in America to cover the expense. He is even arranging for their transportation."

"The Americans, through the British Ambassador, have inquired how soon we could move the Jews under our control to ports for pickup. We have decided to move them all out through the port of Trieste. That is a more centrally located port for us and will provide for a shorter, quicker journey to Palestine. So the whole operation will go more quickly," responded Goerdeler.

"But, how soon can we actually begin the operation?" Rommel asked. "The quicker we can accomplish this operation and get it behind us the better."

"The Americans still have a fairly large number of transport ships as well as warships in the Mediterranean Sea since the British withdrew most of theirs. And they have informed us that they can have the first ship here in a week and one every other day thereafter until all the Jews are moved."

"That is *gut*. Very *gut*," responded Rommel.

"The American Jews," continued Goerdeler, "have requested that we move the victims of the concentration camps to the port as quickly as possible and they will furnish us trucks and fuel on the first ships to help move them. But I must add, *Herr* Chancellor, that ever since the word of this operation has got out, thousands of Jews have started walking towards Trieste. In some places the roads are jammed with people and with little provisions. It is causing problems in some areas as they try to live off the land."

"Perhaps," added Adenauer, "we could ask the Americans to airlift supplies to these people along the roads."

"But," objected one of the generals, "that would mean American aircraft would be violating our airspace."

"That is true, General," responded Adenauer, "however, I doubt the Americans are going to try and bomb us with their transport planes, especially if they are escorted by our ME-262s."

Everyone chuckled at the thought.

"Alright," replied Rommel, "ask the Americans if they will supply these refugees, and thank them for their offer to provide trucks. I am sure we can put them to good use. What about the other so-called 'Undesirables'?"

"*Herr* Chancellor, it is my opinion," offered Adenauer, "that the others, that is, the insane and certain religious or ethnic groups be returned to their native lands and provided for there. If they are reluctant to return, the Italians have agreed to accept them on Sardinia. The island is about two hundred sixty-five kilometers long and one hundred twenty wide. With a population of less than half a million, it has plenty of room for more settlers. There is good farmland in the Campidano plain, where grains, olives, grapes and tobacco are grown. There is also considerable livestock raising in the mountainous regions. The mining of lead, zinc, copper, and salt are also important industries. So, the new immigrant workers would be of benefit to the economy."

"*Wunderbar!*" responded Rommel. "I agree with your proposals. What about the rest of you *Herren*?"

Everyone agreed, although several had reservations about the gypsies and their nomadic way of life fitting in on Sardinia. Nevertheless, they agreed that, with the island being generally mountainous, the gypsies could probably find a home there.

Ten days later the first American liner pulled into Trieste. On board was Bernard Baruch to oversee the emigration. With him were several who would eventually become the future leaders of Israel.

Within three weeks, thousands of Jews began disembarking in the port of Haifa, Palestine, as each day another transport arrived from Trieste. By the end of the third week, the Arab leaders became alarmed as they envisioned their homeland being overrun by foreign Jews. Riots soon broke out in several places and English troops were called in to curb the disturbances. In response the Jews began to smuggle in arms. It was only a matter of time until the English would no longer be able to control the explosive situation.

BERLIN

A month later Rommel met again with his cabinet and military leaders to further discuss problems facing the nation. Turning to the military situation, Rommel asked for a report from *Feldmarschall* Witzleben, his Commander-in-Chief of all military forces.

"General Speidel," began Witzleben, "reports that all is quiet on our frontier with the Russians. However, there has been a slight buildup of Russian forces since their war with the Japanese ended. But nothing of any significance. The occupied lands are generally calm and General Speidel has been able to reduce our military presence there. Again, the general population appears to be more interested in rebuilding their countries than in the politics. Since the Poles are potentially the largest problem, Admiral Doenitz suggested, and I agreed, to give the Polish naval yard at Danzig a contract to build our first post-war freighter. It will provide hundreds of jobs for the Poles. Our own shipyards at Lubeck and Kiel are still in ruins, and we do not have the manpower nor the financial resources to rebuild them at this time. The Poles, on the other hand, will rebuild the Danzig shipyard at their own expense."

"That sounds like a good plan," agreed Walter Funk, the Minister of Economics. "As long as Poland is essentially under our control, the rebuilding of Danzig is to our advantage."

Rommel next turned to former *Feldmarschall* Friedrich von Paulus, now the ambassador to the Soviet Union. "It is good to have you back with us Friedrich," smiled Rommel. "How are things going in the Soviet Union?"

"It is good to be back home for a while, *Herr* Chancellor. *Danke*, for inviting me to this meeting. I can tell you that working with the Bolsheviks is a difficult task. They are suspicious ... no, paranoid is a better word, about everything going on in the world. Some of their leaders believe it is just a matter of time until we join up with the Americans and attack them again. However, Molotov is much more reasonable than Stalin was. He has assured me that all of our prisoners of war have been returned to us, even though it is less than twenty percent of all those captured. Whether or not he is telling the truth can't be determined. I have also heard some very disturbing news. American traitors have passed on to the Bolsheviks the secrets of manufacturing atomic devices, and they could now have such a weapon within a year or two."

"*Ach*, that is bad news," responded Rommel.

"*Ja*, it is. But, I don't believe we have anything to fear from the Bolsheviks in the foreseeable future. Due to the enormous destruction to their country and the loss of over fifteen million of their people, it will take years for them to recover. Their problem is compounded by the fact that they refuse to accept much aid from the Americans. However, once the Bolsheviks acquire atomic weapons, I believe the western democracies will become more convinced that they are a threat and not a true ally."

"That may well be," observed Rommel. "But, from what I have seen so far, it may take us years to rebuild as well. It is too bad we didn't get rid of Hitler sooner and end the war before we were so badly damaged."

With that, Walter Funk, the Minister of Finance, spoke up. "If I may, *Herr* Chancellor? I am pleased to inform you that we have imposed wage and price controls throughout the country, and as a result our inflation rate has dropped to one third of a percent per month. Also, our foreign trade, limited as it is, is now slightly in our favor. Ferdinand Porsche has changed over his factories that were building the military *Kübelwagen* and is building a small automobile on the same chassis. He has named it the *Volkswagen*. He expects it to become the Ford of Germany, an automobile that everyone can afford. It is beginning to sell very well not only in Germany but throughout all of Europe. Also, if we remove our occupational forces from the Western European countries, that should lead to an increase in trade with the rest of the world and with the United States in particular."

Turning to his Foreign Minister, Rommel asked, "*Herr* Adenauer, have you had time to put together a plan for the ending of our occupation of the Western European countries?"

"*Ja*, we do have a plan that we would like to present."

"*Wunderbar*, let's hear it."

"We believe that we should convene a conference with the political leaders of France. France, is, by far, the largest of the occupied countries. After working out an agreement with them, we could then convene another conference with representatives from all of the other countries involved. After presenting our agreement with France, the other smaller countries would be more likely to agree to the same terms."

"That sounds reasonable. Do you have a plan to present to France?"

"*Jawohl, Herr* Chancellor. The Foreign Ministry has been in several conferences with our Defense and Economic Ministries. Any agreement with the western nations must take into account our financial arrangements as well as our own defense. We feel that since we won the war, there is no need to unduly jeopardize either aspect."

"I agree," responded Rommel. "Please continue."

Adenauer walked over to a wall chart, which he pulled down.

"These are the terms we propose: From a monetary point of view, our *Reichsmarks* will continue to be the common currency throughout Western Europe. However, in order to encourage the French to return what gold reserves they managed to ship out of the country at the beginning of the war, they would be allowed to mint gold or silver Francs. Now that the American dollar has replaced the British Pound Sterling, as the strongest currency in the world, we propose to use the American $35.00 per ounce of gold, as a basis for both the Reichsmark and Franc. This would mean a gold Franc would be worth approximately $0.07."

"I suppose you plan to work out the same type of arrangements with the other western countries?"

"That is correct. By the same ratio, a Danish gold or silver Krone would be worth $0.27; the Norwegian Krone, $0.45; the Belgian Belga, $0.17;. the Dutch Guilder $0.68 and the Italian Lira $0.09. The value of our own *Reichsmark* would be set at $0.40."

"Less than the Norwegian Krone or Dutch Guilder?" questioned Rommel.

"I am afraid so, *Herr* Chancellor. The realities of global finances are not what we would always like. And we must remember that the foreign currencies must be in gold. Our currency will not be backed by gold, so in trade with other nations outside of our control, the Reichsmark very possibly may be valued even less. We may be forced to trade with nations like England and America with the monies of our satellite countries until we can build up some sort of gold reserve of our own.

"Of course, it is impractical to mint gold coins in such small denominations. The coins would be so small they would easily be lost. So when we work out the details with the financial leaders of the occupied countries, we will require that their coins be in multiples of their basic unit of currency. The denomination should have a value of approximately a quarter ounce of gold. Smaller denominations will be made in Reich currency.

"We will also require that fifty percent of the total French imports be from us. This will probably be the most difficult point to negotiate, but it is very important to our economic recovery.

"Although it was beyond the scope of this study, it may be to our advantage to permit the occupied countries to our east to also mint their own gold currency. But that is for future consideration.

"We also propose to allow France to retain control of their

overseas colonies, if they can. Of course, several of their colonies like Madagascar were seized by the British early in the war. However, the colonies that France still controls will provide France directly, and ourselves indirectly with much needed raw materials. The same goes of course, for the Dutch and Belgian colonies.

"I will now let *Feldmarschall* Witzleben address the military aspects of treaties," concluded Adenauer.

"From a military point of view," commenced the Commander-in-Chief of the military, "we propose the following: First, the French Army will be limited to no more than 250,000 troops. Second, the French Air Force be limited to no more than one hundred fighter aircraft and no bombers. Third, the French Navy will be limited to no more than twenty destroyers and one aircraft carrier. We feel that these three constraints should allow France to control their colonies while posing no real threat to us. And finally, the French government must agree not to enter into any military pact or treaty with any other country. The same type of arrangements will be offered to the other countries, but modified somewhat to better fit the situation of each individual country."

After a short discussion, the proposed plan was approved by the group. Furthermore, it was decided to hold the first meeting with the French leaders within thirty days, and similar meetings with all the other countries involved, once every sixty days thereafter.

"One last issue, before we adjourn. What is the status of the trials of those who committed gross crimes during the war like the *Kommandants* of the extermination camp for example?" inquired Rommel.

"General Schlabrendorf will address that issue," said Adenauer.

General Schlabrendorf had attempted to kill Hitler by himself in 1943, by planting on bomb on Hitler's aircraft. Unfortunately, the bomb never went off, and Schlabrendorf was never connected to the plot.

Schlabrendorf stood up and walked over to his wall chart. "Of the known ninety-four S.S. Generals involved," he began, "we have determined that thirty-two were killed in action or of wounds they received. Two were executed by Hitler. Nine died of natural causes while on duty. Sixteen have committed suicide, many of which were after the overthrow of Hitler. We have twenty-six in custody and five are unaccounted for. They have probably escaped to South America. We have all of the commanders of the concentration camps and most of their staffs and guards. We also have most of the aides of the General Staff and S.S. leadership. As you are aware, none of those at Goering's party survived. We are of the opinion that all of the rest of these people should be tried for their crimes. However, it might be months or perhaps even years, until we track down all of the other S.S and Gestapo leaders. Unfortunately, the more we investigate, the more people we find to have been involved. We plan to hold two trials within three months."

"Two trials?" inquired Rommel.

"*Ja*, we have decided to hold one trial for all of the military defendants at one time, and another for all of the civilian defendants. But, there will be no individual trials for any one civilian. We feel it is to our advantage to get these trials over with as quickly as possible. Most of the crimes are of a common nature, anyway."

"Excellent! I can see the wisdom in your decisions," replied Rommel.

"After we withdraw from the western countries," continued Schlabrendorff, "we will allow the respective countries to try any of their own collaborators, as they see fit."

"By the way," asked Rommel, "how many of these people are you holding? There must be dozens."

"It is difficult to draw the line on who should be charged and who shouldn't. But we have a total of one hundred seventy-six individuals, including Mildred Gillars, Rita Louise Zucca, the one called Axis Sally. We also have William Joyce, better known as Lord Haw Haw, Jane Anderson, or Lady Haw Haw, and the American Lord Haw Haw, Douglas Chandler. They all were either English or Americans who broadcast propaganda for us during the war."

"What are you going to do about the foreign propagandists?"

"We feel it would be in our best interest to turn them over to the Allies, and let them decide what to do with them."

"I hope they are not too harsh with 'Axis Sally'," responded Rommel, "when I was over the *Afrika Korps*, we all, that is both sides, often had an unofficial cease fire when she came on the air in the evening from Rome. Everyone, including myself, listened to her. Many of her comments were so ludicrous and absurd that her show was the best comedy we had. At times we could even hear the English and Americans laughing across no man's land, and we all enjoyed the American music she played between her talks."

Everyone nodded their heads in agreement and then burst into laughter at the thought of the entire German leadership stopping to listen to their own propagandists.

"I wonder," speculated someone, "if Hitler listened to them and what he thought?"

"I'm sure Goebbels did," said another, "and he must have thought they were doing a good job. Otherwise he would have stopped the broadcasts."

"But don't you think he realized that no one on the Allied side believed any of it? They never bothered to jam the transmissions or forbid their men from listening to any of the propagandists."

"I think," resumed Rommel, "that Goebbels and all the rest of the Nazi hierarchy were so involved in their own propaganda that they actually came to believe it themselves. By the way, where are you holding these people?"

"We have moved all of the previous inmates out of the Dachau Concentration Camp and thought it only fitting that these criminals experience the same accommodations they imposed on others. Also, since Dachau is just outside of Munich, which was the birthplace of the Nazi Party, we thought that is where it should also end."

"Well I have no problem with that," smiled Rommel, "as long as you don't have the former inmates as guards."

"We did consider that, but decided that would be going a little too far," laughed General Schlabrendorff.

"Who did you say would be invited to attend these trials?" asked Adenauer.

"We thought we would allow up to five representatives from each of our former enemies, as well as five from the countries still under our control. Also, testimonies will be allowed from former inmates."

"This could be an ugly trial," observed Adenauer. "We are

essentially hanging out all our dirty linen to be seen by the whole world."

"That is true, *Herr* Minister," agreed Rommel. "But I see no way of avoiding it. If we don't do it now, the truth will eventually get out and we would look worse than ever."

Everyone nodded in agreement.

"While we are on the subject of our secrets," Rommel went on, "there is one last thing we must address. I have decided, and I hope you will all agree, that we must immediately discontinue the research and production of atomic weapons, as well as the development of long-range rockets. The rocket test facility in Argentina must be dismantled as quickly as possible, before it is discovered. If the rest of the world were to discover that we had gone back on our previous agreements, we, as a nation, would never be trusted again. And, in the case of the test facility in Argentina, the Americans could and probably would destroy it as soon as it is detected.

"However, I have been talking to Willy Ley, the writer of space articles. He suggested to me that, given the chance, I should propose to the Americans that we pool our resources and develop a rocket capable of placing artificial satellites into orbit around the earth. In fact, both he and Dr. von Braun believe it is even within our means to make Jules Verne's story of men going to the moon come true before the end of the century."

"That does capture the imagination, but don't you think that it's a little far-fetched?" commented one member of the group.

"Nevertheless," said Adenauer, "I'll contact Juan Peron, the President of Argentina, and tell him of our decision. We will offer assistance in the dismantling of the facility if he wants."

STUTTGART

The first meeting between the new German government and French leaders was held on July 1, 1949. Representing the French were Marshall Petain, the head of the existing French Vichy Government, Felix Gouin, Georges Bidault, Vincent Auriol, Rene Coty, and General Charles de Gaulle. de Gaulle, much to the disgust of the Germans, had been selected by the others to be their leader and chief spokesman.

Representing the German Government were: Foreign Minister Adenauer; *Feldmarschall* Witzleben, Commander-in-Chief of the Military; Walter Bech, Minister of Finance; and several of their staff members.

Adenauer opened the meeting by informing the Frenchmen that the new German Government was considering giving more autonomy to several of the Western European countries. The purpose of the meeting was to discuss this possibility with France first, since it was the largest of the occupied countries.

After the opening, General de Gaulle flew into a tirade on the existing French situation. He demanded that Germany make restitution for the damage sustained by France and wanted the immediate return of the industrial Saar Basin to France..

After listening a few minutes to de Gaulle as he went on, Adenauer stood and brought an end to the tirade by saying, "*Monsieurs*, I am sorry that you are under the impression that we have met here to resume the Treaty of Versailles. The General seems to have forgotten that we won the war this time and not him. Therefore, I can see no purpose in continuing this meeting. *Auf Wiedersehen*!" The German representatives all followed Adenauer out of the room.

"You hot headed fool!" exclaimed Petain to de Gaulle. "Our chance to get a little freedom, and you throw it away with your big mouth!"

"Need I remind you *Monsieur*," retorted de Gaulle, "that you are the one that sold out to the Nazis and became their stooge. I carried on the struggle."

As the two argued back and forth, Felix Gouin nodded to his other associates and they all arose and walked out of the room leaving de Gaulle and Petain alone with their argument. Once outside the room, Gouin spoke up, "*Monsieurs*, it is obvious to me that we will get nowhere with the Germans as long as we have those two albatrosses around our neck. Petain will go along with everything the Germans propose. In fact, he probably already has their proposal committed to memory. De Gaulle, on the other hand, will compromise on nothing."

"I think you are correct in your assessment," agreed Rene

Coty. "If we are to reach any kind of a reasonable agreement with the Germans, both Petain and de Gaulle must go."

"I wonder where the Germans went?" speculated Gouin.

"They couldn't have gotten very far," observed Coty. "Do either of you speak German better than I? We could ask one of the German guards down the hall there about where they are."

"I can do that," volunteered Vincent Auriol as he turned and walked over to the guards. Returning to the group he said, "The guard said they are probably in their office at the top of the stairs."

"Good. Shall we go talk to them now?" asked Gouin.

"I think we had better," responded Coty.

As the three men approached the upstairs office, the guard at the door smiled at them and opened the door. "Please go right in," he said, "I think you are expected."

As they entered the room, the Germans who were all working around a table, looked up. "Well, that certainly didn't take you very long. We thought before you got here we would have time to complete the proposal we are presenting to the Italians in two weeks. But, this is fine. Please sit down."

For the next five days the groups worked back and forth until an agreement was finally reached. In the interim de Gaulle was placed under house arrest. For the most part, the French were forced to accept the German proposal. However, the French were successful in arguing that the size of their navy be increased to include an additional four capital warships so they could better control their overseas colonies.

On the fourteenth of July to commemorate Bastille Day, the last of the German troops left French soil, and Auriol Vincent was elected President of the Fourth Republic. One of his first acts was to officially arrest Henri Petain and try him for treason. After a military trial that lasted only three days, he was found guilty of treason and sentenced to death.

General Charles de Gaulle presented another problem. As the leader of the Free French during the war and in the later futile defense of Italy, he was, indeed, a hero of the Republic. Yet Vincent knew de Gaulle's arrogance would be a constant threat if DeGaulle remained in France. After meeting with his advisors it was decided to offer de Gaulle the Office of Governor General of the French territories of Algeria and French Morocco. Realizing this would give him control over a vast area with little interference from Paris, de Gaulle gladly accepted the offer.

After the agreement was consummated with the French, the negotiations with The Netherlands, Belgium, Luxembourg, Denmark, and Norway went much smoothly. Italy, because it had at one time been an Ally, was allowed a much larger military than the others. Germany looked to the Italians to be a strong buffer on their southern flank.

Queen Wilhelmina of The Netherlands returned from exile and started forming a new government, as did King Haakon VII of Norway, King Frederick IX of Denmark, and Prince Charles of Belgium. In Italy a referendum voted for a republic to be formed. The following month, Luigi Einaudi was elected Premier.

As the Germans completed their withdrawal from the western countries, those countries began to arrest all their citizens who had collaborated with the Nazis. Norway convicted Vidkun Quisling of treason. He was executed along with several of his aides. The Netherlands did the same to Anton Mussert and his cohorts, and Denmark executed Clausen. The French not only quickly executed Pierre Laval and Henri Petain and their aides, but also many of the leaders of the French secret police in the Vichy government.

BERLIN

In Berlin on November 1, 1949, Feldmarschall *Fabian* von Schlabreendorff and Generals Claus von Stauffenberg and Alexis von Roemme, convened the trials of those Nazis accused of war crimes. The three generals were commissioned to be the judges and jury for the trials.

All of the countries of Western Europe including Great Britain sent their foreign ministers to witness the proceedings. The United States sent Secretary of State, John Foster Dulles and Chief Justice, Fred M. Vinson. The Russians, although invited to send representatives, had little use for western-style justice and even less for the German style and so they sent no one, but they did allow several Russian witnesses, who were requested by the prosecution, to attend.

During the next six months hundreds of military and civilian Nazi leaders were tried, including Ernst Kaltenbrunner, the S.S. general who commanded the Reich Main Security Office. Kaltenbrunner was found guilty of crimes against humanity and condemned to death, along with all of the other S.S. Generals. Alfred Rosenberg, the Nazi Commissar of the Occupied Eastern Territories and chief anti-Jewish ideologist for Hitler, was also condemned to death. Hans Frank, the Nazi governor of Poland who was responsible for the atrocities committed there, was condemned to death, as was Wilhelm Frick the governor of Bohemia and Moravia. Julius Streicher the chief anti-Jewish Propagandist was also sentenced to death. Fritz Sauckel, commander of the slave labor program in Germany, was condemned to death along with all of the Commandants of the concentration camps. Dr. Robert Ley, the Director of Labor, escaped trial by hanging himself. Hans Fritzche, one of Goebbel's chief propagandists was acquitted, along with Franz von Papen, Hitler's Vice Chancellor during the early days of the Nazi government. Both men had no direct part in any of the crimes.

Ilse Koch, "The Bitch of Buchenwald" and wife of Karl Doch the Commandant of Buchenwald, was the only woman tried and was sentenced to twenty-five years imprisonment. Albert Speer, the Minister of Armaments received a sentence of twenty years for his role in the use of extensive slave labor throughout the Nazi armament industry. Artur Seyss-Inquart, the governor of The Netherlands, was sentenced to death. Constantin von Neurath, the governor of Czechoslovakia, received a sentence of fifteen years in prison, and Baldur von Schirach the governor of Austria received twenty years.

One hundred twenty-three senior S.S. and *Wehrmacht* officers were found guilty of "crimes against humanity" and sentenced to five to twenty years of imprisonment.

At the end of the trial of the Nazi military and civilian leaders, Rommel's government surprised all of the Allied observers by indicting and putting on trial the leadership of the huge German chemical combine, *I.G. Farbenindustrie*, along with those of the great Krupp Works.

As the twenty-six industrialists filed into the court room,

Secretary of State Dulles turned to Chief Supreme Court Justice Vinson and said, "This is amazing, Fred, can you imagine our government trying the entire leadership of U. S. Steel or Dupont?"

"No, I can't," responded Vinson. "But they evidently know much more about I.G. Farben than we do."

During the war, it was known that the Nazis were producing in several plants, synthetic oil and rubber from coal, which was plentiful in both Germany and conquered Poland. In fact, these facilities were bombed many times during the war. During the three weeks of the trial it came to be known that Farben had built two plants, one for synthetic oil and one for synthetic rubber just several miles from the notorious Auschwitz concentration camp.

From testimonies given by former inmates who survived the ordeal, it was revealed that under the direction of Walter Duerrfeld, I. G. Farben's chief engineer in charge of construction, over ten thousand inmates of Auschwitz were forced to work long hours in all kinds of weather on the construction of the two plants. Each morning the weakened workers were forced to march the four kilometers from the concentration camp to the work sites and then back at the end of the day. Due to the harsh treatment the inmates received at the camp and the lack of sufficient food, dozens of workers died everyday while on the job. Although there were always plenty of replacement workers, Farben was continually having to train the new workers.

Finally, in order to increase efficiency, and to protect the billion *Reichsmarks* Farben had invested in the two facilities, Hermann Schmitz, the President of I.G. Farben, testified that, in July of 1942, the management of I. G. Farben decided to approach the Nazis on the possibility of the company building its own concentration camp for the workers.

Under questioning, Schmitz testified that he had explained the advantages of such a proposition to S.S. Major Rudolf Hoess, the camp Commandant at Auschwitz. Schmitz testified that he had reasoned the inmates would not be drained of their already-limited physical energy by the long marches to and from the main concentration camp to the construction sites. By eliminating the marches there would be more time to work on the projects.

Furthermore, security would be made more efficient by eliminating the marches which required more S.S. guards than were required at the work sites.

Another reason, which Schmitz said he did not point out to Hoess, was that with a greater efficiency in the work force, the facilities would be completed at a reduced cost and production could start that much sooner.

Schmitz went on, "Once the authorities agreed to our plan, we commenced to build the facility, which we named *Monowitz*, which of course, was a facetious name. Under the terms of the agreement, I. G. Farben was to be responsible for the housing, feeding, and health of the inmates; the S.S. was charged with the security, punishment and supply of inmates."

When asked how much Farben invested in the camp, Schmitz stated, "Over five million *Reichsmarks*. But it was thought to be a modest amount to protect the billion *Reichsmarks* that had been invested to date."

He also testified that once the plants were completed, Otto Ambros was appointed to be the supervisor of the synthetic rubber plant and Heinrich Buetefisch the supervisor of the petroleum plant.

From the records available it was determined that over three hundred thousand concentration camp inmates worked at the I. G. Farben Plants at Auschwitz and at least twenty five thousand were essentially worked to death.

At the close of the fifth, and final day, of the trial, all of the Allied representatives who witnessed the trials were invited to a dinner at the British Embassy. Following the dinner, the group retired to a large reception room and discussed the trial.

"How would the United States Supreme Court rule in a case like this, Justice Vinson?" asked the British Foreign Secretary.

"It is a difficult and complex case, perhaps unprecedented in history," responded Vinson. "The defense made a good case in pointing out that the company had little choice but to conform to the Nazi slave labor program. If they had refused to become an oppressor, the company would probably have become a victim itself, with the government taking over the company and running it with their own men. On the other hand, where do you draw the line in refusing to do evil at the risk of your own life?"

"Refresh my memory of history," asked Secretary Dulles. "What did the United States do to the superintendent of the Confederate Andersonville Prison in Georgia after the Civil War?"

"Let's see," responded Vinson. "What was his name? Oh, yes, Major Wirz. Henry Wirz. After the war, he was tried by a military court, convicted of murder, and hanged. As I recall, almost fourteen thousand of the fifty thousand that were sent to Andersonville died there. Of course, the records of the Union prisons were not much better. About fifteen percent of all Union prisoners died in captivity compared to a little over twelve percent of the southern prisoners. But, with the superior hospitals, physicians, medicines and foods the North had, one would think there should have been an even greater disparity in favor of the Union."

"Were any of the Union camp commanders tried for their treatment of Confederate prisoners?" someone asked.

"Not that I am aware of," replied Vinson. "I guess that's one of the advantages of being the victor. That's what makes this trial unique. It is the Germans trying their own. If we had won this war, something like this trial probably would have taken place. But, under the circumstances, I didn't expect of the Germans."

Everyone nodded in agreement.

Three days later, the court reconvened with their verdict. Judge Fabian von Schlabrendorff ordered the twenty-four executives of I. G. Farben to stand as he read the verdicts. The verdicts were:

Otto Ambros, the superintendent of the synthetic rubber plant, was found guilty of slavery and mass murder and sentenced to imprisonment for eight years.

Walter Duerrfeld, the chief engineer in charge of construction of the plant, was found guilty of slavery and mass murder and sentenced to imprisonment for eight years.

Fritz ter Meer, Farben's chief scientist, was found guilty of slavery and mass murder and sentenced to imprisonment for seven years.

Karl Krauch, the Nazi *Kommandant* for chemical production, was found guilty of slavery and mass murder and sentenced to imprisonment for six years.

Heinrich Buetefisch, superintendent of the synthetic oil plant, was found guilty of slavery and mass murder and sentenced to imprisonment for six years.

Herman Schmitz, the President of the company, and Georg von Schnitzler, one of the senior members of the managing board of directors, were found guilty of plunder and spoliation and sentenced to imprisonment for five years.

The court also found the remaining members of the board of directors guilty of plunder and spoliation. However, not wanting to completely cripple the management of the company, which was one of the most important industries in the country, the court did not sentence them to imprisonment, but fined them each twenty-five thousand *Reichsmarks* and allowed them to return to work at I. G. Farber.

Both Baron Gustav Krupp and his son Alfred, were tried and found guilty of slavery. However, due to the Baron's poor physical and mental condition he was acquitted. Alfred, who had assumed sole ownership of the company in 1943, was sentenced to twelve years imprisonment and confiscation of all of his property.

All the civilians found guilty and sentenced to imprisonment were informed they were to be sent to the island of Sardinia, where they would be interned in several large prisons built apart from the areas where the *"undesirables"* had been exiled.

At the conclusion of the trial, the court judges asked the American and British representatives to approach the bench. As they did, Judge von Schlabrendorff addressed the men. "*Herren*, as we conclude these proceedings, my associates and I have decided to leave several cases for your countries to handle. As you are aware, we have several of your citizens who collaborated with us during the war. I am referring to the Americans Rita Zucca, commonly referred to as 'Axis Sally', Douglas Chandler, who I believe you referred to as the American Lord Haw Haw, his companion Jane Anderson or Lady Haw Haw, and Mildred Gillars whose nickname I don't remember, and Ezra Pound. We also have the Englishman, William Joyce or Lord Haw Haw. All of these individuals were, as you know, propagandists for the Nazi regime."

"We are very much aware of them and their activities," responded John Foster Dulles.

"Since they are, or were, citizens of your two countries, it is our opinion that they should be turned over to your governments for trial, rather than standing trial here. Do you agree?"

"Yes, at least speaking for the United States, we would like to have our people," replied Dulles.

"As would we," added Clement Attlee, the British Prime Minister.

POST WAR EVENTS

On the January 2, 1950, the first open and free election was held in Germany since Hitler seized complete control of the country in 1934, after the death of President Paul von Hindenburg. Erwin Rommel easily won the election with eighty two percent of the vote. The newly reorganized Socialist and Communist parties divided the balance.

Two weeks later as a part of the swearing-in ceremonies a brief biography of Rommel was read by the famous movie actress, Marlene Dietrich, who had been born in Germany but fled the country when the Nazis seized control. Since the end of the war Marlene had been on a personal campaign to help obtain world wide recognition of the new German Republic. Now, upon the urging of several of her family members still loving in Germany and with the encouragement of several officials of the new German government, Marlene had once again returned to the city of her birth.

In the biography Marlene in her deep throaty voice told of Erwin Rommel being born on November 15, 1891 in the small town of Heidenheim near Elm in Southern Germany. She told about how his father and grandfather had both been schoolteachers specializing in mathematics. His mother was the daughter of a former president of the state government of Wurttemberg. Influenced by his father's knowledge of mathematics, Marlene explained how young Rommel dreamed of becoming an engineer and although he was not from an upper class Prussian family he was admitted to the officer's military academy at Danzig. In January of 1912 at the age of twenty-one he was commissioned into the army. However, while attending the academy, Rommel met a young attractive language student by the name of Lucie Maria Mollin. Rommel was introduced to Lucie by one of his student colleagues who was her cousin. The Mollin family were well to do Prussian landowners but were not opposed to her seeing Erwin, and up and coming cadet in the prestigious academy.

When the Great War broke out in August of 1914 Rommel was called up to serve on the Western Front and served with distinction. Marlene told how in 1916, while on a leave, Erwin proposed to Lu, as he called her, and she accepted. They were married before Erwin returned to the front. After the war Erwin remained in the army and as Germany went through terrible economic times, Erwin wrote about his exploits during the war in a booklet call *Infantry Attack* in an effort to supplement their income.

In 1928 their first and only child, Manfred, was born. Marlene had Manfred, who was still in the military, stand and be acknowledged by the crowd.

After the Nazis sized control of Germany, Hitler read Rommel's *Infantry Attack* and was impressed by the officer's ideas. As a result Rommel advanced quickly through the ranks and became on of the few general officers not of the Prussian class. In order not to offend the non-German visitors, Marlene passed over Rommel's exploits during the recent war and turned the time back over to several of the civilian German leaders, who explained that without Rommel's backing the overthrow of Hitler might never have succeeded. They also praised him for his present leadership.

At the conclusion of the program, Marlene agreed to sing *Edelweiss*.

After his election, Rommel formally resigned from the military after serving for forty years and devoted himself to the rebuilding of the new German Empire. But new problems were arising. In Asia, the Communists under Mao Tse-tung and the

Kuomintang government under Chiang Kai-shek had managed to drive the Japanese out of China, and then immediately resumed fighting among themselves for control of the country, with the Communists winning. In mid-1949 the Russians successfully tested an atomic device and then broke their treaty with the Japanese and drove them into two small pockets around Vladivostok and Pusan in Southern Korea. After defeating Tojo at the battle of Vladivostok, the Japanese surrendered and Tojo was executed by the Russians. The Russians then, like the Japanese before them, established puppet governments in both Mongolia and Korea.

The Americans occupied all of the Japanese Home Islands as well as the Kuril Islands up to the fiftieth parallel, but returned all of the Island of Sakhalin, which the Japanese had seized in the Russo-Japanese War of 1905.

By 1950, most of the world powers, including the United States, recognized the new German Government and trade resumed with all of Western Europe once again. Rommel, like Hitler, saw before him the potential threat of the Bolsheviks and began to strengthen the fortifications along the Russian border. The Russians responded in kind.

EPILOGUE

The great I. G. Farben chemical complex, with its strong ties to Bayer and the other German chemical and pharmaceutical companies never did fully recover after the removal of their head management. This forced Rommel to commute the sentences of all of the leaders to aid in rebuilding this critical industry.

Rommel, himself, did not live to complete his six year term as Chancellor. He died unexpectedly on the 14th of October, 1954, just before his sixty-third birthday. His Foreign Secretary, Konrad Adenauer, succeeded him as Chancellor of the German Republic.

General Eisenhower retired to his farm at Gettysburg, Pennsylvania where he lived the rest of his life.

In 1952 President Dewey ran again for the Presidency. He selected General Douglas MacArthur as his running mate. They were easily re-elected.

Joseph Kennedy never re-entered the political arena after his defeat. He retired to his estate in Massachusetts where he continued to manage his vast business ventures and began grooming his sons for future political offices.

General George Patton was killed in an automobile accident as he was on his way to the Rome airport for a flight back to the United States, during the American withdrawal from Italy.

Captain Bernhard Rogge was persuaded by the new government to come out of retirement. He was promoted to the office of Lieutenant Admiral and placed on the Staff of Grand Admiral Karl Doenitz, who retained his position as senior officer over the Kreigsmarine. Rogge held the position for ten years, until his retirement.

Vyacheslav Molotov continued as the Premier of the Soviet Union into the 1960s. During his administration he lead the USSR into the Atomic Age, was instrumental in the Communist conquest of China and spread of Communism throughout the world.

Ensign Fritz Stuben was promoted to the office of *Kapitän* and assigned to the staff of the Baltic fleet at Kiel. He married Debbie

Johnson, who joined the nursing staff of the general hospital in Kiel.

Captain Ruth Lewis returned to England, where she worked in a military hospital that specialized in the treatment of the victims of the atomic attack at Normandy. She eventually met and married a doctor who also worked at the hospital. Her brother, who was aboard the destroyer *Swift* which never returned from Normandy, was presumed killed when the destroyer sank at Normandy.

Airmen Stewart and Cooper both survived the war and returned to their homes where they married their high school sweethearts.

Rita Zucca, better known as "Axis Sally", served just nine months for her propaganda activities. She was given a light sentence since her broadcasts, though unintentional, were considered more entertaining than demoralizing. Upon her release she moved to Italy where she lived the rest of her life.

Mildred Gillars, who went by the name "Midge", was found guilty of treason due to the vicious propaganda she broadcasted. She remained in prison until 1961.

Douglas Chandler, who was known as the "American Lord Haw Haw" and to the amusement of his audience always began each of his propaganda broadcasts with, "Misinformed, misgoverned friends and compatriots", was also found guilty of treason and sentenced to life imprisonment.

Jane Anderson, or "Lady Haw Haw," escaped arrest in Germany, and was never found or heard from again.

Ezra Pound was declared psychologically unfit to stand trial for treason and was confined to a mental hospital until his release in 1958. After his release he, like Rita Zucca, returned to live in Italy.

The British were not so forgiving with Will Joyce or "Lord Haw Haw." He was tried for treason, found guilty and hanged.

Ilse Koch, "The Bitch of Buchenwald," was sentenced to life imprisonment, but could not handle incarceration, and soon committed suicide in Aichach women's prison in Bavaria.